THE WORK OF MOURNING

THE WORK OF
MOURNING

JACQUES DERRIDA

EDITED BY
PASCALE-ANNE BRAULT AND MICHAEL NAAS

THE UNIVERSITY OF CHICAGO PRESS
CHICAGO AND LONDON

The University of Chicago Press, Chicago 60637
The University of Chicago Press, Ltd., London
© 2001 by The University of Chicago
All rights reserved. Published 2001
Paperback edition 2003
Printed and bound by CPI Group (UK) Ltd,
Croydon, CR0 4YY

English language only.

24 23 22 21 20 19 18 17   4 5 6 7 8
ISBN: 978-0-226-50249-6

Library of Congress Cataloging-in-Publication Data

Derrida, Jacques.
    The work of mourning / Jacques Derrida ; edited by
Pascale-Anne Brault and Michael Naas.
        p.   cm.
Includes bibliographical references.
ISBN 0-226-14316-3 (cloth : alk. paper)
    1. Derrida, Jacques—Friends and associates.
2. Philosophers—Biography.   3. Eulogies.   I. Brault,
Pascale-Anne.   II. Naas, Michael.   III. Title.
    B2430.D483 W67 2001
    194—dc21

                                             00-012995

CONTENTS

1.   The biographical sketches are by Kas Saghafi.

v

ACKNOWLEDGMENTS

The impetus for this book was a conference held on October 7, 1996, at DePaul University on the themes of mourning and politics in the work of Jacques Derrida. We offer our heartfelt thanks to David Krell, who organized the conference and provided us with a forum for discussing this topic with Jacques Derrida, and to Peg Birmingham, who first suggested the idea of collecting these texts into a single volume. Their support and collegiality have been invaluable in the preparation of this work.

Of the fifteen translations gathered here, eight have been previously published. We are grateful to Kevin Newmark (and Columbia University Press), Samuel Weber (and the Louisiana State University Press), and Leonard Lawlor (and *Philosophy Today*) for allowing us to republish their translations of Derrida's texts on de Man, Riddel, and Deleuze. Our thanks also to Boris Belay for making his translation of "Lyotard and *Us*" available to us for this volume, and to Stanford University Press, *Critical Inquiry,* and Northwestern University Press for permission to reprint our own previously published translations of the texts on Foucault, Kofman,

Levinas, Marin, and Barthes. All but the Foucault and Kofman texts are published here in their entirety, these being abridged only in those places where they depart significantly from the central themes of the volume. The complete version of these texts can be found in *Resistances of Psychoanalysis* and *The Sarah Kofman Reader,* both from Stanford University press.

We owe a truly inestimable debt to Kas Saghafi of DePaul University for compiling the biographies and bibliographies in this volume. His exceptional library sleuthing skills and exemplary attention to detail have helped put Derrida's words of remembrance into the context of the lives and works of these thinkers. Kas has asked us to thank here in his name the excellent staff at the DePaul University Library, particularly Marilyn Browning, John Rininger, and Denise Rogers, for their unsparing and professional assistance. Kas's efforts, and those of the library staff at DePaul, have helped make this collection of works of mourning a genuinely collective work of memory.

Our special thanks to Françoise Marin and Christiane Mauve for the biographical information they were kind enough to share with us concerning their late husbands, Louis Marin and Michel Servière, and to Didier Cahen, who made available to us an unpublished letter by Derrida on Edmond Jabès and helped write the biographical sketch on the poet. Our thanks as well to Pleshette DeArmitt, David Krell, and Alan Schrift for their many excellent suggestions on the penultimate draft of this work.

We would also like to express our gratitude to the University Research Council at DePaul University, along with DePaul's College of Liberal Arts and Sciences, and especially its dean, Michael Mezey, for their generous support of this project over the past couple of years.

Finally, we offer our deepest thanks to Jacques Derrida, who not only accepted our request to collect these very personal reflections on friends and colleagues into a single volume but encouraged us throughout with a grace and generosity beyond measure.

To Reckon with the Dead: Jacques Derrida's Politics of Mourning

> *Philia* begins with the possibility of survival.
> Surviving—that is the other name of a mourning
> whose possibility is never to be awaited.
>
> *Politics of Friendship*

One must always go before the other. In the *Politics of Friendship,* Jacques Derrida demonstrates that this is the law of friendship—and thus of mourning.[1] One friend must always go before the other; one friend must always die first. There is no friendship without the possibility that one friend will die before the other, perhaps right before the other's eyes. For even when friends die together, or rather, at the same time, their friendship will have been structured from the very beginning by the possibility that one of the two would see the other die, and so, surviving, would be left to bury, to commemorate, and to mourn.

---

1. Jacques Derrida, *Politics of Friendship,* trans. George Collins (New York: Verso, 1997).

While Jacques Derrida has formalized this law in numerous texts over the past few decades, he has also had to undergo or bear witness to it, as friends—and there are now many of them—have gone before him, making explicit or effective the structural law that will have determined all his friendships from the beginning. Over the past couple of decades, then, Derrida has not only continued to develop in a theoretical fashion this relationship between friendship and mourning but has, on several occasions, and in recent years with greater and greater frequency, been called upon to respond at a determined time and place to an unrepeatable event—the death of a friend. Each time this has occurred, Derrida has tried to bear witness to the singularity of a friendship, to the absolute uniqueness of his relationship with a friend, in a form that varies between a word or letter of condolence, a memorial essay, a eulogy, and a funeral oration. Each time, he has tried to respond to a singular event, a unique occasion, with words fit for the friend—words that inevitably relate life and friendship to death and mourning. This volume gathers together these various responses, written over a period of some twenty years, in order to draw attention to a series of questions and aporias concerning what we have risked calling Jacques Derrida's "politics of mourning."

The idea of bringing these texts together first grew out of a conference with Jacques Derrida at DePaul University in October of 1996 on the theme of mourning and politics. During that conference, it became clear that while these texts were not originally destined to share the same space, they have come to resemble a sort of corpus within the corpus of Derrida. Having prevailed upon Jacques Derrida to allow us to gather these texts of mourning into a single volume, we have asked in essence for a sort of reckoning between them. From the very first of these essays, "The Deaths of Roland Barthes," written in 1981, Derrida has been concerned with the relationship between the singularity of death and its inevitable repetition, with what it means to reckon with death, or with the dead, with all those who were once close to us but who are no longer, as we say, "with us," or who are "with us" only insofar as they are "in us." By bringing these various tributes together under a single cover, by drawing up a sort of account of those whom Derrida has mourned, we have in effect asked each of these texts to reckon not only with the singular death that each addresses but with one another, and with the inevitable repetition and betrayal that each represents in relation to the others.

To reckon: that is to say, to recount, relate, or narrate, to consider, judge, or evaluate, even to estimate, enumerate, and calculate. Such a reckoning is perhaps to be expected when it comes to politics, where accounts must be given, judgments rendered, and calculations made. But when it comes to mourning, to texts of mourning, texts written after the deaths of close friends and dear colleagues, to ask for a reckoning, to ask someone not only to recount but to take account, even to calculate, may seem indecent or at the very least lacking in taste. If we have persisted, then, in asking for such a reckoning, it has been in order to learn something more from Jacques Derrida about taste, about a taste for death and about taste in death or mourning, about whether one can ever be politic in mourning, and whether it makes any sense to talk of a politics of mourning. In these introductory pages we would simply like to give a brief overview of these texts in order to raise a few questions about the necessity of such reckoning, of taking stock of the dead, of calculating and negotiating between them, of giving them their due in a language that is repeatable, even predictable, and that perhaps cannot help but commit what is called near the end of Proust's *Remembrance of Things Past* a kind of "posthumous infidelity."[2]

Risking the impolitic, we have gathered together not those texts that speak of the work of mourning, of phantoms and specters, in a more or less theoretical fashion but those that enact the work of mourning—and of friendship—in a more explicit way, texts written after the deaths of friends and colleagues to recall their lives and work and bear witness to a relationship with them. Written over the past two decades on figures well known in France and the United States (Roland Barthes, Paul de Man, Michel Foucault, Louis Althusser, Edmond Jabès, Louis Marin, Sarah Kofman, Gilles Deleuze, Emmanuel Levinas, and Jean-François Lyotard), as well as figures less well known (Max Loreau, Jean-Marie Benoist, Joseph Riddel, and Michel Servière), these texts not only speak of or about mourning but are themselves texts *of* or *in* mourning.

We realize that in drawing attention to these so very personal texts we run the risk of a sort of morbid taste or shameless curiosity. Yet these are, after all, public texts, published texts, which most likely could not be radically distinguished from other works of Derrida. We have, however, for reasons of both tact and coherence, excluded from this series of public texts about public figures those texts that mourn more private figures, such as family members, even though works like "Circumfession" and *Memoirs of the Blind* have themselves been published, and thus made public, and probably could not in all rigor be completely distinguished from these other texts of mourning.[3]

2. Marcel Proust, *Remembrance of Things Past,* trans. C. K. Scott Moncrieff, Terence Kilmartin, and Andreas Mayor (New York: Random House, 1981), 3:940.

3. See Jacques Derrida, "Circumfession," in *Jacques Derrida,* by Geoffrey Bennington and Jacques Derrida, trans. Geoffrey Bennington (Chicago: University of Chicago Press,

By gathering these works of mourning—by incorporating them—into a single volume, we hope to make even more apparent the ways in which the oeuvre or corpus of Derrida has, to cite Proust once more, come to resemble "a huge cemetery in which on the majority of the tombs the names are effaced and can no longer be read," a cemetery where some of the names are nonetheless still legible because of these acts of mourning and friendship, even if these names mask or refer to others that have long been obscured.[4] We will ultimately be asking, therefore, about the encryption of names and friends in an oeuvre, about the way in which an oeuvre does not simply grow larger but thickens with time, ages, comes to have time written across it, becomes wrinkled, furrowed, or folded, its volume worked over like a landscape or, indeed, like a cemetery.

While the texts of mourning that Jacques Derrida has written over the past twenty years on friends from Roland Barthes to Jean-François Lyotard seem to agree with and confirm much that is said about writing and death in so many early texts,[5] it is a banal but nonetheless incontrovertible observation that these texts could not have been written before they were. For them to have been written, time was required—and not just the passing but the ravages of time, time for one's teachers to begin to pass away, and then one's colleagues and friends, slowly at first, but then with an ever-increasing regularity. This is all so commonplace, and yet how does one reckon it, and what does it do to an oeuvre? Does it give it not simply a chronology but, perhaps, a temporality, not simply a signification but a force?

If these essays in and on mourning appear very much in accord with several early essays, they are surely not wholly continuous with or already contained within them, as if there were a sort of teleology to the Derridean corpus, as if a kind of biological preformationism were at work in his

1993) (hereafter abbreviated as *C*), and *Memoirs of the Blind,* trans. Pascale-Anne Brault and Michael Naas (Chicago: University of Chicago Press, 1993).

4. Proust, *Remembrance of Things Past,* 3:940. While Derrida might find such a claim about his corpus highly problematic, he would not find it totally foreign, for he himself has cited a similar phrase in a relatively recent text on Jean-Paul Sartre in which Sartre cites this well-known phrase of Proust (see "'Il courait mort': Salut, salut: Notes pour un courrier aux *Temps Modernes,*" *Les Temps Modernes* 51 [March–May 1996]: 7–54).

5. See, for example, Jacques Derrida, "Signature Event Context," in *Margins of Philosophy,* trans. Alan Bass (Chicago: University of Chicago Press, 1982), 309–30, or pt. 1 of *Of Grammatology,* trans. Gayatri Chakravorty Spivak (Baltimore: Johns Hopkins University Press, 1974). For a fascinating analysis of Derrida's work on art and mourning, see David Farrell Krell, *The Purest of Bastards: Works of Mourning, Art, and Affirmation in the Thought of Jacques Derrida* (University Park: Pennsylvania State University Press, 2000).

oeuvre. It is precisely this kind of teleology that Jacques Derrida takes issue with in his 1963 essay "Force and Signification," where, in a critique of Jean Rousset's analysis of the aesthetics and temporality of Proust, he opposes a teleology and a theology of signification to a new thinking of force.[6] We will thus not be asking here about an unfolding meaning to the Derridean corpus, a meaning implicit already in the beginning though not yet revealed, but about the intrusion of the unexpected and the unanticipated in an oeuvre, about what happens when proper names become engraved on tombs, each name joining the others and yet each naming a singular mourning. We will be asking about the force of time and the time of force, about the relation between force and language, between time and the force of mourning.

In conformity with the genre, Derrida begins many of these powerful and moving texts by admitting how difficult it is to speak at such a moment of mourning, difficult to get the words out and difficult to find the right words. "So much to say, and I don't have the heart for it today. So much to say about what has happened to us . . . with the death of Gilles Deleuze" (192). Three years after writing these words for the newspaper *Libération,* Derrida writes in that same paper, just hours after receiving word of Jean-François Lyotard's death: "I feel at such a loss, unable to find public words for what is happening to us, for what has left speechless all those who had the good fortune to come near this great thinker—whose absence will remain for me, I am certain, forever unthinkable" (214).

In mourning we find ourselves at a loss, no longer ourselves, as if the singular shock of what we must bear had altered the very medium in which it was to be registered. But even if the death of a friend appears unthinkable, unspeakable, we are nonetheless, says Derrida, called upon to speak, to break the silence, to participate in the codes and rites of mourning. "Speaking is impossible," writes Derrida in the wake of Paul de Man's death, "but so too would be silence or absence or a refusal to share one's sadness."[7]

6.   See Jacques Derrida, "Force and Signification" in *Writing and Difference,* trans. Alan Bass (Chicago: University of Chicago Press, 1978), 3–30.

7.   Jacques Derrida, *Memoires for Paul de Man,* rev. ed., trans. Cecile Lindsay, Jonathan Culler, Eduardo Cadava, and Peggy Kamuf (New York: Columbia University Press, 1989), xvi (hereafter abbreviated as *M*).

And so Derrida broke the silence, first in 1981, following the death of Roland Barthes, and thirteen more times between then and now. He thus did what he thought he would never do; having spoken so often of death, of the theme of death, having written on so many occasions of those whom he knew living but who had subsequently died, Derrida had more or less vowed never to speak just after the death of a friend:

> What I thought impossible, indecent, and unjustifiable, what long ago and more or less secretly and resolutely I had promised myself never to do . . . was to write *following the death,* not after, not long after the death *by returning* to it, but just following the death, *upon or on the occasion of the death,* at the commemorative gatherings and tributes, in the writings "in memory" of those who while living would have been my friends, still present enough to me that some "declaration," indeed some analysis or "study," would seem at that moment completely unbearable. (49–50)

In all these essays of mourning Derrida is acutely aware of the dangers involved in speaking of the dead in the wake of their death, the dangers of using the dead, and perhaps despite one's own best intentions, for one's own ends or purposes. It is a question of both tact or taste and ethical responsibility. Derrida's "Circumfession" is emblematic in this regard. Writing in 1989 and 1990 about or "for" his mother, who, though still living, no longer recognizes him, and who, though she had never really read him in the past, is now blind and near death and so surely will not read him in the future, Derrida speaks of feeling "guilty for publishing her end," for "exhibiting her last breaths and, still worse, for purposes that some might judge to be literary" (*C,* 25, 36).

Perhaps even more disturbing, and even more common, than these "literary" purposes are the personal or political uses to which a death is put with the intent not simply of reckoning but of winning or scoring points. Derrida thus recalls the desire on the part of some "still to maneuver, to speculate, to try to profit or derive some benefit, whether subtle or sublime, to draw from the dead a supplementary force to be turned against the living" (51). Whereas Derrida might rather easily avoid these more egregious forms of bad taste or bad faith, he finds others more difficult to avoid or even recognize. Derrida thus speaks in several of these works of the dangers inherent in what might appear to be simple acts of fidelity, dangers inherent in all commemorative gatherings and tributes, all funeral orations. "There are of course lesser offenses, but offenses nonetheless: to pay homage with an essay that treats the work or a part of the work bequeathed to us, to talk on a theme that we confidently believe would have interested the author who has passed away (whose tastes, curiosities, and projects should, it seems, no longer surprise us). Such a treatment would indeed point out the debt, but it would also pay it back" (51).

If there are dangers in speaking of the deceased in a certain way, there are equally grave dangers in speaking of one's own relations with them, in offering, as Derrida says in his homage to Jean-François Lyotard, "an homage in the form of a personal testimony, which always tends toward reappropriation and always risks giving in to an indecent way of saying 'we,' or worse, 'me'" (225). In other words, there is always in mourning the danger of narcissism, for instance, the "egotistical" and no doubt "irrepressible" tendency to bemoan the friend's death in order to take pity upon oneself by saying, as Derrida was tempted to say after the death of Althusser: "A whole part of my life, a long, rich, and intense stretch of my living self has been interrupted today, comes to an end and thus dies with Louis in order to continue to accompany him, as in the past, but this time without return and into the depths of absolute darkness" (115).

The funeral oration is a genre beset on all sides by bad faith, self-delusion, and, of course, denial. For even when we use the dead for some end or purpose of our own, even when we speak to the dead simply to ask for their forgiveness, it is often because we do not wish to admit that the dead can no longer respond to us, can no longer, for example, offer us their forgiveness. Even though "nothing is more unbearable or laughable than all the expressions of guilt in mourning, all its inevitable spectacles" (44), even though it appears "naive and downright childish to come before the dead to ask for their forgiveness" (44), since the admission of guilt seems aimed always at its expiation, at giving oneself a good conscience, Derrida himself does not refrain from expressing regret at having let certain things cloud a friendship or at having been too discreet in the declaration of his admiration or affection. He writes in his essay on Jean-Marie Benoist, "I blame myself for this more than ever today, and for having taken these things much more seriously than they deserved to be, as if death were not keeping watch" (110).

Political calculation, personal retaliation, narcissism, attempts at achieving a good conscience—these are just some of the dangers to which these texts are, by their very nature, exposed. But can one ever write with perfect tact or in perfect taste? In "Circumfession" Derrida dreams of one day writing with a syringe rather than a pen, so that all he would have to do is find the right vein and let the writing come on its own, a writing that would no longer have to choose, inscribe, and calculate, that would be "without any labor or responsibility, without any risk of bad taste or violence" (C, 12). This is, of course, just a dream, for it seems that for

Jacques Derrida there never is any writing without responsibility, without an other to whom it must respond. In each of these texts of mourning, then, Jacques Derrida must struggle to avoid such bad taste, to refrain from using a death for his own advantage. That is, he must continue to reckon.

And what is our own responsibility in reading these texts of mourning? Can we ourselves avoid using them for our own purposes, either simply to add to our knowledge or, more perversely, to satisfy our curiosity about the deaths of famous teachers, writers, thinkers, and philosophers and the reactions they elicited from Jacques Derrida? Since we are reading texts that mourn the passing of people who, in most cases, were not our own friends or colleagues, are we not destined—are we perhaps not even invited—to use these deaths and the lessons learned from them to understand the deaths of those dear to us?

By pronouncing these texts of mourning in a public forum, by publishing them, Jacques Derrida has, it seems, made unavoidable this slippage from one death to another, this repetition and transference of the rhetoric and perhaps even the sentiments of mourning. We cannot mourn for those another has mourned—or at least not in the same way. They could not have touched us in the same way, and so we betray them in reading—though this betrayal will have been made possible, if not inevitable, as we will see, by the very publicity, the very readability, of mourning's inscription.

Despite all the dangers of the genre, all the dangers of memory and recognition, Derrida remembers and pays tribute. He recalls not only what is public but what is personal, not only what concerns us all but what concerned only him. In several of these texts, Derrida recounts personal memories of the deceased: traveling on a plane to Baltimore with Roland Barthes, driving through Chicago with his son and Paul de Man, recounting stories with Sarah Kofman at dinner, speaking with Louis Althusser and Jean-François Lyotard for the last time on the telephone, receiving a final letter from Michel Servière. He recounts and recalls but then asks in almost every case about the tact or taste of doing so, trying in each case to avoid the insidious pathos of personal memory.

One way to temper this pathos is to refuse to present a picture of one's relations with the friend that excludes all difference or conflict. Derrida thus often says that he owes it to the truth, and "so as not to give in too much to the genre" (56), not to whitewash the stormy aspects of his friendships. He thus speaks openly of the difficulties in his friendship with Foucault beginning in 1972, and of his differences with Althusser, Max Loreau, and Jean-Marie Benoist. In each case, however, he wishes to reaffirm that none of these difficulties ever jeopardized his "friendship" or "admiring attention," that none of this "ever compromised in the least the foundation of [the] friendship" (116).

Trying to bear witness to a unique friendship without giving in to some narcissistic "we" or "me," being willing to return to the troublesome aspects of the past without wanting to claim the "last word" on it (98), Derrida lays out not so much a middle ground as a series of aporias, aporias that, curiously, do not paralyze speech but inhabit and mobilize it. In his essay on Roland Barthes, for example, Derrida wonders whether fidelity to the friend consists in reading or acting like him, or in giving to him or to his memory something completely different and unexpected. The answer, it seems, is to be found not in dissolving the aporia but in clarifying and undergoing it: "I was searching *like him,* as him, for in the situation in which I have been writing since his death, a certain mimetism is at once a duty (to take him into oneself, to identify with him in order to let him speak within oneself, to make him present and faithfully to represent him) and the worst of temptations, the most indecent and most murderous. The gift *and* the revocation of the gift, just try to choose" (38).

Derrida suggests that it is only "in us" that the dead may speak, that it is only by speaking *of* or *as* the dead that we can keep them alive. "To keep alive, within oneself," asks Derrida, "is this the best sign of fidelity?" (36), and he seems to answer in the affirmative, so long as we understand that this "within oneself" is always already a response to the friend we mourn. "Each time," writes Derrida, we must acknowledge "our friend to be gone forever, irremediably absent . . . for it would be unfaithful to delude oneself into believing that the other living *in us* is living *in himself*" (*M,* 21).

Fidelity thus consists in mourning, and mourning—at least in a first moment—consists in interiorizing the other and recognizing that if we are to give the dead anything it can now be only in us, the living. Derrida writes in "By Force of Mourning," in the context of a reading of Louis Marin's work: "ever since psychoanalysis came to mark this discourse, the image commonly used to characterize mourning is that of an interiorization (an idealizing incorporation, introjection, consumption of the other)" (159).[8]

---

8. Derrida writes in *Memoires for Paul de Man:* "Memory and interiorization: since Freud, this is how the 'normal' 'work of mourning' is often described. It entails a movement in which an interiorizing idealization takes in itself or upon itself the body and voice of the other, the other's visage and person, ideally *and* quasi-literally devouring them" (*M,* 34). For a more developed analysis of the relationship between introjection and incorporation in mourning, see "Fors: The Anglish Words of Nicolas Abraham and

Not to recognize the intractable reality that the dead are now only "in us" would be not only a form of denial but a betrayal of the dead friend, a failure to accede to the unique event the friend has undergone. "He is no more, he whom we see in images or in recollection. . . . And nothing can begin to dissipate the terrifying and chilling light of this certainty. As if respect for this certainty were still a debt, the last one, owed to the friend" (159–60). The dead can and must be only "for us," and everything we receive from and give to them will remain among ourselves. In the text written "for" Roland Barthes, Derrida reminds himself that the thoughts he dedicates and destines for Barthes "will no longer reach him, and this must be the starting point of my reflection" (35). What we must recognize in every funeral oration, in every memorial gathering and tribute, is that everything we say of and even to the friend "remains hopelessly *in* us or *between* us the living, without ever crossing the mirror of a certain speculation." In other words, "All we seem to have left is memory . . ." (*M*, 32–33).

Even the proper name seems to refer, in the wake of death, not to the deceased but only to him or her in us, in memory. "When I say Roland Barthes it is certainly him whom I name, him beyond his name. But since he himself is now inaccessible to this appellation, since this nomination cannot become a vocation, address, or apostrophe . . . it is him in me that I name, toward him in me, in you, in us that I pass through his name" (46).

But what does it mean to say that the dead are "in" us? Reflecting on Louis Marin's final book on the powers of the image, Derrida describes the topology and orientation of this supposed interiority of the mourning self before demonstrating their limits in the very assumption of a limit. "When we say 'in us,' when we speak so easily and so painfully of inside and outside, we are naming space, we are speaking of a visibility of the body, a geometry of gazes, an orientation of perspectives. *We are speaking of images.* . . . [The other] appears only as the one who has disappeared or passed away, as the one who, having passed away, leaves 'in us' only images" (159). Mourning consists in recognizing that the dead are now only "in us," now only images "for us." And yet there is a limit to this interiorization, one that comes not from some impermeability of a boundary between two homogeneous spaces but from a different organization of space. For the part that is "in us" comes before and is greater than the whole, that is, comes before and is greater than us; the part that is seen by us first sees

---

Maria Torok," Derrida's foreword to Abraham and Torok's *Wolf Man's Magic Word*, trans. Nicholas Rand (Minneapolis: University of Minnesota Press, 1986), xi–xlviii.

and looks at us as our origin and our law. Derrida argues throughout these essays that the living are who they are only in and through these others, their interiority, even their narcissism, constituted always in relation to them, their memory itself formed, as Derrida writes remembering Louis Althusser, "only through this movement of mourning" (115). Though "the modes of interiorization or of subjectification that psychoanalysis talks about are in some respects undeniable in the work of mourning" (159), interiorization is never completed and, because of this reorganization of space, remains in the end impossible. According to Derrida, interiorization cannot—must not—be denied; the other is indeed reduced to images "in us." And yet the very notion of interiorization is limited in its assumption of a topology with limits between inside and out, what is ours and what is the other. "Roland Barthes looks at us . . . and we do not do as we please with this look, even though each of us has it at his disposal, in his own way, according to his own place and history. It is within us but it is not ours; we do not have it available to us like a moment or part of our interiority" (44). Derrida invokes throughout these essays of mourning the possibility of an interiorization of what can never be interiorized, of what is always before and beyond us as the source of our responsibility. This is the "unbearable paradox of fidelity" (159). The look that is "in us" is not ours, as the images within us might seem to be. We look at the dead, who have been reduced to images "in us," and we are looked at by them, but there is no symmetry between these gazes. There is thus a "dissymmetry that can be interior-ized only by exceeding, fracturing, wounding, injuring, traumatizing the interiority that it inhabits or that welcomes it through hospitality, love, or friendship" (160). In other words, "Ghosts: the concept of the other in the same . . . the completely other, dead, living in me" (41–42).

In mourning, we must recognize that the friend is now both only "in us" and already beyond us, in us but totally other, so that nothing we say of or to them can touch them in their infinite alterity. The other who has been reduced to images looks at us, looks "in us," but at an infinite remove. "We are all looked at, I said, and each one singularly, by Louis Marin. He looks at us. *In us*. . . . He is completely other, infinitely other, as he has always been, and death has more than ever entrusted him, given him over, distanced him, in this infinite alterity" (161). The friend must be interiorized, but the singular alterity or "infinite transcendence" that marked our friendship and constituted the very friendship of the friend cannot. "Upon the death of the other we are given to memory, and thus to interiorization, since the other, outside us, is now nothing. And with the dark light of this nothing, we learn that the other resists the closure of our interiorizing memory. . . . death constitutes and makes manifest the limits of a *me* or an *us* who are obliged to harbor something that is greater and other than them; something *outside of them within them*" (*M*, 34). We can thus understand why Derrida in *Memoires for Paul de Man* would say that "the possibility of the impossible" commands "the whole rhetoric of mourning," and why the aporia of mourning dictates that "success fails" and "failure succeeds" (*M*, 34–35). "For this is the law, the law of mourning, and the law of the law, always in mourning, that it would have to fail in order to succeed. In order to succeed, it would well have to *fail*, to fail *well*. . . . And while it is always promised, it will never be assured" (144). The work of mourning is thus not one kind of work among others; it remains, says Derrida, "the name of a problem. For if mourning works, it does so only to dialectize death, a death that Roland Barthes *called* 'undialectical'" (50).

We thus return to the question of responsibility and fidelity, of how to mourn and how to speak in mourning, how to bear the aporia, the impossible choice between two infidelities. "Is the most distressing, or even the most deadly infidelity that of a *possible mourning* which would interiorize within us the image, idol, or ideal of the other who is dead and lives only in us? Or is it that of the impossible mourning, which, leaving the other his alterity, respecting thus his infinite remove, either refuses to take or is incapable of taking the other within oneself, as in the tomb or the vault of some narcissism?" (*M*, 6).

This is the aporia in which we are left at the death of a friend, the aporia in which we are caught when every successful strategy of mourning would well have to fail, an aporia that becomes most palpable at the death of the friend but was already in force well before. For the mourning that follows death had already been prepared and anticipated—and thus had already begun—well before death itself, the anticipation of death coming "to hollow out the living present that precedes it" (151). Indeed, friendship would be but another name for this anticipation, for "that twilight space of what is called mourning: the mourning that follows death but also the mourning that is prepared and that we expect from the very beginning to follow upon the death of those we love. Love or friendship would be nothing other than the passion, the endurance, and the patience of this work" (146). Mourning begins before death, already with friendship—and, in some cases, even before "friendship proper." Derrida invokes both friendship and mourning in relation to Edmond Jabès even before actually meeting him, that is, after having only read him: "There was already in this first reading a certain experience of apophatic silence, of absence, the desert, paths opened up off all the beaten tracks, deported memory—in short, mourning, every impossible mourning. Friendship had thus already come to be reflected in mourning, in the eyes of the poem, even before friendship—I mean before the friendship that later brought us together" (122).

We began by saying that one friend must always go before the other, that one must always die first. For Derrida, this is not just some law of destiny to which we all must succumb but a law of friendship that friends must acknowledge. Derrida begins his text in memory of Jean-Marie Benoist, "To have a friend, to look at him, to follow him with your eyes, to admire him in friendship, is to know in a more intense way, already injured, always insistent, and more and more unforgettable, that one of the two of you will inevitably see the other die" (108). There is "no friendship without this knowledge of finitude," says Derrida in *Mémoires for Paul de Man,* "and everything that we inscribe in the living present of our relation to others already carries, always, the signature of *memoirs-from-beyond-the-grave*" (*M,* 28–29). The aporia of mourning in which we seem to be caught following the death of the friend, at the end of a living relationship, is already there, virtually at work, from the very inception of that friendship. Writing in the wake of Sarah Kofman's death, Derrida explains that a knowledge of her death, of her possible death, filled the very air their friendship breathed: "From the first moment, friends become, as a result of their situation, virtual survivors, actually virtual or virtually actual, which amounts to just about the same thing. Friends know this, and friendship breathes this knowledge, breathes it right up to expiration, right up to the last breath" (171).

We prepare for the death of a friend; we anticipate it; we see ourselves already as survivors, or as having already survived. To have a friend, to call him or her by name and to be called by him or her, is already to know that one of the two of you will go first, that one will be left to speak the name of the other in the other's absence. Again, this is not only the ineluctable law of human finitude but the law of the name. As Derrida has shown in numerous texts, the name is always related to death, to the structural possibility that the one who gives, receives, or bears the name will be absent from it. We can prepare for the death of the friend, anticipate it, repeat or iterate it before it takes place, because "in calling or naming someone while he is alive, we know that his name can survive him and *already survives him*" (*M,* 49); we know that "the name begins during his life to get along without him, speaking and bearing his death each time it is pronounced . . ." (*M,* 49). Mourning thus begins already with the name. "Even before the unqualifiable event called death, interiority (of the other in me, in you, in us) had already begun its work. With the first nomination, it preceded death as another death would have done.

The name alone makes possible the plurality of deaths" (46). Yet another aporia. For while the proper name "alone and by itself forcefully declares the unique disappearance of the unique," it also bespeaks the *possible* death—or deaths—of the one who bears it, saying "death even while the bearer of it is still living." It *says* death, and so lends itself already to the work of mourning, to all the "codes and rites" that work to take away the "terrifying" privilege of the proper name to declare "the singularity of an unqualifiable death" (34). The proper name speaks the singularity of death, and, in speaking, already repeats that singularity, already survives it. "The name races toward death even more quickly than we do," says Derrida in his text remembering Joseph Riddel, "we who naively believe that we bear it. . . . It is in advance the name of a dead person" (130).

In "The Deaths of Roland Barthes," Derrida insists on recalling that "Roland Barthes is the name of someone who can no longer hear or bear it" (45). Indeed, death appears to sever the name from the bearer of it; it is the event or operation that lifts or peels the name off the body that once bore it. But as Derrida recalls some sixteen years after this text on Barthes, in the context of an analysis of Sarah Kofman's last work on the relationship between the book and the body, the corpus and the corpse, this operation severing the name from the body is already at work among the living. The operation "proper to death" happens everywhere a name can be cited or used without or in place of the body. It becomes possible with the very giving of a name, and so happens to us "all the time, especially when we speak, write, and publish" (179). The name is separable from the body, the corpus from the corpse. This is the case when others use or speak our name, either before or after our death, but also when we ourselves use our name. Derrida comments on Michel Servière's work on the signature: "a signature not only signs but speaks to us always of death," of "the possible death of the one who bears the name" (136).

Though many of these claims and propositions about the proper name or signature can be found, as we said, in innumerable early works of Derrida, never have they been put to the test as they are in the texts gathered in this volume. In 1999, for example, Derrida recalls a phrase written some nine years earlier by Jean-François Lyotard in a text that was, in some sense, destined for or addressed to him. He recalls this curious phrase, "there shall be no mourning," one year after the death of Lyotard, in part to show that the very possibility of reading it, not only in 1999 but already in 1990, was determined by the structural possibility that its addressor, as well as—for no one knew who would in fact go first—any of its addressees, and first of all Derrida, would be absent from it. "Readability bears this mourning: a phrase can be readable, it must be able to become readable, up to a certain point, without the reader, he or she, or any other place of reading, occupying the ultimate position of addressee. This mourning provides the first chance and the terrible condition of all reading" (220).

In mourning, the unqualifiable event is repeated; the proper name bespeaks a singular death and yet allows us to speak of that death, to anticipate and prepare for it, to read it. Derrida begins his text on Emmanuel Levinas, "For a long time, for a very long time, I've feared having to say *Adieu* to Emmanuel Levinas" (200). Though the text was clearly written in the emotion immediately following Levinas's death in December of 1995, this opening indicates that certain words must have already been half-formed, that mourning must have already been at work, virtually at work, long before, no doubt as long as there was friendship.

We thus imagine, even before the fact, a world without the friend or without us, a world that will have absorbed either absence. And yet when the event itself comes, the event we thought we knew and had prepared ourselves for, it hits us each time uniquely—like the end of the world. "What is coming to an end, what Louis [Althusser] is taking away with him, is not only something or other that we would have shared at some point or another, in one place or another, but the world itself, a certain origin of the world—his origin, no doubt, but also that of the world in which I lived, in which we lived a unique story" (115). In "each death" there is an end of the world, the phrase "each death" suggesting that the end of the world can come more than once. For Jacques Derrida, it came at least three times in the year 1990 alone. The world, the whole world, is lost, and then, impossibly, the catastrophe is repeated. Speaking after the death of Jean-Marie Benoist, Derrida recalls how "death takes from us not only some particular life within the world . . . but, each time, without limit, someone through whom the world, and first of all our own world, will have opened up in a both finite and infinite—mortally infinite—way" (107). And again in 1990, the same year he spoke of the end of the world in the deaths of Althusser and Benoist, Derrida writes after the death of Max Loreau: "each time it is nothing less than an origin of the world, each time the sole world, the unique world" (95).

In "each death" there is an end of the world, and yet the rhetoric of mourning allows us to speak of this end and multiply it, both to anticipate it and repeat it—with regard not only to one friend, one proper name, but many, one death after another. The "death of the other" is the "first death" (204), as Levinas says, and yet the first death gets repeated. With *each first death* the whole world is lost, and yet with each we are called to reckon our losses.

Each time we mourn, then, we add another name to the series of singular mournings and so commit what may be called a sort of "posthumous infidelity" with regard to the others. Even worse, if friendship is always structured by the possibility that one friend will die before the other, then simply to have friends—more than one—would already be to commit this infidelity. The infidelity that occurs after death will have begun already before it. The singular friendship, the singular mourning, the first mourning, will have already been repeated; posthumous infidelity would thus structure all our friendships from the very beginning.

If our friendships, and thus our mournings, end up being inscribed or iterated in a series relating each unique death to others, then this series would also appear fatally to presage other mournings of its kind. This would be yet another form of infidelity, another way of reckoning, against which Jacques Derrida struggles in each of these texts. Though "each death is unique" (193), as Derrida writes in his text on Deleuze, though each strikes us as the first death, as the end of the world, can we not predict what future mournings will look like for Jacques Derrida, what reserve will be found in them, what texts cited—on death, or force, or absence?

Inasmuch as Jacques Derrida has himself written not just one but several texts of mourning, the betrayal of the unique other, of the friend, appears not only spoken about but enacted, played out. Already in "The Deaths of Roland Barthes," the question of the iteration of death is posed, and it is put to the test in all the texts of mourning that follow. We began by saying that Derrida has tried "each time" to respond to the death of a friend with words fit for that friend, words that inevitably relate life and friendship to death and mourning. But how does one respond to a singular event "each time," and how is one's response compromised if, "each time," it ends up relating life and friendship to death and mourning? How can one mourn the singular event all the while knowing that there have been and probably will be other friends to mourn, other singular events to which to respond?

In his *Politics of Friendship* Derrida explores the question of the number of friends it is good or possible to have, following a line of investigation from the *Nicomachean Ethics,* where Aristotle claims that we can have true friendship with only a few.[9] If friendship is essentially related to mourning, how many friends may we or are we able to mourn? What happens when one friend must "each time" go before the other, when a singular relation with a friend ends up being repeated, put into relation with others, compared and contrasted—in a word, reckoned—with others

9.   See Aristotle, *Nicomachean Ethics,* 1171a ff.

that are, we have to assume, just as unique? What happens when the unique death is taken up into all the codes and rituals of mourning, when the singular event comes to be marked by the designated spaces and times of mourning, when all talk of death comes to be inflected by a prescribed rhetoric? Can there be other words in which to mourn?

Because of the possibility, indeed the ineluctability, of iteration, we should perhaps not assume that we can ever identify with absolute certainty the object of our mourning. For we might think we are mourning one friend when we are in fact mourning another, or think we are mourning a colleague when we are in fact, or in addition, mourning a child, or, as we see in the essay on Barthes, a mother. Or perhaps all our mournings are but iterations of the one death that can never be identified—the first death, the total, undialectical death—so that what is mourned is a singularity that exceeds any proper name, making posthumous infidelity the very work of mourning. Perhaps what we mourn is thus always nothing other than our very ability to identify, our mastery over the other and over death, as we yield to a force that is not ours, a force that always exceeds the rhetoric of mourning.

In "The Deaths of Roland Barthes," the first essay in this collection and the one that, to borrow a word from it, "irradiates" and punctuates all the others, announcing, in a sense, all these other deaths, Derrida analyzes the "metonymic force" that allowed Barthes's analysis of his own mother's death in one of his last works to become meaningful *for us*. This force, he argues, while able to assure "a certain generality to the discourse," that is, while able to make it understandable to us, is also what makes it "poignant to us," striking and piercing for us. Such a force cannot simply be "mistaken for something that facilitates the movement of identification," for "the alterity remains almost intact; that is the condition" (58).

It is this metonymic force of alterity—along with the movement of identification that "almost" immediately inscribes it—that allows what is poignant and striking in each of these deaths of Jacques Derrida to be repeated. And it is this force, along with the moment of reckoning that accompanies it, that, at the end of two decades, allows all these so striking deaths to be put into a series, gathered together not only into a volume but into something like a "generation." In his 1995 text on the death of Gilles Deleuze, Derrida writes: "Each death is unique, of course, and therefore unusual. But what can be said about the unusual when, from Barthes to Althusser, from Foucault to Deleuze, it multiplies, as in a series, all these uncommon ends in the same 'generation'?" (193). Derrida goes on to speak of those of "my 'generation'" who were fortunate enough to share their thought and time with Deleuze. Indeed it seems that Derrida has been in the process of mourning an entire "generation" of French and American intellectuals in philosophy, literature, and literary theory. But can one really speak of mourning a "generation," the singularity of a generation, or would this be yet another way of reckoning and thus betraying all the singularities within it? What is the force of time or language that allows the unique death to become absorbed, evaluated, compared, or reckoned, to become simply part of an epoch or part of what we call—with this "terrible and somewhat misleading word"—a "'generation'"? (193). Derrida's use of quotation marks already puts us on guard, alerting us to his suspicion that it would not be difficult "to show that the times of those who seem to belong to the same epoch, defined in terms of something like a historical frame or social horizon, remain infinitely heterogeneous and, to tell the truth, completely unrelated to one another" (55).

And yet, near the end of a "generation," time appears marked by a different rhythm, as "you reach an age . . . where more and more friends leave you" (108), so that, even if terrible and misleading, this word perhaps speaks a certain truth about the gathering force of memory and mourning. For it is no doubt this multiplication of deaths within a generation, this metonymic force of mourning, that allows us to identify a generation in the first place, and the multiplication of deaths within and across generations that allows us to gather and compare our various responses to death and to identify them as already belonging to a *genre*.

While these texts vary greatly in form, from letters of condolence addressed to family members to eulogies read at the grave site, from words of tribute first published in newspapers in the hours immediately following a death to memorial essays read at colloquia a few or even many months after the death, and while any rigorous analysis of these texts would have to reckon with all the differences in tone, style, audience, and context, these texts are nonetheless part of a recognizable genre, even if there is no single apt term to describe it. Attentive as always to questions of style and genre, Derrida reflects in these essays on the very genre of the eulogy or funeral oration, all the while himself giving orations or eulogies, pronouncing them, working within the codes and tropes of such speech acts and yet referring throughout to what exceeds them. Derrida has thus opted, it seems, to forsake or abandon neither the concept of mourning given to us by psychoanalysis nor the genre of the funeral oration that has been handed down to us in the West from at least the time of Pericles. Eulogizing the singularity of the friend, he has tried to inhabit and inflect both the concept and the genre of mourning differently. He has tried to reinvent, always in public and always in context, that is, always from within, a better politics of mourning.

Near the end of a "generation," then, we have these texts, gathered together, selected by means of certain criteria, already part of a genre. And yet the genre of the eulogy or funeral oration is not one genre among others but the one that, it could be argued, opens up the possibility of a political space to accommodate all the others. Though it is beyond the scope of this introduction, which has focused essentially on the politics *in* or *of* mourning, to show how politics or the political is related to or perhaps even arises *out of* mourning, out of the rites and rituals of mourning, it is important to note that Derrida is not unaware of these larger stakes. In *Aporias* he writes: "In an economic, elliptic, hence dogmatic way, I would say that there is no politics without an organization of the time and space of mourning, without a topolitology of the sepulcher, without an anamnesic and thematic relation to the spirit as ghost, without an open hospitality to the guest as *ghost,* whom one holds, just as he holds us, hostage.[10] In the long essay in this volume devoted to Lyotard, Derrida speaks of Lyotard's own analyses, in *The Differend* and elsewhere, of the political dimensions of the funeral oration. Since Plato's *Menexenus,* or since the funeral oration of Pericles that Plato parodies in this dialogue, politics is related to, or founded on, mourning. In the Athenian context, for example, it is related to a rhetoric of mourning that tries to complete or even foreclose mourning by lifting death up, sublating it in the fulfillment and glory of the "beautiful death."

The genre of the funeral oration is thus more than a powerful genre within an already given social and political context; it constitutes or consolidates the very power of that context, with all the promises and risks this entails. In his essay on Barthes, Derrida says he himself was tempted, out of a kind of fidelity to Barthes, who was a master of the genre of looking at genres, to analyze the genre of funeral tributes and declarations, not necessarily its historical origins but "what in this century has come to replace the funeral oration . . . the corpus of declarations in newspapers, on radio and television . . . the rhetorical constraints, the political perspectives, the exploitations by individuals and groups, the pretexts for taking a stand, for threatening, intimidating, or reconciling" (51). Derrida does not carry out such an analysis in any of these texts. One could, however, on the basis of these texts, ask a number of political, social, or historical questions that Derrida does not, questions not only about the

10.   Jacques Derrida, *Aporias,* trans. Thomas Dutoit (Stanford: Stanford University Press, 1993), 61–62. In *Specters of Marx,* trans. Peggy Kamuf (New York: Routledge, 1994), xix, Derrida speaks of learning to live with ghosts or specters as a *"politics* of memory, inheritance, and generations."

practices of mourning in the West, and particularly in France, but about, for example, the role of the intellectual in French society, or the place of the university in France and the constitution of its members. The fact, for instance, that only one woman—Sarah Kofman—is spoken of here surely tells us something about the educational institutions in France during the twentieth century. The role the United States has played in the intellectual itineraries of several thinkers spoken of here, from de Man to Lyotard to Derrida himself, is also noteworthy. And one is constantly reminded in reading these texts and the biographies appended to them just how much this "generation" has been marked in one way or another by two world wars and by the event named "Auschwitz." There would be much to say as well about the kinds of death gathered here, from deaths in relative old age by "natural causes," to premature deaths from sudden illnesses, to accidents, AIDS, and suicide.

As we have seen, there are numerous dangers inherent in the genre of the funeral oration—not the least of which is precisely that it is a genre. For "the discourse of mourning is more threatened than others, though it should be less, by the generality of the genre" (95). It should be less threatened because it is each time a response to an absolutely unique event, so that any recourse to common usage or convention seems either "intolerable or vain," and silence appears to be "the only rigorous response" (72, 95). And yet, as we have seen, since 1981 Derrida has refused silence, and so has opened himself and his words up to the generality of the genre, to an unavoidable rhetoric of mourning. Even to approach the death of a friend as an example of "impossible mourning" would be to betray the uniqueness of that friend, as one attempts to transfer what is unique and poignant, as Derrida says in his essay on Sarah Kofman, "onto someone else," or worse, "onto some conceptual generality that would not be Sarah, Sarah Kofman herself" (172).

Despite all the dangers of the genre, of genres in general, these texts of mourning enact many of the rhetorical gestures of other eulogies or words of remembrance: in each case, Derrida at once bears witness to a unique, personal relationship with the deceased and pays tribute to their public life and accomplishments, their words and deeds, sometimes even attempting to draw inspiration from the way they approached life and death in word and deed. Derrida is, of course, well aware of both the danger and the necessity of speaking not simply of the dead, of the "dead themselves," but of their works, their deeds, or their signature. In his analysis of a short text written by Sarah Kofman just before her death, Derrida speaks of the repression—the no doubt irrepressible repression—involved in speaking of the works of the deceased rather than the deceased themselves, of the book rather than the body, of the corpus rather than corpse, and yet, following Kofman's analysis, Derrida sees in this tendency not simply a form of repression but an affirmation of life. There is surely a kind of infidelity in the biography or obituary, which tries to encapsulate a life, to reduce the dead to their accomplishments, to a series of dates and places, but Derrida courts this infidelity (as do we in the biographical accounts accompanying these texts), noting dates and places, works and days, not so as to absorb the singularity of the deceased into some literary or philosophical history but so as to mark their unique time and place among us, the only ones they ever had and will ever have. The singularity and punctuality of the date ("In 1930 Levinas . . .") can, of course, be reduced to history, but before such a reduction they are the inscriptions of an event.

Again as a concession to the genre, Derrida cites in every one of these texts the words of the dead—and often at length. But considering all that has been said about interiorization and the status of the other "in us," it would seem that citation is actually being used here as a form of textual interiorization, that the words of the dead are being incorporated not merely to become part of the text, to be "in it," but to act as that point of infinite alterity "within" the text, to act as its law. It would seem that Derrida's "rhetoric of mourning" is borrowing from the schema of interiorization in order to convert citation from a gesture simply dictated by the genre into another consequence of the metonymic force of mourning.

Because there is no first death available to us, no *protos thanatos* to become the sole and incomparable object of our mourning, iteration is unavoidable, the slippage between deaths inevitable, our language for speaking about these deaths repeatable and, thus, open to citation.[11] In "Circumfession" Derrida himself follows the mourning of another, citing words of Augustine in the first person, and in another language, as he mourns the death of his own mother: "Ego silebam et fletum frenabam" [I remained silent and restrained my tears] (*C*, 20). Derrida is himself, at this point, tending to his own dying mother, trying to put into words what

---

11.   In the *Lysis* Socrates objects in the course of a conversation about the nature of friendship that if the friend is always a friend for the sake of something else, then they will be forced to follow the chain of friends back to the "original friend [*prōton philon*],for whose sake all the other things can be said to be friends." This would mean that all those others whom they had cited as friends for the sake of that one friend "may be deceiving us like so many phantoms of it, while that original thing may be the veritable friend [*alēthōs philon*]" (Plato, *Lysis,* trans. W. R. M. Lamb [Cambridge, Mass.: Harvard University Press, 1983], 219c–d).

is to come; he thus turns to Augustine for words about silence and tears to address his own imminent loss. Yet it is not just Augustine's mother's death, or his own mother's, that he seeks to address in this way, but his own. For through the tears he tries to restrain in mourning for his mother he sees, foresees, his own children faced with his own death: "I weep like my own children on the edge of my grave" (*C*, 41). In his own tears, in Augustine's, there are already those of his children—the tears of yet another generation. Throughout this text, citation appears as the vehicle by which Derrida both recalls Augustine's singular mourning for his mother, for her alone, and links this mourning to others, allowing for both singularity and relation, something absolutely unique and yet nonetheless shared.

The interiorization of the friend in mourning, the reduction of that friend to signs and images "in us," is thus paralleled, it seems, by Derrida's use and incorporation of citation in these texts of mourning, as if, in a first moment, such citation would allow Derrida to let the friend speak, to give the one he is mourning the last word. Derrida writes near the beginning of his text for Louis Marin, "Let us begin by letting him speak. Here are a few words, his words, that say something difficult to understand" (143), and he then cites Marin's words on force and the mourning of force. In his text on Levinas, he says, "allow me once again to let Emmanuel Levinas speak, him whose voice I would so much love to hear today when it says that the 'death of the other' is the 'first death,' and that 'I am responsible for the other insofar as he is mortal'" (204).[12]

Is there, then, we might ask, a law of citation to which we must answer and before which we are responsible? What are the responsibilities of citation, of adorning, concealing, or protecting oneself beneath quotation marks? To whom or what are we responsible in mourning? To the friend him- or herself? To his or her words? His or her memory? What is the best way of remaining faithful? In remembering Sarah Kofman, Derrida says he was "tempted to approach Sarah's last text" in order "to make linger, these last words leaving her lips" (175). Are we responsible for endlessly citing or repeating the words of others so as to allow them to live on? Or are we responsible to something else, to the unique gesture that first produced such words and allowed such citations? Do we cite merely to repeat the words of the other, or do we do so in order to enact or reenact an inimitable gesture, a singular way of thinking, a unique manner of speaking? If the latter, then the quotation would in each case

12.   Later in this text Derrida actually stages a brief "conversation" between Blanchot and Levinas by citing Blanchot's words from *The Infinite Conversation* about Levinas—an incorporation or interiorization of an interiorization.

mark a limit, the place where the inimitable gesture of the dead friend becomes inscribed, and thus repeatable, comparable to other gestures, put into a series, perhaps even reckoned as part of a "generation." Each time, citation would mark the beginning of a unique and singular life as well as its brutal interruption.

Now, it is not insignificant that in citing the dead in these texts it is often an explicit reference to death or mourning that Derrida recalls. For in each of these works Derrida mourns not only a friend but a writer or thinker who inevitably had something to say about death or mourning. Hence, Derrida turns in these essays to the deceased's own words about death (Foucault, Deleuze, Levinas), or mourning (Marin, Lyotard, Benoist), or the relationship between death and literature (Althusser, de Man, Jabès, Loreau, Riddel) or photography (Barthes) or painting (Kofman, Servière). Citing the one who is no longer, borrowing from them what they have to say about mourning or death, appears to be a way of bearing witness to the friend so as to say or enact with their own words an Adieu, or rather, an "Adieu"—itself a citation, since it was Emmanuel Levinas, Derrida recalls, who "will have taught [him] to think or to pronounce [this word] otherwise" (200).

Citing works on death and on mourning, Derrida frequently turns here to the last words of the dead, that is, to their final works, those written just before death that speak of death in general or, uncannily, of the anticipated or intimated death of their author. In "The Deaths of Roland Barthes," Derrida writes, just after having cited Barthes on the death of his mother and on his own death: "I could feel a sort of autobiographical acceleration, as if he were saying, 'I feel that I have little time left.' . . . While still living, he wrote a death of Roland Barthes by himself" (52). In "I'm Going to Have to Wander All Alone," Derrida cites a passage in which Deleuze is speaking not only of death but, in some sense, of the very manner of his death (192). Citing the other speaking of death, of their own death, here allows the dead a sort of *survivance,* a kind of living on, not only after their death, their actual death, but even before, as if they were already living on posthumously before their death, as if they had found a way not simply to utter some prophetic intimation of their own death but to enact the impossible speech act from Poe cited at the beginning of *Speech and Phenomenon:* "I am dead."

Yet the question of fidelity and responsibility remains. In a first moment, citation seems to be a way of avoiding the indecency or irresponsibility of speaking simply *of* the dead, *of* them as a subject or object. Whence the possibility of simply citing them, of letting them speak without interference or interruption. But to do only this would be to offer no real recognition or tribute, no genuine gift to the other. Derrida writes in his text for Barthes, reformulating, it seems, one of the aporias of mourning into an aporia of the *rhetoric* of mourning:

> Two infidelities, an impossible choice: on the one hand, not to say anything that comes back to oneself, to one's own voice, to remain silent, or at the very least to let oneself be accompanied or preceded in counterpoint by the friend's voice. Thus, out of zealous devotion or gratitude, out of approbation as well, to be content with *just quoting,* with just accompanying that which more or less directly comes back or returns to the other, to let him speak, to efface oneself in front of and to follow his speech, and to do so right in front of him. But this excess of fidelity would end up saying and exchanging nothing. It returns to death. It points to death, sending death back to death. On the other hand, by *avoiding all quotation,* all identification, all rapprochement even, so that what is addressed to or spoken of Roland Barthes truly comes from the other, from the living friend, one risks making him disappear again, as if one could add more death to death and thus indecently pluralize it. We are left then with having to do and not do both at once, with having to correct one infidelity by the other. From one death, the other: is this the uneasiness that told me to begin with a plural? (45; our emphasis)

By citing the other, by recalling the other's words and then cutting them off, Derrida attempts to negotiate the passage between these two infidelities. The work or labor of mourning would seem to consist in attempting to dialectize, as Roland Barthes said, the undialectical death, and in so doing, to be faithful by means of betrayal. Speaking at a memorial gathering for Jean-François Lyotard in 1999, one year after his death, Derrida again gives voice to the double imperative to let the friend speak, him alone, and yet not leave him alone as he speaks: "A double injunction, then, contradictory and unforgiving. How to leave him alone without abandoning him?" (225).

And so Derrida cites and interrupts the citation, the point of this interruption, the intersection of these two infidelities, being perhaps the point or force that wounds us, that pierces us, the *punctum* or point of singularity that will have organized or given force to the friend's work. It is this point, perhaps, and not their words, that Derrida mourns, so that citing and interrupting the words of the dead is the only way, the only chance, for the *punctum* to make its mark. "I return to this because *punctum* seems to say, to let Barthes himself say, the point of singularity, the traversal of discourse toward the unique, the 'referent' as the irreplaceable other, the one who was and will no longer be" (56).

Everything would thus be interiorized save that which touches us most—that which is most poignant. In *Camera Lucida,* the text in which Barthes develops his theory of the *punctum* and the *studium* in relation to the photographic image, a text written not long after Barthes's mother's death, the photograph that strikes him most, the "Winter Garden Photograph" of his mother as a child, is the one photograph described by Barthes that is not reproduced in the text, that is not framed, cited, or incorporated by it. For it can exist, he says, only for him: a singular photograph, a singular death, a *punctum* that strikes and wounds only him. And yet, as soon as it strikes, as soon as it makes its mark, in words if not in images, the singular death is pluralized, opening up a space and time that can be read and so reckoned with other times and other deaths.

In his analysis of Barthes's book, Derrida calls this photograph that does not appear, that is not incorporated or interiorized into the text, the *punctum* that irradiates the entire field or *studium* of the book. It is beyond every frame, escapes every interiorization, and yet makes possible the series of photographs and the relations that Barthes finds between them. Similarly, in each of the texts of mourning gathered here, there is an interiorization of what cannot be interiorized, a citation punctuated or bordered by that which gives this volume its force of mourning. One might thus think of Derrida's essay on Barthes as not only the first in the series but the *punctum* of the entire collection. As the first of these essays on the deaths of friends and colleagues, it has itself become repeated and pluralized, its themes and claims as well as its gestures and rhetoric, so that the plurality of "deaths" in its title already names the deaths of all these others.

"Each time"—a phrase that we now see both marks a site of iteration and substitution and punctuates a singular time and place—one must speak so as to give voice to the friend's singularity, so as to respond both for and to the alterity that first makes one's response possible. Whence the desire, and the responsibility, to speak not only *of* but *with* or even *to* the dead, the desire to tear the fabric of language that would reduce the dead to the living, the other to the same. Though we must recognize that death has made the friend inaccessible except "in us," that the other whose name I still use can no longer "become a vocation, address, or apostrophe" (46), our desire to speak again *to* the other, to the other uniquely, corresponds nonetheless to a responsibility. Such a responsibility is secretly acknowledged, it appears, by the very genre of the eulogy or funeral oration, where one is allowed to "speak familiarly to the other who keeps silent, calling upon him without detour or mediation, apostrophizing him, even greeting him or confiding in him" (200). Though this may seem to be done merely out of "respect for convention," "simply part of the rhetoric of oration," it also testifies to the need "to traverse speech at the very point where words fail us, since all language that would return to the self, to us, would seem indecent, a reflexive discourse that would end up coming back to the stricken community, to its consolation or its mourning, to what is called, in a confused and terrible expression, 'the work of mourning'" (200). In another concession to the genre, then, Derrida speaks not only *of* but *to* the friend. Always a response to a unique occasion, always occasioned by others and by events that are beyond his control, the eulogy or funeral oration provides Derrida with the occasion to bear witness to the singularity of the friend in the midst of all these iterable codes by means of a unique apostrophe. Even if, within the genre, this apostrophe is always a "supplementary fiction, for it is always the dead in me, always the others standing around the coffin whom I call out to . . . [the] caricatured excess, the overstatement of this rhetoric at least pointed out that we ought not to remain among ourselves. The interactions of the living must be interrupted, the veil must be torn toward the other, the other dead *in us* though other still" (51–52).[13] The eulogy or word of condolence, pronounced always at the limits of life and death, provides the unique occasion to turn to the dead—"in us though other still"—one last time in tribute, in memory, one last time in friendship.

Such a turn to the friend is, in the end, all we have to give. And if this turn is not completely ours, that is why it is a gift. For in turning toward the friend who has died, we turn not as already constituted beings toward someone outside us, or simply inside us as part of our interiority, but toward our law, toward what first forms our very interiority. As Derrida says of Louis Althusser, "he hears me only inside me, inside us (though we are only ever *ourselves* from that place within us where the other, the mortal other, resonates)" (117). It is only through memory and mourning that we become ourselves, indebted even before we can owe anything to ourselves. "Louis Marin is outside and he is looking at me, he himself, and I am an image for him. At this very moment. There where I can

13.   Thus, even when one speaks a final time *to* the dead and not simply *of* them, it is only to the dead *in us* that we speak. Though Derrida says he wishes to say adieu to Levinas *himself,* he knows that he must "call his name, his first name, what he is called at the moment when, if he no longer responds, it is because he is responding in us, from the bottom of our hearts, in us but before us, in us right before us—in calling us, in recalling to us: *à-Dieu.*"

say *cogito, sum,* I know that I am an image for the other and am looked at by the other, even and especially by the mortal other. . . . Louis Marin is looking at me, and it is for this, for him, that I am here this evening. He is my law, the law, and I appear before him, before his word and his gaze" (160).

Yet another danger in mourning, perhaps the greatest, is that when the friend has died, when he or she has become infinitely distanced from us, we tend to forget this law and shy away from this gaze. We have seen how, for Derrida, the mourning that follows death is prepared for and anticipated even before death, how this anticipation is the very time of friendship. But after the event of death, after the singular event, the loss that had been anticipated risks becoming strikingly present, leveled off, in a word, reckoned. We recall what Maurice Blanchot, speaking of Georges Bataille, writes near the very end of *Friendship,* an exemplary text of mourning and of friendship. While it might seem that in death the friend becomes truly other, even more than they were in life, Blanchot seems to suggest the opposite, for "when the event itself comes, it brings this change: not the deepening of the separation but its erasure; not the widening of the caesura but its leveling out and the dissipation of the void between us where formerly there developed the frankness of a relation without history."[14]

The drama, it seems, is not so much that we lose the friend after death but that we can no longer lose them; they who were once so distant become all too close, too close because now only within us—in us as a part of us and of history and no longer as the singularity that called us out of ourselves and first made us responsible before them. What Blanchot seems to suggest is that the apostrophe becomes more and more effaced as the friend becomes absorbed by history, their name put alongside others in a series, compared and analyzed, in short, reckoned—gathered together in a volume. Since we can no longer turn toward them, no longer say "Adieu" to them in an apostrophe, they become simply present to us, no longer our friend but just another name in the cemetery, or just another figure in the pantheon of French and American intellectuals of the past few decades.

By gathering these texts of mourning into a volume, by reading, analyzing, even dissecting them as we have done here, we inevitably avert our gazes from the dead to Derrida's words about them, avoiding the corpse in order to learn from the corpus. And yet what else can we

14.   Maurice Blanchot, *Friendship,* trans. Elizabeth Rottenberg (Stanford: Stanford University Press, 1997), 292.

do? In a special issue of a journal dedicated to the memory of Sarah Kofman, Derrida recalls Kofman's comments on Rembrandt's painting *The Anatomy Lesson* in order to describe the very situation in which he and the others participating in the memorial issue have found themselves. Like the doctors attending the anatomy lesson, they are looking at books rather than the body, "as if, by reading, by observing the signs on the drawn sheet of paper, they were trying to forget, repress, deny, or conjure away death—and the anxiety before death" (176). This, it seems, is the risk the living must always run. Since 1981 Derrida has run it numerous times, and from the very first words of the very first text. Indeed the "indecent" and somewhat "violent" title "The Deaths of Roland Barthes" already seemed to suggest that Derrida was "resisting the unique," trying to avoid, deny, or efface Barthes's unique death in the plural; but "how do we speak otherwise and without taking this risk? Without pluralizing the unique or generalizing what is most irreplaceable in it?" (58–59).

How else do we speak and how else do we let the dead speak? At the death of a friend, we feel it is almost indecent to speak, and yet the substitution of the name for the body, of the corpus for the corpse, appears to be the only chance the dead have left. That is why Derrida so often cites the dead in these texts and, near the end of so many of them, turns to the dead for a final word. While the bodies of these friends and thinkers have been spirited away, their bodies of work remain; they remain with us, though it is not certain that we understand or can ever completely understand them, that is, interiorize them. Just as, for Derrida, those whom he calls "friends" remain in some way "forever unknown and infinitely secret" (225), just as the debt that binds him to them is "in some sense incalculable" (224), so the works of these friends remain unknown and our debt to them incalculable, undecided, open to a future. Because Derrida always recognizes not only the systematicity and coherence of a corpus but its openness, its unpredictability, its ability to hold something in reserve or surprise for us, one of the ways he pays tribute to a work is by bearing witness not just to what it has taught us but to the questions it has opened up and left us. Derrida concludes his text on Foucault and his *History of Madness:* "What we can and must try to do in such a situation is to pay tribute to a work this great and this uncertain by means of a question that it itself raises, by means of a question that it carries within itself, that it keeps in reserve in its unlimited potential, one of the questions that can thus be deciphered within it, a question that keeps it in suspense, holding its breath—and, thus, keeps it alive" (88). The question keeps the text open, keeps it alive, assures it a future, or at least opens it toward the future, so long as we are ready and willing to take it up, patient enough to read and reread it. "In the end this is the question Marin leaves us. It is with this question that he leaves us, like rich and powerless heirs, that is, both provided for and at a loss" (144). We are the heirs of questions, Derrida suggests, responsible for and before them; only by remembering them, by returning to them, are we to have a future. Speaking "in memory" of Paul de Man, Derrida thus promises to "speak of the future, of what is bequeathed and promised to us by the work of Paul de Man" (*M,* 19). Hence Derrida's insistence in so many of these texts that we go back and reread what we have already read, take up again what has been left us. He writes of Max Loreau: "I am rereading him right now in wonder, better no doubt than ever before. I would like to quote everything, read or reread everything aloud. Everyone can— everyone should—do this" (99). "For me everything still remains to come and to be understood" (170), says Derrida of Sarah Kofman's work after her death. Derrida thus reads and rereads, analyzes and questions, and then often ends by citing the words of his friend one final time. He says at the end of his eulogy of Althusser, "I wish now to turn it over to him, to let him speak. For another last word, once again his" (118). Again in conformity with the genre, Derrida recalls the words of the deceased in an attempt to hear them or bring them back to speak to us one last time. And in each case he asks whether it is politic to be doing this, whether he is acting with tact or in good taste, whether he is being faithful to the friendship he mourns.

In each of these texts of mourning, Derrida begins by saying that he is at a loss, that he cannot find the words. We have seen how "this being at a loss also has to do with a duty: to let the friend speak, to turn speech over to him, his speech, and especially not to take it from him, not to take it in his place—no offense seems worse at the death of a friend" (95). And yet, as we have also seen, this duty is countered by another, the duty to pay tribute to the friend in one's own words, to give something back, even when speaking in such circumstances is almost indecent, in bad taste. Thus Derrida speaks, for in speaking, in giving an account, in reckoning with the dead, and with the rhetoric of mourning, that which exceeds the account, the apostrophe that refuses to be absorbed by any reckoning, by any of the rites of mourning, is given the chance to come on the scene for an impossible performative. Such is the duty of the friend, a duty whose call must always be met, and yet one the friend must never get used to. Derrida writes in his essay devoted to Jean-Marie Benoist: "One should not develop a taste for mourning, and yet mourn we *must.* We *must,* but we must not like it—mourning, that is, mourning *itself,* if such a thing exists" (110).

One must respond even when one does not have the heart or is at a loss, lacking the words; one must speak, even reckon, so as to combat all the forces that work to efface or conceal not just the names on the tombstones but the apostrophe of mourning. Derrida's oeuvre or corpus, assuming that it can be identified as such and that it is singular, has become marked throughout by these performatives, marked by proper names that recall the unique, many uniques, and that give to this oeuvre a certain temporality and force of mourning it did not and could not have had years ago. Like the photograph, which, as Roland Barthes says in *Camera Lucida*, "is literally an emanation of the referent," its unique force the result of being not a representation of the referent but a record of its having been there "on that day," an imprint of its very light on the day of reckoning, this volume is filled to the point of being consumed by the light of these extinguished luminaries.[15] And this is perhaps its force, its force of mourning, a force that "gathers" only by dispersing more and more of the Pleiades into the night, by interiorizing and recalling a singular incandescence that no volume and no memory can contain.

Each time Derrida is faced with having to speak in mourning, one imagines him saying to himself with words that resemble those of another, "A reckoning? No, no reckonings. Never again."[16] And yet, each time, he will have reckoned, and reckoned with what is always beyond all reckoning, eliciting in so many of us who remain to read him an incalculable gratitude.

---

15.   Roland Barthes, *Camera Lucida: Reflections on Photography,* trans. Richard Howard (New York: Hill and Wang, 1981), 80–82.

16.   See Maurice Blanchot, *The Madness of the Day,* trans. Lydia Davis (Barrytown, N.Y.: Station Hill Press, 1981), 18.

CHAPTER I

ROLAND BARTHES

NOVEMBER 12, 1915—MARCH 26, 1980

Acclaimed literary critic and essayist Roland Barthes was born in Cherbourg, into what he described as a "bourgeois family," to a Protestant mother, Henriette Binger, and a Catholic father, Louis Barthes. Barthes was scarcely a year old when his father, a naval lieutenant, died in combat in the North Sea. Much of Barthes's childhood was spent in Bayonne, in the southwest of France, until he moved to Paris in 1924, where his mother earned a modest living as a bookbinder. From 1930 to 1934 Barthes attended the Lycées Montaigne and Louis-le-Grand, obtaining two baccalaureates. He then studied classics and French literature at the University of Paris, Sorbonne, and founded the Groupe de théâtre antique.

Throughout his life Barthes suffered bouts of ill health, the most devastating being an illness in his left lung that first began in 1934 and would affect the next ten years of his life, dashing his hopes of ever attending the Ecole Normale Supérieure. In 1937 he was exempted from military service after contracting tuberculosis. Despite his poor health, Barthes visited Hungary and Greece before starting to teach at the lycée of Biarritz in 1939.

He eventually obtained a *licence de lettres classiques* in 1939 and a *diplôme d'études supérieures* (based on his work on Greek tragedy) from the Sorbonne in 1941. From 1940 to 1941 he taught intermittently at the Lycées Voltaire and Carnot in Paris. A relapse of his pulmonary tuberculosis in 1942 caused him to enter the Sanatorium Saint Hilaire in the Isère region. He spent the next five years in and out of various sanatoriums and convalescing in Paris. During these years he read Michelet voraciously, developed an interest in existentialism, and wrote for Camus's journal, *Combat*. Due to his ill health, the future professor at the Collège de France and renowned expert in semiology was never able to take the *agrégation* exam and never held a degree higher than a *certificat de licence* in grammar and philology (obtained in 1943).[1]

With improved health, Barthes taught French at the Institut Français in Bucharest, Romania (1948), and at the University of Alexandria in Egypt (1949–50), before returning to France. Between 1952 and 1954 he wrote a regular column for *Les lettres nouvelles* and cofounded a radical journal, *Théâtre populaire*. From 1952 to 1959 he worked at the Centre National de la Recherche Scientifique, doing research in lexicology and sociology. His first book, *Writing Degree Zero*, appeared in 1953, followed by *Michelet* (1954) and *Mythologies* (1957), all of which displayed innovative uses of Saussurean structural linguistics.

In 1960 he entered the Ecole Pratique des Hautes Etudes, where, in 1962, he became director of studies in the "sociology of signs, symbols, and representations." A year after the publication of his controversial *On Racine* (1963), Raymond Picard, a professor at the Sorbonne and editor of the Pléiade edition of Racine's works, published a pamphlet criticizing Barthes. The ensuing "war of the critics" (Barthes responded in *Criticism and Truth* in 1966) had the unintended result of increasing Barthes's burgeoning reputation.

In the early 1960s Barthes befriended members of the journal *Tel Quel* (to which he also often contributed), in particular Philippe Sollers and Julia Kristeva (who became his student in 1965). In 1966 he visited Japan for the first time and attended the famous conference at Johns Hopkins

1.   Geoffrey Bennington offers the following explanation of the *agrégation:* "The *agrégation* is a competitive examination that qualifies successful candidates for higher teaching posts. Success in this examination guarantees the candidate a state job for life, and it is consequently highly prized. A first stage of the examination consists in written papers; those achieving a high enough mark in these move on to the oral examination at which the final results are decided" (Geoffrey Bennington and Jacques Derrida, *Jacques Derrida,* trans. Geoffrey Bennington [Chicago: University of Chicago Press, 1993], 329).

in Baltimore along with a number of other leading French intellectuals, including Jacques Derrida. From 1969 to 1970 Barthes lectured at the Mohamed V University of Rabat in Morocco and later taught rhetoric at the University of Geneva.

His famous essay "The Death of the Author" appeared in 1968, around the same time he began criticizing structuralism in his seminars. In the early 1970s Barthes published a string of innovative books: *S/Z* (1970; a reading of Balzac's novella "Sarrasine"), *Empire of Signs* (1970), *Sade/Fourier/Loyola* (1971), *New Critical Essays* (1972), and *The Pleasure of the Text* (1973). His interest in painting, in particular Giuseppe Arcimboldo, Erté, and Cy Twombly, also dates from the same period. In 1972 Barthes met the young film director André Téchiné, who would become a lifelong friend. (Barthes played a minor role, as William Thackeray, in Téchiné's *Les soeurs Brontë* [1978]). In 1974 Barthes accompanied Sollers and Kristeva on their trip to China and became a champion of the *nouveau roman,* especially the work of Robbe-Grillet and Sollers (Barthes's *Sollers, Writer* appeared in 1979).

The 1970s saw Barthes's increasing rise to prominence with the publication of an "autobiography," *Roland Barthes by Roland Barthes* (1975), after which he made several radio and television appearances. Barthes was then appointed to the chair of "literary semiology" at the Collège de France (his inaugural lecture, delivered in January 1977, was later published as *Leçon*). He conducted a number of important radio interviews during this time with Bernard-Henri Lévy and Jean-Marie Benoist and, from 1978 to 1979, contributed a regular column to *Le nouvel observateur. A Lover's Discourse,* published in 1977, became a best-seller, and Barthes appeared on Bernard Pivot's popular television show *Apostrophe.* In 1978 a colloquium was devoted to Barthes's work at Cerisy-la-Salle (at that time, an honor usually bestowed only upon the deceased).

The death of Barthes's mother on October 25, 1977 was a devastating blow from which Barthes, according to his own account, never fully recovered. His last book, *Camera Lucida,* written partly in memory of his mother, was published in 1980. On February 25, 1980, after leaving a luncheon organized by Jack Lang for the presidential candidate François Mitterand, Barthes was hit by a truck while crossing the rue des Ecoles near the Collège de France. He was taken to the Salpêtrière Hospital where he was treated for trauma and later developed severe pulmonary complications. Already handicapped by chronic respiratory problems, Barthes died on the afternoon of March 26, 1980.

How to reconcile this plural? How to concede, grant, or accord it? And to whom? How to make it agree or bring it into accord? And with whom?[1] And such questions must also be heard with an ear to music. With a confident obedience, with a certain abandon that I feel here in it, the plural seems to follow: an order, after the beginning of an inaudible sentence, like an interrupted silence. It follows an order and, notice, it even obeys; it lets itself be dictated. It asks (for) itself. And as for myself, at the very moment I allowed myself to order a plural for these deaths, I too had to give myself over to the law of the name, the law of numbers.[2] No objection could resist it, not even the modesty immediately following an uncompromising and punctual decision, a decision that takes place in the almost no time of a (camera's) click: it will have been like this, uniquely, once and for all. And yet I can scarcely bear the apparition of a title in this place. The proper name would have sufficed, for it alone and by itself says death, all deaths in one. It says death even while the bearer of it is still living. While so many codes and rites work to take away this privilege, because it is so terrifying, the proper name alone and by itself forcefully declares the unique disappearance of the unique—I mean the singularity of an unqualifiable death (and this word "unqualifiable" already resonates like a quotation from one of Roland Barthes's texts I will reread later). Death inscribes itself right in the name, but *so as* immediately to disperse itself there, so as to insinuate a strange syntax—in the name of only one to answer (as) many.

●

I do not yet know, and in the end it really does not matter, if I will be able to make it clear why I must leave these thoughts for Roland

Reprinted, with changes, from "The Deaths of Roland Barthes," translated by Pascale-Anne Brault and Michael Naas, in *Continental Philosophy* 1 (1987): 259–96. Republished in *Philosophy and Non-Philosophy since Merleau-Ponty,* edited by Hugh J. Silverman (Evanston, Ill.: Northwestern University Press, 1997), 259–96. Copyright © 1988 by Hugh J. Silverman. Northwestern University Press edition published 1997 by arrangement with Hugh J. Silverman. All rights reserved. First French publication, "Les morts de Roland Barthes," *Poétique* 47 (September 1981): 269–92. Republished in *Psyché,* by Jacques Derrida (Paris: Galilée, 1987), 273–304.

1. Derrida is working here with several different meanings of the verb *accorder:* to bring into harmony or accord; to concede, grant, admit, or avow; to put in grammatical agreement; to tune.—*Trans.*

2. *La loi du nom* (the law of the name) suggests *la loi du nombre* (the law of numbers, the rule of the majority).—*Trans.*

Barthes fragmentary, or why I value them for their incompleteness even more than for their fragmentation, more for their pronounced incompleteness, for their punctuated yet open interruption, without even the authoritative edge of an aphorism. These little stones, thoughtfully placed, only one each time, on the edge of a name as the promise of return.

●

These thoughts are *for him,* for Roland Barthes, meaning that I think of him and about him, not only of or about his work. "For him" also suggests that I would like to dedicate these thoughts to him, give them to him, and destine them for him. Yet they will no longer reach him, and this must be the starting point of my reflection; they can no longer reach him, reach all the way to him, assuming they ever could have while he was still living. So where do they go? To whom and for whom? Only for him in me? In you? In us? For these are not the same thing, already so many different instances, and as soon as he is in another the other is no longer the same, I mean the same as himself. And yet Barthes himself is no longer there. We must hold fast to this evidence, to its excessive clarity, and continually return to it as if to the simplest thing, to that alone which, while withdrawing into the impossible, still leaves us to think and gives us occasion for thought.

●

(No) more light, leaving something to be thought and desired.[3] To know or rather to accept that which leaves something to be desired, to love it from an invisible source of clarity. From where did the singular clarity of Barthes come? From where did it come *to him,* since he too had to receive it? Without simplifying anything, without doing violence to either the fold or the reserve, it always *emanated* from a certain point that yet was not a point, remaining invisible in its own way, a point that I cannot locate—and of which I would like, if not to speak, at least to give an idea of what it remains for me.

---

3.   *Plus de* can mean both "more" and "no more." This undecidability is discussed by Alan Bass in a translator's note in Derrida's *Margins of Philosophy* (Chicago: University of Chicago Press, 1982), 219.—*Trans.*

•

To keep alive, within oneself: is this the best sign of fidelity? Uncertain whether I was in fact going to what is most living, I just read two of his books I had never read before. I thus secluded myself on this island as if to convince myself that nothing had been finalized or had come to an end. And so I believed this, and each book told me what to think of this belief. I had, for quite different reasons, postponed reading these two books, the first and the last. First, *Writing Degree Zero:* I understood better its force and necessity beyond all that had previously turned me away from it, and it was not only because of the capital letters, the connotations, the rhetoric, and all the signs of an era from which I had then thought I was *taking leave* [*sortir*] and from which it seemed necessary to take and rescue [*sortir*] writing. But in this book of 1953, as in those of Blanchot to which he often refers us, the movement that I awkwardly and mistakenly call the taking leave or the exit [*la sortie*] is underway. And second, *Camera Lucida,* whose time and tempo accompanied his death as no other book, I believe, has ever kept watch over its author.

•

For a first and a last book, *Writing Degree Zero* and *Camera Lucida* are fortunate titles. A terrible fortune, vacillating terribly between chance and predestination. I like to think of Roland Barthes now, as I endure this sadness, that which is mine today and that which I always thought I felt in him, a sadness that was cheerful yet weary, desperate, lonely, refined, cultivated, epicurean, so incredulous in the end, always letting go without clinging, endless, fundamental and yet disappointed with the essential. I like to think of him in spite of the sadness as someone who never renounced any pleasures [*jouissance*] but, so to speak, treated himself to them all. And I feel certain—as families in mourning naively say—that he would have liked this thought. Or to put it differently, the image of the I of Barthes would have liked this thought, the image of the I of Barthes that Barthes inscribed in me, though neither he nor I is completely in it. I tell myself now that this image likes this thought in me, that it rejoices in it here and now, that it smiles at me. Ever since reading *Camera Lucida,* Roland Barthes's mother, whom I never knew, smiles at me at this thought, as at everything she breathes life into and revives with pleasure. She smiles at him and thus in me since, let's say, the Winter Garden Photograph, since the radiant invisibility of a look that he describes to us only as clear, so clear.

•

For the first time, then, I read the first and last Barthes, with the welcomed naïveté of a desire, *as if* by reading the first and last without stopping, back to back, as a single volume with which I would have secluded myself on an island, I were finally going to see and know everything. Life was going to continue (there was still so much to read), but a history was perhaps going to come together, a history bound to itself, History having become Nature through this collection, *as if* . . .

•

I just capitalized Nature and History. He used to do it almost all the time. He did it frequently in *Writing Degree Zero,* and from the very beginning: "No one can without formalities pretend to insert his freedom as a writer into the resistant medium of language because, behind the latter, the whole of History stands unified and complete in the manner of a Natural Order."[4] And again in *Camera Lucida:* "this couple who I know loved each other, I realize: it is love-as-treasure that is going to disappear forever; for once I am gone, no one will any longer be able to testify to this: nothing will remain but an indifferent Nature. This is a laceration so intense, so intolerable, that, alone against his century, Michelet conceived of History as love's Protest."[5] These capital letters that I myself used out of mimetism, he too played with, in order to mime and, already, to quote. They are quotation marks ("this is how you say"), which, far from indicating an hypostatization, actually lift up and lighten, expressing disillusionment and incredulity. I believe, in the end, that he did not believe in this opposition (Nature/History), or in any others. He would use them only for the time of a passage. Later, I would like to show that the concepts that seemed the most squarely opposed, or opposable, were put in play by him, the one *for* the other, in a metonymic composition. This light way of mobilizing concepts by playing them against one another could frustrate a certain logic while at the same time resisting it with the greatest force, the greatest force of play.

4.   Roland Barthes, *Writing Degree Zero,* trans. Annette Lavers and Colin Smith (New York: Hill and Wang, 1983), 9–10 (hereafter abbreviated as *WDZ*).

5.   Roland Barthes, *Camera Lucida: Reflections on Photography,* trans. Richard Howard (New York: Hill and Wang, 1981), 94 (hereafter abbreviated as *CL*). The French title is *La chambre claire* (Paris: Seuil, 1980).

•

As if: I read these two books *one after the other,* as if the negative of an idiom were finally going to appear and develop before my eyes, as if the pace, step, style, timbre, tone, and gestures of Roland Barthes—so many obscurely familiar signatures, already recognizable among all others—were all of a sudden going to yield their secret to me as one more secret hidden behind the others (and I call *secret* not only what is intimate but a certain way of doing things: the inimitable); I read these two books as if the unique trait were all of a sudden going to appear in full light.[6] And yet I was so grateful for what he said about the "unary photograph," which works naturally against itself as soon as it negates the "poignant" in the "studied," the *punctum* in the *studium.* I was dreaming: as if the point of singularity, even before becoming a line, though continuously asserting itself from the first book right up to that which in the last book was its interruption, resisting in different ways, though resisting nonetheless, the mutations, upheavals, or displacements of terrain, the diversity of objects, of corpora and contexts, as if the insistence of the invariable were finally going to be revealed to me as it is in itself—and in something like a detail. Yes, it was from a detail that I asked for the ecstasy of revelation, the instantaneous access to Roland Barthes (to him and him alone), a free and easy access requiring no labor. I was expecting this access to be provided by a detail, at once very visible and hidden (too obvious), rather than by the great themes, subjects, theories, or strategies of writing that, for a quarter of a century, I thought I knew and could easily recognize throughout the various "periods" of Roland Barthes (what he called "phases" and "genres" in *Roland Barthes by Roland Barthes*). I was searching *like him,* as him, for in the situation in which I have been writing since his death, a certain mimetism is at once a duty (to take him into oneself, to identify with him in order to let him speak within oneself, to make him present and faithfully to represent him) and the worst of temptations, the most indecent and most murderous. The gift *and* the revocation of the gift, just try to choose. Like him, I was looking for the *freshness* of a reading in relation to detail. His texts are familiar to me but I don't yet know them—that is my certainty—and this is true of all writing that matters to me. This word "freshness" is his and it plays an essential role in the axiomatics of *Writing Degree Zero.* The interest in detail was also his. Benjamin saw in the analytic enlargement of the fragment or minute signifier a point of intersection between the era of psychoanalysis

---

6. The word *trait* can be heard here and in what follows in several different senses: as line, trace, feature, reference, draught, or even musical passage.—*Trans.*

and that of technical reproduction, in cinematography, photography, and so on. (Moving through, extending beyond, and exploiting the resources of phenomenological *as well as* structural analysis, Benjamin's essay[7] and Barthes's last book could very well be the two most significant texts on the so-called question of the Referent in the modern technological age.) The word *punctum,* moreover, translates, in *Camera Lucida,* one meaning of the word "detail": a point of singularity that punctures the surface of the reproduction—and even the production—of analogies, likenesses, and codes. It pierces, strikes me, wounds me, bruises me, and, first of all, seems to concern only me. Its very definition is that it addresses itself to me. The absolute singularity of the other addresses itself to me, the Referent that, in its very image, I can no longer suspend, even though its "presence" forever escapes me, having already receded into the past. (That is why the word "Referent" could be a problem if it were not reformed by the context.) This solitude, which rends the fabric of the same, the networks or ruses of economy, addresses itself to me. But it is always the singularity of the other insofar as it comes to me without being directed towards me, without being present to me; and the other can even be "me," me having been or having had to be, me already dead in the future anterior and past anterior of my photograph. And, I would add, in my name. Although it seems, as always, only lightly marked, this range of the dative or accusative that addresses to *me* or destines for *me* the *punctum* is, I think, essential to the very category of the *punctum,* at least as it is put to work in *Camera Lucida.* If we were to bring together two different aspects or exposures of the same concept, then it would appear that the *punctum* aims at *me* at the instant and place where I aim at it; it is thus that the punctuated photograph pricks me, points me. On its minute surface, the same point divides of itself: this double punctuation disorganizes right from the start both the unary and the desire that is ordered in it. First exposure: "It is this element that rises from the scene, shoots out of it like an arrow, and pierces me. A Latin word exists to designate this wound, this prick, this mark made by a pointed instrument: the word suits me all the better in that . . ." (*CL,* 26). (This is the form of what I was looking for, something that *suits him,* that concerns only him; as always, he claims to be looking for what comes *to him* and suits him, what agrees with him and fits him like a garment; and even if it is a ready-made garment, and only in fashion for a certain time, it must conform to the inimitable *habitus* of a unique body; thus to choose one's words, whether new or very old, from the storeroom

7.   Walter Benjamin, "The Work of Art in the Age of Mechanical Reproduction," in *Illuminations,* trans. Harry Zohn (New York: Schocken Books, 1969), 217–51.

of languages, as one picks out a garment, taking everything into account: the season, fashion, place, fabric, shade, and cut.) "The word suits me all the better in that it also refers to the notion of punctuation, and because the photographs I am speaking of are in effect punctuated, sometimes even speckled with these sensitive points; precisely, these marks, these wounds are so many *points*. This second element that will disturb the *studium* I shall therefore call *punctum;* for *punctum* is also: sting, speck, cut, little hole—and also a cast of the dice. A photograph's *punctum* is that accident that pricks me, points me (but also bruises me, is poignant to me)" (*CL,* 26–27). This parenthesis does not enclose an incidental or secondary thought: as it often does, it lowers the voice—as in an *aside*—out of a sense of modesty. And elsewhere, several pages later, *another exposure.* "Having thus reviewed the *docile interests* that certain photographs awaken in me, I deduced that the *studium,* in so far as it is not traversed, lashed, striped by a detail (*punctum*) that attracts or distresses me, engenders a very widespread type of photograph (the most widespread in the world), which we might call the *unary photograph*" (*CL,* 40).

•

His *manner,* the way in which he displays, plays with, and interprets the pair *studium/punctum,* all the while explaining what he is doing by giving us his *notes*—in all of this we will later hear the music. This manner is unmistakably his. He makes the opposition *studium/punctum,* along with the apparent "versus" of the slash, appear slowly and cautiously in a new context, without which, it seems, they would have had no chance of appearing. He gives to them or he welcomes this chance. The interpretation can at first appear somewhat artificial, ingenuous, elegant perhaps, but specious, for example, in the passage from the "point" to the "pointing me" [*me poindre*] to the "poignant," but little by little it imposes its necessity without concealing the artifact under some putative nature. It demonstrates its rigor throughout the book, and this rigor becomes indistinguishable from its productivity, from its performative fecundity. He makes it *yield* the greatest amount of meaning, of descriptive or analytic power (phenomenological, structural, and beyond). The rigor is never rigid. In fact, the supple is a category that I take to be indispensable to any description of Barthes's manners. This virtue of suppleness is practiced without the least trace of either labor or labor's effacement. He never did without it, whether in theorization, writing strategies, or social intercourse, and it can even be read in the graphics of his writing, which I read as the extreme refinement of the civility he locates, in *Camera Lucida* and while speaking of his mother, at the limits of the moral and even above it. It is a suppleness that is at once *liée,* linked, and *déliée,* unlinked, flowing, shrewd, as one says of writing or of the mind. In the liaison as well as in the undoing of the liaison, it never excludes accuracy, what is just right [*justesse*]—or justice; it must have secretly served him, I imagine, even in the impossible choices. The conceptual rigor of an artifact remains supple and playful here, and it lasts the time of a book; it will be useful to others but it suits perfectly only the one who signs it, like an instrument that can't be lent to anyone, like the unique history of an instrument. For above all, and in the first place, this apparent opposition (*studium/punctum*) does not forbid but, on the contrary, facilitates a certain *composition* between the two concepts. What is to be heard in "composition"? Two things that compose together. First, separated by an insuperable limit, the two concepts compromise with one another. They compose together, the one *with* the other, and we will later recognize in this a *metonymic* operation; the "subtle beyond" of the *punctum,* the uncoded beyond, composes with the "always coded" of the *studium* (*CL,* 59, 51). It belongs to it without belonging to it and is unlocatable within it; it is never inscribed in the homogeneous objectivity of the framed space but instead inhabits or, rather, haunts it: "it is an addition [*supplément*]: it is what I add to the photograph and *what is none the less already there*" (*CL,* 55). We are prey to the ghostly power of the supplement; it is this unlocatable site that gives rise to the *specter.* "The *Spectator* is ourselves, all of us who glance through collections of photographs—in magazines and newspapers, in books, albums, archives. . . . And the person or thing photographed is the target, the referent, a kind of little simulacrum, any *eidolon* emitted by the object, which I should like to call the *Spectrum* of the Photograph, because this word retains, through its root, a relation to 'spectacle' and adds to it that rather terrible thing that is there in every photograph: the return of the dead" (*CL,* 9). As soon as the *punctum* ceases to oppose the *studium,* all the while remaining heterogeneous to it, as soon as we can no longer distinguish here between two places, contents, or things, it is not entirely subjugated to a concept, if by "concept" we mean a predicative determination that is distinct and opposable. This concept of a ghost is as scarcely graspable in its self [*en personne*] as the ghost of a concept. Neither life nor death, but the haunting of the one by the other. The "versus" of the conceptual opposition is as unsubstantial as a camera's click. "*Life/Death:* the paradigm is reduced to a simple click, the one separating the initial pose from the final print" (*CL,* 92). Ghosts: the concept of the other in the same, the *punctum* in the *studium*, the completely other, dead, living in me. This concept of the photograph *photographs* every conceptual opposition; it captures a relationship of haunting that is perhaps constitutive of every "logic."

•

I was thinking of a second meaning of *composition*. In the ghostly opposition of two concepts, in the pair S/P, *studium/punctum*, the composition is also the music. One could open here a long chapter on Barthes as musician. In a note, one would begin by locating a certain analogy between the two heterogeneous elements S and P. Since this relation is no longer one of simple exclusion, since the punctual supplement parasites the haunted space of the *studium*, one would discretely suggest, parenthetically, that the *punctum* gives rhythm to the *studium*, that it "scans" it. "The second element will break (or scan) the *studium*. This time it is not I who seek it out (as I invest the field of the *studium* with my sovereign consciousness), it is this element that rises from the scene, shoots out of it like an arrow, and pierces me. A Latin word exists . . . *punctum*" (*CL,* 26). With the relationship to scansion already stressed, music returns, from some other place, at the bottom of the same page. Music and, more precisely, composition: the analogy of the classical sonata. As he often does, Barthes is in the process of describing his way of proceeding, of giving us an account of what he is doing while he is doing it (what I earlier called his notes). He does so with a certain cadence, progressively, according to the tempo, in the classical sense of tempo; he marks the various stages (elsewhere he emphasizes in order to stress and, perhaps, to play point counter point, or point counter study: "*at this point in my investigation*" [*CL,* 55]). In short, he is going to let us hear, in an ambiguous movement of humility and defiance, that he will not treat the pair of concepts S and P as essences coming from outside the text in the process of being written, essences that would then lend themselves to some general philosophical signification. They carry the truth only within an irreplaceable musical composition. They are motifs. If one wishes to transpose them elsewhere, and this is possible, useful, and even necessary, one must proceed analogically, though the operation will not be successful unless the other opus, the other system of composition, itself also carries these motifs in an original and irreplaceable way. Hence: "Having thus distinguished two themes in Photography (for in general the photographs I liked were constructed in the manner of a classical sonata), I could occupy myself with one after the other" (*CL,* 27).

•

It would be necessary to return to the "scansion" of the *studium* by a *punctum* that is not opposed to it even though it remains completely other, a *punctum* that comes to stand in or double for it, link up to it, and compose with it. I am thinking of a musical composition in counterpoint, of all the sophisticated forms of counterpoint and polyphony, of the fugue.

•

The Winter Garden Photograph: the invisible *punctum* of the book. It does not belong to the corpus of photographs he exhibits, to the series of examples he displays and analyzes. Yet it irradiates the entire book. A sort of radiant serenity comes from his mother's eyes, whose brightness or clarity he describes, though we never see. The radiance composes with the wound that signs the book, with an invisible *punctum*. *At this point,* he is no longer speaking of light or of photography; he is seeing to something else, the voice of the other, the accompaniment, the song, the accord, the "last music": "Or again (for I am trying to express this truth) the Winter Garden Photograph was for me like the last music Schumann wrote before collapsing, that first *Gesang der Frühe* that accords with both my mother's being and my grief at her death; I could not express this accord except by an infinite series of adjectives" (*CL,* 70). And elsewhere: "In a sense I never 'spoke' to her, never 'discoursed' in her presence, for her; we supposed, without saying anything of the kind to each other, that the frivolous insignificance of language, the suspension of images must be the very space of love, its music. Ultimately I experienced her, strong as she had been, my inner Law, as my feminine child" (*CL,* 72).

•

For him, I would have wanted to avoid not evaluation (if this were possible or even desirable) but all that insinuates itself into the most implicit evaluation in order to return to the coded (once again to the *studium*). For him I would have wanted, without ever succeeding, to write at the limit, as close as possible to the limit but also beyond the "neutral," "colorless," "innocent" writing of which *Writing Degree Zero* shows at once the historical novelty and the infidelity. "If the writing is really neutral . . . then Literature is vanquished. . . . Unfortunately, nothing is more unfaithful than a colorless writing; mechanical habits are developed in the very place where freedom existed, a network of set forms hem in more and more the pristine freshness of discourse" (*WDZ*, 78). It is not a question here of vanquishing literature but of preventing it from neatly and cleverly sealing up the singular and flawless wound (nothing is more unbearable or laughable than all the expressions of guilt in mourning, all its inevitable spectacles).

•

To write—to him, to present to the dead friend within oneself the gift of his innocence. For him, I would have wanted to avoid, and thus spare him, the double wound of speaking of him, here and now, as one speaks of one of the living *or* of one of the dead. In both cases I disfigure, I wound, I put to sleep, or I kill. But whom? Him? No. Him in me? In us? In you? But what does this mean? That we remain among ourselves? This is true but still a bit too simple. Roland Barthes looks at us (inside each of us, so that each of us can then say that Barthes's thought, memory, and friendship concern only us), and we do not do as we please with this look, even though each of us has it at his disposal, in his own way, according to his own place and history. It is within us but it is not ours; we do not have it available to us like a moment or part of our interiority. And what looks at us may be indifferent, loving, dreadful, grateful, attentive, ironic, silent, bored, reserved, fervent, or smiling, a child or already quite old; in short, it can give us any of the innumerable signs of life or death that we might draw from the circumscribed reserve of his texts or our memory.

•

What I would have wanted to avoid for him is neither the Novel nor the Photograph but something in both that is neither life nor death, something he himself said before I did (and I will return to this—always the promise of return, a promise that is not just one of the commonplaces of composition). I will not succeed in avoiding this, precisely because this *point* always lets itself be reappropriated by the fabric it tears toward the other, because the studied veil always mends its way. But might it not be better not to get there, not to succeed, and to prefer, in the end, the spectacle of inadequacy, failure, and, especially here, truncation? (Is it not derisory, naive, and downright childish to come before the dead to ask for their forgiveness? Is there any meaning in this? Unless it is the origin of meaning itself? An origin in the scene you would make in front of others who observe you and who also play off the dead? A thorough analysis of the "childishness" in question would here be necessary but not sufficient.)

•

Two infidelities, an impossible choice: on the one hand, not to say anything that comes back to oneself, to one's own voice, to remain silent, or at the very least to let oneself be accompanied or preceded in counterpoint by the friend's voice. Thus, out of zealous devotion or gratitude, out of approbation as well, to be content with just quoting, with just accompanying that which more or less directly comes back or returns to the other, to let him speak, to efface oneself in front of and to follow his speech, and to do so right in front of him. But this excess of fidelity would end up saying and exchanging nothing. It returns to death. It points to death, sending death back to death. On the other hand, by avoiding all quotation, all identification, all rapprochement even, so that what is addressed to or spoken of Roland Barthes truly comes from the other, from the living friend, one risks making him disappear again, as if one could add more death to death and thus indecently pluralize it. We are left then with having to do and not do both at once, with having to correct one infidelity by the other. From one death, the other: is this the uneasiness that told me to begin with a plural?

•

Already, and often, I know that I have written *for him* (I always say "him," to write, to address, or to avoid "him"); well before these fragments. For him: but I insist here on recalling, for him, that there is today no respect, no living respect, that is, no living attention paid to the other, or to the name alone now of Roland Barthes, that does not have to expose itself without respite, without weakness, and without mercy to what is too transparent not to be immediately exceeded: Roland Barthes is the name of someone who can no longer hear or bear it. And he will receive nothing of what I say here of him, for him, to him, beyond the name but still within it, as I pronounce his name that is no longer his. This living attention here comes to tear itself toward that which, or the one who, can no longer receive it; it rushes toward the impossible. But if his name is no longer his, was it ever? I mean simply, uniquely?

•

The impossible sometimes, by chance, becomes possible: as a utopia. This is in fact what he said before his death, though for him, of the Winter Garden Photograph. Beyond analogies, "it achieved for me, utopically, *the impossible science of the unique being"* (*CL*, 71). He said this uniquely, turned toward his mother and not toward the Mother. But the poignant singularity does not contradict the generality, it does not forbid it from having the force of law, but only arrows it, marks, and signs it. Singular plural. Is there, then, already in the first language, in the first mark, another possibility, another chance beyond the pain of this plural? And what about metonymy? And homonymy? Can we suffer from anything else? Could we speak without them?

•

What we might playfully call the *mathesis singularis,* what is achieved for him "utopically" in front of the Winter Garden Photograph, is impossible and yet takes place, utopically, metonymically, as soon as it marks, as soon as it writes, even "before" language. Barthes speaks of utopia at least twice in *Camera Lucida.* Both times between his mother's death and his own— that is, inasmuch as he entrusts it to writing: "Once she was dead I no longer had any reason to attune myself to the progress of the superior Life Force (the race, the species). My particularity could never again universalize itself (unless, utopically, by writing, whose project henceforth would become the unique goal of my life)" (*CL*, 72).

•

When I say Roland Barthes it is certainly him whom I name, him beyond his name. But since he himself is now inaccessible to this appellation, since this nomination cannot become a vocation, address, or apostrophe (supposing that this possibility revoked today could have ever been pure), it is him in me that I name, toward him in me, in you, in us that I pass through his name. What happens around him and is said about him remains between us. Mourning began at this point. But when? For even before the unqualifiable event called death, interiority (of the other in me, in you, in us) had already begun its work. With the first nomination, it preceded death as another death would have done. The name alone makes possible the plurality of deaths. And even if the relation between them were only analogical, the analogy would be singular, without common measure with any other. Before death without analogy or sublation, before death without name or sentence, before that in front of which we have nothing to say and must remain silent, before that which he calls "my total, undialectical death" (*CL*, 72), before the last death, all the other movements of interiorization were at once more and less powerful, powerful *in an other way,* and, *in an other way,* more and less certain of themselves. More inasmuch as they were not yet disturbed or interrupted by the deathly silence of the other that always comes to recall the limits of a speaking interiority. Less inasmuch as the appearance, the initiative, the response, or the unforeseeable intrusion of the living other *also* recalls this limit. Living, Roland Barthes cannot be reduced to that which each or all of us can think, believe, know, and already recall of him. But once dead, might he not be so reduced? No, but the chances of the illusion will be greater *and* lesser, other in any case.

•

"Unqualifiable" is another word I borrow from him. Even if I transpose and modify it, it remains marked by what I read in *Camera Lucida.* "Unqualifiable" there designated a way of life—it was for a short time his, after his mother's death—a life that already resembled death, one death before the other, more than one, which it imitated in advance. This does not prevent it from having been an accidental and unforeseeable death, outside the realm of calculation. Perhaps this resemblance is what allows us to transpose the unqualifiable in life into death. Hence the *psyche* (the soul). "It is said that mourning, by its gradual labor, slowly erases pain; I could not, I cannot believe this; because for me, Time eliminates the emotion of loss (I do not weep), that is all. For the rest, everything has remained motionless. For what I have lost is not a Figure (the Mother), but a being; and not a being, but a *quality* (a soul): not the indispensable, but the irreplaceable. I could live without the Mother (as we all do, sooner or later); but what life remained would be absolutely and entirely *unqualifiable* (without quality)" (*CL,* 75). "A soul"—come from the other.

•

La chambre claire, the light room, no doubt says more than *camera lucida,* the name of the apparatus anterior to photography that Barthes opposes to *camera obscura.* I can no longer not associate the word "clarity," wherever it appears, with what he says much earlier of his mother's face when she was a child, of the distinctness or luminosity, the "clarity of her face" (*CL,* 69). And he soon adds: "the naive attitude of her hands, the place she had docilely taken without either showing or hiding herself."

•

Without either showing or hiding herself. Not the Figure of the Mother but his mother. There should not be, there *should* not be, any metonymy in this case, for love protests against it ("I could live without the Mother").

•

Without either showing or hiding herself. This is what took place. She had already taken her place "docilely," without initiating the slightest activity, according to the most gentle passivity, and she neither shows nor hides herself. The possibility of this impossibility derails and shatters all unity, and this is love; it disorganizes all studied discourses, all theoretical systems and philosophies. They must decide between presence and absence, here and there, what reveals and what conceals itself. Here, there, the unique other, his mother, appears, that is to say, without appearing, for the other can appear only by disappearing. And his mother "knew" how to do this so innocently, because it is the "quality" of a child's "soul" that he deciphers in the pose of his mother who is not posing. Psyche without mirror. He says nothing more and underscores nothing.

•

He speaks, moreover, of clarity as the "evidential power" of the Photograph (*CL,* 47). But this carries both presence and absence; it neither shows nor hides itself. In the passage on the *camera lucida,* Barthes quotes Blanchot: "The essence of the image is to be altogether outside, without intimacy, and yet more inaccessible and mysterious than the thought of the innermost being; without signification, yet summoning up the depth of any possible meaning; unrevealed yet manifest, having the absence-as-presence that constitutes the lure and fascination of the Sirens" (*CL,* 106).[8]

•

He insists, and rightly so, upon the adherence of the "photographic referent": it does not relate to a present or to a real but, in an other way, to the other, and each time differently according to the type of "image," whether photographic or not. (Taking all differences into account, we

8.   Maurice Blanchot, *Le livre à venir* (Paris: Gallimard, 1959), 25.

would not be reducing the specificity of what he says about photography were we to find it pertinent elsewhere: I would even say everywhere. It is a matter of at once acknowledging the possibility of suspending the Referent [not the reference], wherever it is found, including in photography, and of suspending a naive conception of the Referent, one that has so often gone unquestioned.)

•

Here is a brief and very preliminary classification drawn simply from common sense: there are, in the *time* that relates us to texts and to their presumed, nameable, and authorized signatories, at least three possibilities. The "author" can already be dead, in the usual sense of the term, at the moment we begin to read "him," or when this reading orders us to write, as we say, about him, whether it be about his writings or about himself. Such authors whom we never "knew" living, whom we never met or had a chance to like or love (or the opposite), make up by far the greatest number. This asymbiosis does not exclude a certain modality of the contemporaneous (and vice versa), for it too implies a degree of interiorization, an a priori mourning rich in possibility, a whole experience of absence whose originality I cannot really describe here. A second possibility is that the authors are living when we are reading them, or when this reading orders us to write about them. We can, knowing that they are alive, and this involves a bifurcation of the same possibility, know them or not, and once having met them, "love" them or not. And the situation can change in this regard; we can meet them after having begun to read them (I have such a vivid memory of my first meeting with Barthes), and there are any number of means of communication to bring about the transition: photographs, correspondence, hearsay, tape recordings, and so on. And then there is a "third" situation: at the death and after the death of those whom we also "knew," met, loved, and so forth. Thus, I have had occasion to write about or in the wake of those texts whose authors have been dead long before I read them (for example, Plato or John of Patmos) or whose authors are still living at the time I write, and it would seem that this is always the most risky. But what I thought impossible, indecent, and unjustifiable, what long ago and more or less secretly and resolutely I had promised myself never to do (out of a concern for rigor or fidelity, if you will, and because it is in this case *too* serious), was to write *following the death,* not after, not long after the death *by returning* to it, but just following the death, *upon or on the occasion of the death,* at the commemorative gatherings and tributes, in the writings "in memory" of those who while living would have been my friends, still present enough to me that some "declaration," indeed some analysis or "study," would seem at that moment completely unbearable.

But then what, silence? Is this not another wound, another insult? To whom?

Yes, to whom and of what would we be making a gift? What are we doing when we exchange these discourses? Over what are we keeping watch? Are we trying to negate death or retain it? Are we trying to put things in order, make amends, or settle our accounts, to finish unfinished business? With the other? With the others outside and inside ourselves? How many voices intersect, observe, and correct one another, argue with one another, passionately embrace or pass by one another in silence? Are we going to seek some final evaluation? For example, to convince ourselves that the death never took place, or that it is irreversible and we are protected from a return of the dead? Or are we going to make the dead our ally ("the dead with me"), to take him by our side, or even inside ourselves, to show off some secret contract, to finish him off by exalting him, to reduce him in any case to what can still be contained by a literary or rhetorical performance, one that attempts to turn the situation to its advantage by means of stratagems that can be analyzed interminably, like all the ruses of an individual or collective "work of mourning"? And this so called "work" remains here the name of a problem. For if mourning works, it does so only to dialectize death, a death that Roland Barthes *called* "undialectical" ("I could do no more than await my total, undialectical death") (*CL,* 72).

•

A piece [*morceau*] of myself like a piece of the dead [*mort*]. In saying "the deaths" are we attempting to dialectize them or, as I would want, the contrary—though we are here at a limit where wanting is, more than ever, found wanting. Mourning and transference. In a discussion with Ristat about the "practice of writing" and self-analysis, I remember him saying: "Self-analysis is not transferential, and it is here that psychoanalysts would perhaps disagree." No doubt. For there is, no doubt, still transference in self-analysis, particularly when it proceeds through writing and literature, but it plays in an other way, or plays more—and the difference in play is essential here. When we take the possibility of writing into account, another concept of transference is needed (that is, if there ever was one).

•

For what was earlier called "following the death," "on the occasion of the death," we have a whole series of typical solutions. The worst ones—or the worst in each of them—are either base or derisory, and yet so common: still to maneuver, to speculate, to try to profit or derive some benefit, whether subtle or sublime, to draw from the dead a supplementary force to be turned against the living, to denounce or insult them more or less directly, to authorize and legitimate oneself, to raise oneself to the very heights where we presume death has placed the other beyond all suspicion. There are of course lesser offenses, but offenses nonetheless: to pay homage with an essay that treats the work or a part of the work bequeathed to us, to talk on a theme that we confidently believe would have interested the author who has passed away (whose tastes, curiosities, and projects should, it seems, no longer surprise us). Such a treatment would indeed point out the debt, but it would also pay it back; and one would tailor one's remarks according to the context. For example, in *Poétique,* to stress the essential role Barthes's works have played and will continue to play in the open field of literature and literary theory (this is legitimate, one has to do it, and I am doing it now). And then, perhaps, to undertake some analysis, as an exercise made possible and influenced by Barthes (an initiative that would gain approval in us through the memory of him). For example, to analyze a genre or discursive code, or the rules of a particular social arrangement, and to do so with his meticulousness and vigilance, which, as uncompromising as they were, still knew how to yield with a certain disabused compassion, a nonchalant elegance that would make him give up the fight (though I sometimes saw him get angry, for reasons of ethics or fidelity). But what "genre"? Well, for example, what in this century has come to replace the funeral oration. We could study the corpus of declarations in newspapers, on radio and television; we could analyze the recurrences, the rhetorical constraints, the political perspectives, the exploitations by individuals and groups, the pretexts for taking a stand, for threatening, intimidating, or reconciling. (I am thinking of the weekly newspaper that, upon Sartre's death, dared to put on trial those who deliberately, or simply because they were away, had said nothing or had said the wrong thing. Using their photographs to bring them to justice, the newspaper accused them all in the headline of still being afraid of Sartre.) In its classical form, the funeral oration had a good side, especially when it permitted one to call out directly to the dead, sometimes very informally [*tutoyer*]. This is of course a supplementary fiction, for it is always the dead in me, always the others standing around the coffin whom I call out to. But because of its caricatured excess, the overstatement of this rhetoric at least pointed out that we ought not to remain among ourselves. The interactions of the living must be interrupted, the veil must be torn toward the other, the other dead *in us* though other still, and the religious promises of an afterlife could indeed still grant this "as if."

•

The deaths of Roland Barthes: *his* deaths, that is, those of his relatives, those deaths that must have inhabited him, situating places and solemn moments, orienting tombs in his inner space (ending—and probably even beginning—with his mother's death). *His* deaths, those he lived in the plural, those he must have linked together, trying in vain to "dialectize" them before the "total" and "undialectical" death; those deaths that always form in our lives a terrifying and endless series. But how did he "live" them? No answer is more impossible or forbidden. Yet a certain movement had quickened in those last years; I could feel a sort of autobiographical acceleration, as if he were saying, "I feel that I have little time left." I must concern myself first with this thought of a death that begins, like thought and like death, in the memory of the idiom. While still living, he wrote a death of Roland Barthes by himself. And, finally, *his* deaths, his texts on death, everything he wrote, with such insistence on displacement, on death, on the theme of Death, if you will, if indeed there is such a theme. From the Novel to the Photograph, from *Writing Degree Zero* (1953) to *Camera Lucida* (1980), a certain thought of death set everything in motion, or rather set it traveling, on a sort of journey toward the beyond of all closed systems, all forms of knowledge, all the new scientific positivisms whose novelty always tempted the *Aufklärer* and discoverer in him, though only for a time, the time of a passage, the time of a contribution that, after him, would become indispensable. And yet he was already elsewhere, and he said so; he would speak openly about this with a calculated modesty, with a politeness that revealed a rigorous demand, an uncompromising ethic, like an idiosyncratic destiny naively assumed. In the beginning of *Camera Lucida* he tells—and tells himself—of his "discomfort" at always

> being the subject torn between two languages, one expressive,
> the other critical; and at the heart of this critical language, be-
> tween several discourses, those of sociology, of semiology, and of
> psychoanalysis—but [I tell myself] that, by ultimate dissatisfaction
> with all of them, I was bearing witness to the only sure thing that

was in me (however naive it might be): a desperate resistance to
any reductive system. For each time, having resorted to any such
language to whatever degree, each time I felt it hardening and
thereby tending to reduction and reprimand, I would gently leave it
and seek elsewhere: I began to speak differently. (*CL,* 8)

The beyond of this journey is no doubt the great headland and enigma
of the Referent, as it has been called for the past twenty years, and death
is clearly not in this for nothing (it will be necessary to return to this in
another tone). In any case, as early as *Writing Degree Zero,* all this passes
through the Novel and "The Novel is a Death" (*WDZ,* 38)—the beyond
of literature as literature, literary "modernity," literature producing itself
and producing its essence as its own disappearance, showing and hiding
itself at the same time (Mallarmé, Blanchot, among others): "Modernism
begins with the search for a Literature that is no longer possible. Thus we
find, in the Novel too, this machinery directed towards both destruction
and resurrection, and typical of the whole of modern art. . . . The Novel
is a Death; it transforms life into destiny, a memory into a useful act,
duration into an orientated and meaningful time" (*WDZ,* 38–39). And
it is the modern possibility of photography (whether art or technique
matters little here) that combines death and the referent in the same
system. It was not for the first time, and this conjugation of death and
the referent did not have to wait for the Photograph to have an essential
relationship to reproductive technique, or to technique in general, but the
immediate proof given by the photographic apparatus or by the structure
of the *remains* it leaves behind are irreducible events, ineffaceably original.
It is the failure, or at any rate the limit, of all that which, in language,
literature, and the other arts seemed to permit grandiose theories on
the general suspension of the Referent, or of what was classified, by a
sometimes gross simplification, under that vast and vague category. By
the time—at the instant—that the *punctum* rends space, the reference and
death are in it together in the photograph. But should we say reference
or referent? Analytical precision must here be equal to the stakes, and the
photograph puts this precision to the test: in the photograph, the referent
is noticeably absent, suspendable, vanished into the unique past time of its
event, but the reference to this referent, call it the intentional movement of
reference (since Barthes does in fact appeal to phenomenology in this book),
implies just as irreducibly the having-been of a unique and invariable
referent. It implies the "return of the dead" in the very structure of both
its image and the phenomenon of its image. This does not happen in
other types of images or discourses, or indeed of marks in general, at least

not in the same way, the implication and form of the reference taking very different paths. From the beginning of *Camera Lucida* the "disorder" introduced by the photograph is largely attributed to the "unique time" of its referent, a time that does not let itself be reproduced or pluralized, and whose referential implication is inscribed *as such right on* the very structure of the photogram, regardless of the number of its reproductions and even the artifice of its composition. Whence "this stubbornness of the Referent in always being there" (*CL,* 6). "It is as if the Photograph always carries its referent with itself, both affected by the same amorous or funereal immobility. . . . In short, the referent adheres. And this singular adherence . . ." (*CL,* 5–6). Though it is no longer *there* (present, living, real), its *having-been-there* presently a part of the referential or intentional structure of my relationship to the photogram, the return of the referent indeed takes the form of a haunting. This is a "return of the dead," whose spectral arrival in the very space of the photogram indeed resembles that of an emission or emanation. Already a sort of hallucinating metonymy: it is something else, a piece come from the other (from the referent) that finds itself in me, before me, but also in me like a piece of me (since the referential implication is also intentional and noematic; it belongs neither to the sensible body nor to the medium of the photogram). Moreover, the "target," the "referent," the "*eidolon* emitted by the object," the "*Spectrum*" (*CL,* 9), can be me, seen in a photograph of myself: "I then experience a micro-version of death (of parenthesis): I am truly becoming a specter. The Photographer knows this very well, and himself fears (if only for commercial reasons) this death in which his gesture will embalm me. . . . I have become Total-Image, which is to say, Death in person. . . . Ultimately, what I am seeking in the photograph taken of me (the 'intention' according to which I look at it) is Death: Death is the *eidos* of that Photograph" (*CL,* 14–15).

•

Carried by this relationship, drawn or attracted by the pull and character of it (*Zug, Bezug*), by the reference to the spectral referent, Roland Barthes traversed periods, systems, modes, "phases," and "genres"; he marked and punctuated the *studium* of each, passing *through* phenomenology, linguistics, literary mathesis, semiosis, structural analysis, and so on. His first move was to recognize in each of these their necessity or richness, their critical value and light, in order to turn them against dogmatism.

•

I shall not make of this an allegory, even less a metaphor, but I recall that it was *while traveling* that I spent the most time alone with Barthes. Sometimes head to head, I mean face to face (for example on the train from Paris to Lille or Paris to Bordeaux), and sometimes side by side, separated by an aisle (for example on the trip from Paris to New York to Baltimore in 1966). The time of our travels was surely not the same, and yet it was also the same, and it is necessary to accept these two absolute certainties. Even if I wanted or was able to give an account, to speak of him as he was for me (the voice, the timbre, the forms of his attention and distraction, his polite way of being there or elsewhere, his face, hands, clothing, smile, his cigar, so many features that I name without describing, since this is impossible here), even if I tried to reproduce what took place, what place would be reserved for the reserve? What place for the long periods of silence, for what was left unsaid out of discretion, for what was of no use bringing up, either because it was too well known by both of us or else infinitely unknown on either side? To go on speaking of this all alone, after the death of the other, to sketch out the least conjecture or risk the least interpretation, feels to me like an endless insult or wound—and yet also a duty, a duty toward him. Yet I will not be able to carry it out, at least not right here. Always the promise of return.

•

How to believe in the contemporary? It would be easy to show that the times of those who seem to belong to the same epoch, defined in terms of something like a historical frame or social horizon, remain infinitely heterogeneous and, to tell the truth, completely unrelated to one another. One can be very sensitive to this, though sensitive at the same time, on another level, to a being-together that no difference or differend can threaten. This being-together is not distributed in any homogeneous way in our experience. There are knots, points of great condensation, places of high valuation, paths of decision or interpretation that are virtually unavoidable. It is there, it seems, that the law is produced. Being-together refers to and recognizes itself there, even though it is not constituted there. Contrary to what is often thought, the individual "subjects" who inhabit the zones most difficult to avoid are not authoritarian "superegos" with power at their disposal, assuming that Power can be at one's disposal. Like those for whom these zones become unavoidable (and this is first of all their history), they inhabit them, and, rather than ruling there, take from them a desire or an image. It is a certain way of relinquishing authority, a certain freedom in fact, an acknowledged relationship to their own finitude, which, by an ominous and rigorous paradox, confers on them an additional authority, an influence, radiance, or presence that leads their ghost to places where they are not and from which their ghost will never return. It is this, in short, that makes one always ask, more or less explicitly: What does he or she think about this? Not that one is ready to agree that they are right, a priori and in all cases, not that one awaits a verdict or believes in a lucidity without weakness, but, even before looking for it, the image of an evaluation, look, or affect imposes itself. It is difficult to know then who addresses this "image" to whom. I would like to describe, patiently and interminably, all the trajectories of this address, especially when its reference passes through writing, when it then becomes so virtual, invisible, plural, divided, microscopic, mobile, infinitesimal, specular even (since the demand is often reciprocal and the trajectory easily lost), punctual, seemingly on the verge of the zero point even though its exercise is so powerful and so diverse.

•

Roland Barthes is the name of a friend whom, in the end, beyond a certain familiarity, I knew very little, and of whom, it goes without saying, I have not read everything, I mean reread, understood, and so on. And my first response was most often certainly one of approval, solidarity, and gratitude. Yet not always, it seems, and as insignificant as it may be, I must say this so as not to give in too much to the genre. He was, I mean he remains, one of those of whom I have constantly wondered, for almost twenty years now, in a more or less articulated way: What does he think of this? In the present, the past, the future, the conditional, and so on? Especially, why not say it, since this should surprise no one, at the moment of writing. I even told him this once in a letter long ago.

•

I return to the "poignant," to this pair of concepts, this opposition that is not one, the ghost of this pair, *punctum/studium*. I return to this because *punctum* seems to say, to let Barthes himself say, the point of singularity, the traversal of discourse toward the unique, the "referent" as the irreplaceable other, the one who was and will no longer be, who returns like that which will never come back, who marks the return of the dead right on the reproductive image. I return to this because Roland Barthes is the name of that which "points" me, or "points" (to) what I am awkwardly trying to say here. I return to this also in order to show how he himself treated and properly signed this simulacrum of an opposition. He first highlighted the absolute irreducibility of the *punctum,* what we might call the unicity of the *referential* (I appeal to this word so as not to have to choose between reference and referent: what adheres in the photograph is perhaps less the referent itself, in the present effectivity of its reality, than the implication in the reference of its having-been-unique). The heterogeneity of the *punctum* is rigorous; its originality can bear neither contamination nor concession. And yet, in other places, at other times, Barthes accedes to another descriptive demand, let's call it *phenomenological* since the book *also* presents itself as a phenomenology. He accedes to the requisite rhythm of the composition, a musical composition that, to be more precise, I would call contrapuntal. It is indeed necessary for him to recognize, and this is not a concession, that the *punctum* is not what it is. This absolute other composes with the same, with its absolute other that is thus not its opposite, with the locus of the same and of the *studium* (it is the limit of the binary opposition and, undoubtably, of a structural analysis that the *studium* itself might exploit). If the *punctum* is more or less than itself, dissymmetrical—to everything and in itself—then it can invade the field of the *studium,* to which, strictly speaking, it does not belong. It is located, we recall, outside all fields and codes. As the place of irreplaceable singularity and of the unique referential, the *punctum* irradiates and, what is most surprising, lends itself to metonymy. As soon as it allows itself to be drawn into a network of substitutions, it can invade everything, objects as well as affects. This singularity that is nowhere *in* the field mobilizes everything everywhere; it pluralizes itself. If the photograph bespeaks the unique death, the death of the unique, this death immediately repeats itself, as such, and is itself elsewhere. I said that the *punctum* allows itself to be drawn into metonymy. Actually, it induces it, and this is its *force,* or rather than its force (since it exercises no actual constraint and exists completely in reserve), its *dynamis,* in other words, its power, potentiality, virtuality, and even its dissimulation, its latency. Barthes marks this relationship between force (potential or in reserve) and metonymy at certain intervals of the composition that I must here unjustly condense. "However lightning-like it may be, the *punctum* has, more or less potentially, a power of expansion. This power is often metonymic" (*CL,* 45). Further: "I had just realized that however immediate and incisive it was, the *punctum* could accommodate a certain latency (but never any examination)" (*CL,* 53). This metonymic power is essentially related to the supplementary structure of the *punctum* ("it is a supplement") and of the *studium* that receives from it all its movement, even if it must content itself, like the "examination," with turning round the point and never getting down to it.[9] Henceforth, the relationship between the two concepts is neither tautological nor oppositional, neither dialectical nor in any sense symmetrical; it is supplementary and musical (contrapuntal).

•

The metonymy of the *punctum:* scandalous as it may be, it allows us to speak, to speak of the unique, to speak of and to it. It yields the trait that relates to the unique. The Winter Garden Photograph, which he neither shows nor hides, which he speaks, is the *punctum* of the entire book. The mark of this unique wound is nowhere visible as such, but its unlocatable brightness or clarity (that of *his* mother's eyes) irradiates the entire study. It makes of this book an irreplaceable event. And yet only a metonymic force can continue to assure a certain generality to the discourse and offer it to analysis by submitting its concepts to a quasi-instrumental use. How else could we, without knowing her, be so deeply moved by what he said about *his* mother, who was not only the Mother, or a mother, but the only one she was and of whom such a photo was taken "on that day"? How could this be poignant to us if a metonymic force, which yet cannot be mistaken for something that facilitates the movement of identification, were not at work? The alterity remains almost intact; that is the condition. I do not put myself in his place, I do not tend to replace his mother with mine. Were I to do so, I could be moved only by the alterity of the without-relation, the absolute unicity that the metonymic power comes to recall in me without effacing it. He is right to protest against the confusion between she who was his mother and the Figure of the Mother, but the metonymic power (one part for the whole or one name for another) will always come to inscribe both in this relation without relation.

•

The deaths of Roland Barthes: because of the somewhat indecent violence of this plural, one might perhaps think that I was resisting the unique; I would have thus avoided, denied, or tried to efface his death. As a sign of protection or protest, I would have in the process accused and given over

9.   *Tourner autour du point* is a play on *tourner autour du pot,* "to beat around the bush."—*Trans.*

his death to the trial of a studied metonymy. Perhaps, but how do we speak otherwise and without taking this risk? Without pluralizing the unique or generalizing what is most irreplaceable in it, his own death? And didn't he himself speak right up until the very last moment about his death and, metonymically, about his deaths? Didn't he say what is essential (especially in *Roland Barthes by Roland Barthes,* a metonymic title and signature par excellence) about the undecidable vacillation between "speaking and keeping silent"?[10] And one can also remain silent by speaking: "The only 'thought' I can have is that at the end of this first death, my own death is inscribed; between the two, nothing more than waiting; I have no other resources than this *irony:* to speak of the 'nothing to say'" (*CL,* 93). And just before: "The horror is this: nothing to say about the death of one whom I love most, nothing to say about her photograph" (*CL,* 92–93).

•

Friendship: from the few pages at the end of the volume that bears this title, we have no right to take anything for ourselves.[11] What linked Blanchot to Bataille was unique, and *Friendship* expresses this in an absolutely singular way. And yet the metonymic force of even the most poignant writing allows us to *read* these pages, which does not mean however to expose them outside their essential reserve. It lets us think that which it nonetheless never forces open, never shows or hides. Without being able to enter into the absolute singularity of this relationship, without forgetting that only Blanchot could write this and that only of Bataille could he be speaking, without understanding, or in any case without knowing, we can think what is being written here. Though we should not be able to quote, I nonetheless take upon myself the violence of a quotation, especially of one that has been necessarily truncated.

How could one agree to speak of this friend? Neither in praise nor in the interest of some truth. The traits of his character, the forms of his existence, the episodes of his life, even in keeping with the search for which he felt himself responsible to the point

10.   Roland Barthes, *Roland Barthes by Roland Barthes,* trans. Richard Howard (New York: Hill and Wang, 1977), 142 (hereafter abbreviated as *RB*).

11.   Maurice Blanchot, *Friendship,* trans. Elizabeth Rottenberg (Stanford: Stanford University Press, 1997), 289 (hereafter abbreviated as *F*). [As Derrida later explains, both the book and the last section of the book (289–92), which is entirely in italics, bear this title.—*Trans.*]

of irresponsibility, belong to no one. There are no witnesses. Those
who were closest say only what was close to them, not the distance
that affirmed itself in this proximity, and distance ceases as soon as
presence ceases. . . . We are only looking to fill a void, we cannot
bear the pain: the affirmation of this void. . . . Everything we
say tends to veil the one affirmation: that everything must fade
and that we can remain loyal only so long as we watch over this
fading movement, to which something in us that rejects all memory
already belongs.

•

In *Camera Lucida,* the value of *intensity* (*dynamis,* force, latency), which
I have been following, leads to a new contrapuntal equation, to a new
metonymy of metonymy itself, a new metonymy of the substitutive virtue
of the *punctum.* And this is Time. For is not Time the ultimate resource for
the substitution of one absolute instant by another, for the replacement of
the irreplaceable, the replacement of this unique referent by another that
is yet another instant, completely other and yet still the same? Is not time
the punctual form and force of all metonymy—*its instant recourse?* Here
is a passage wherein the passage from one death to another, from that of
Lewis Payne to that of Roland Barthes, seems to pass (between others, dare
one say) through the Winter Garden Photograph. And on the theme of
Time. There is here, in short, a terrifying syntax, from which I pick out
first a singular accord, at the point of transition between S and P: "The
photo is handsome, as is the boy" (*CL,* 96). And here is the passage from
one death to the other:

> I now know that there exists another *punctum* (another "stigma-
> tum") than the "detail." This new *punctum,* which is no longer of
> form but of intensity, is Time, the lacerating emphasis of the *noeme*
> (*"that-has-been"*), its pure representation.
>
>   In 1865, young Lewis Payne tried to assassinate Secretary
> of State W. H. Seward. Alexander Gardner photographed him
> in his cell, where he was waiting to be hanged. The photograph
> is handsome, as is the boy: that is the *studium.* But the *punctum* is:
> *he is going to die.* I read at the same time: *this will be* and *this has
> been;* I observe with horror an anterior future of which death is
> the stake. By giving me to the absolute past of the pose (aorist), the
> photograph tells me death in the future. What *points* me, *pricks* me,

is the discovery of this equivalence. In front of the photograph of my mother as a child, I tell myself: she is going to die: I shudder, like Winnicott's psychotic patient, *over a catastrophe that has already occurred.* Whether or not the subject is already dead, every photograph is this catastrophe. (*CL,* 96)

And further on: "It is because each photograph always contains this imperious sign of my future death that each one, however attached it seems to be to the excited world of the living, challenges each of us, one by one, outside of any generality (but not outside of any transcendence)" (*CL,* 97).

•

Time: the metonymy of the instantaneous, the possibility of the narrative magnetized by its own limit. The instantaneous in photography, the snapshot, would itself be but the most striking metonymy within the modern technological age of an older instantaneity. Older, even though it is never foreign to the possibility of *technē* in general. Remaining as attentive as possible to all the differences, one must be able to speak of a *punctum* in all signs (and repetition or iterability already structures it), in any discourse, whether literary or not. As long as we do not hold to some naive and "realist" referentialism, it is the relation to some unique and irreplaceable referent that *interests* us and animates our most sound and studied readings: what took place only once, while dividing itself already, in the sights or in front of the lens of the *Phaedo* or *Finnegans Wake,* the *Discourse on Method* or Hegel's *Logic,* John's *Apocalypse* or Mallarmé's *Coup de dés.* The photographic apparatus reminds us of this irreducible referential by means of a very powerful telescoping.

•

The metonymic force thus divides the referential trait, suspends the referent and leaves it to be desired, while still maintaining the reference. It is at work in the most loyal of friendships; it plunges the destination into mourning while at the same time engaging it.

•

Friendship: between the two titles, that of the book and that of the final farewell in italics, between the titles and the exergue ("quotations" of

Bataille that speak twice of "friendship"), the exchange is still metonymic, though the singularity does not lose any of its force; quite the contrary.[12]

> I know there are the books. . . . The books themselves refer to an existence. This existence, because it is no longer a presence, begins to be deployed in history, and in the worst of histories, literary history. . . . One wants to publish "everything," one wants to say "everything," as if one were anxious about only one thing: that everything be said; as if the "everything is said" would finally allow us to stop a dead voice. . . . As long as the one who is close to us exists and, with him, the thought in which he affirms himself, his thought opens itself to us, but preserved in this very relation, and what preserves it is not only the mobility of life (this would be very little), but the unpredictability introduced into this thought by the strangeness of the end. . . . I also know that, in his books, Georges Bataille seems to speak of himself with a freedom without restraint that should free us from all discretion—but that does not give us the right to put ourselves in his place, nor does it give us the power to speak in his absence. And is it certain that he speaks of himself? . . . We must give up trying to know those to whom we are linked by something essential; by this I mean we must greet them in the relation with the unknown in which they greet us as well, in our estrangement. (F, 289–91)

•

Where does the desire to date these last lines (the 14th and 15th of September, 1980) come from?[13] The date—and this is always something of a signature—accentuates the contingency or insignificance of the interruption. Like an accident and like death, it seems to be imposed from the outside, "on that day" (time and space are here given together, the conditions of a publication), but it no doubt also indicates another

12. Blanchot begins *Friendship* (ix) with two epigraphs from Bataille: "My complicitous friendship: this is what my temperament brings to other men"; " . . . friends until that state of profound friendship where a man abandoned, abandoned by all of his friends, encounters in life the one who will accompany him beyond life, himself without life, capable of free friendship, detached from all ties."—*Trans.*

13. Derrida is referring here to his own text. First published in *Poétique* in September 1981, it was written about a year before that, approximately six months after Barthes's death in March, 1980.—*Trans.*

interruption. Though neither more essential nor more interior, this interruption announces itself in another register, as another thought of the
same one . . .

•

Having returned from the somewhat insular experience wherein I had
secluded myself with the two books, I look today only at the photographs
in other books (especially in *Roland Barthes by Roland Barthes*) and in
newspapers; I cannot tear myself away from the photographs and the
handwriting. I do not know what I am still looking for, but I'm looking
for it in the direction of his body, in what he shows and says of it, in what
he hides of it perhaps—like something he could not *see* in his writing.
I am looking in these photographs for "details"; I am looking, without
any illusion, I believe, without any indulgence, for something that regards
me, or has me in view, without seeing me, as I believe he says at the end
of *Camera Lucida*. I try to imagine the gestures around what we believe
to be the essential writing. How, for example, did he choose all these
photographs of children and old people? How and when did he choose
these lines for the back cover where Marpa speaks of his son's death?[14]
And what about these white lines on the black background of the inside
cover of *Roland Barthes by Roland Barthes*?[15]

•

Today somebody brought me a note (less than a letter, a single sentence)
that had been destined for me but never given to me twenty-four years ago,
almost to the day. On the eve of a journey, the note was to accompany the
gift of a very singular book, a little book that even today I find unreadable.

14.   Like so many other things that do not survive translation, the passage on the back
      of *La chambre claire* has been omitted in *Camera Lucida*. We thus restore here this
      "gesture around what we believe to be the essential writing": "Marpa was very shaken
      when his own son died, and one of his disciples said to him, 'You have always said
      that everything is an illusion. Is not the death of your son an illusion as well?' And
      Marpa responded, 'Certainly, but the death of my son is a super-illusion.'"—*A Practice
      of the Tibetan Way.*—*Trans.*

15.   In the English edition these handwritten lines of Barthes appear in black on a white
      background and have been incorporated into the opening and closing pages of the text
      rather than printed on the front and back inside covers. Howard translates these two
      inscriptions: "It must all be considered as if spoken by a character in a novel"; "And
      afterward? / —What to write now? Can you still write anything? / —One writes with
      one's desires, and I am not through desiring."—*Trans.*

I know, or I think I know, why this gesture was interrupted. Actually, it was detained (and the little book ended up being placed inside another) as if to preserve the memory of the interruption itself. This interruption, for reasons at once serious and playful, in fact concerns something I would be tempted to call the whole of my life. This note (which I thus received today on the eve of the *same* journey, I mean to the same places) was found by chance, long after the death of the one who destined it for me. Everything is very close to me, the form of the writing, of the signature, these very words. Another interruption makes all this as distant and unreadable as that little, insignificant *viaticum*. But in the interruption, the other, returning, addresses himself to me, in me, the other truly returning, truly ghostly.[16] The paper retains the folds of these twenty-four years; I read the blue writing (and more and more I am sensitive to the color of writing, or at any rate, I am now more aware that I am sensitive to it) of someone who, speaking about death, had told me in a car one day, and I recall these words often: "It will happen to me soon." And it was true.

•

That was yesterday. Today, another strange coincidence: a friend sent me from the United States a photocopy of a text by Barthes that I had never read before ("Analyse textuelle d'un conte d'Edgar Poe," 1973).[17] I will read it later. But while "leafing" through it, I picked out this:

> Another scandal of enunciation is the reversal of the metaphor
> in the letter. It is indeed common to utter the sentence "I am
> dead!" . . . [But] the transposition of the metaphor into the letter,
> *precisely for this metaphor,* is impossible: the utterance "I am dead"
> is, literally, according to the letter, foreclosed. . . . It is a question, if
> you like, of a scandal of language . . . of a performative utterance,
> to be sure, but one that neither Austin nor Benveniste had foreseen
> in their analyses. . . . the extraordinary sentence "I am dead" is by
> no means the incredible statement, but much more radically, the
> *impossible utterance.*

16. *Revenant* as a gerund means "returning" or "coming back," and as a noun, "ghost" or "phantom." Two sections further, Derrida uses the phrase *revenant à la lettre,* which can be translated as "returning to the letter," "literally returning," "ghost to the letter," or even "literally a ghost."—*Trans.*

17. Roland Barthes, "Analyse textuelle d'un conte d'Edgar Poe," in *L'aventure sémiologique* (Paris: Seuil, 1985), 329–59.

●

Would the impossible utterance "I am dead" really never have taken place? He is right when he says that, "literally, according to the letter," it is "foreclosed." Yet one understands it, one hears its so-called literal meaning, even if only to declare it legitimately impossible as a performative utterance. What was he thinking at the moment he referred to "the letter"? Probably, to begin with, that in the idea of death, all other predicates remaining questionable, one might analytically deduce the inability to utter, to speak, to say *I* in the present: a punctual *I,* punctuating in the instant a reference to the self as to a unique referent, this autoaffective reference that defines the very heart of the living. To return from this point to metonymy, to the metonymic force of the *punctum,* without which there would undoubtably be no *punctum* as such. . . . For at the heart of the sadness felt for the friend who dies, there is perhaps this point: that after having been able to speak of death as plural, after having said so often "I am dead" metaphorically or metonymically, he was never able to say "I am dead" literally or according to the letter. Were he to have done so, he would have again given in to metonymy. But metonymy is no mistake or falsehood; it does not speak untruths. And literally, according to the letter, there is perhaps no *punctum.* Which makes all utterances possible but does not reduce suffering in the least; indeed, it is even a source, the unpunctual, illimitable source of suffering. Were I to write *revenant à la lettre* and were I to try to translate it into another language . . . (All these questions are also questions of translation and transference.)

●

I: the pronoun [*pronom*] or the first name [*prénom*], the assumed name [*prête-nom*] of the one to whom the *utterance* "I am *dead*" can never happen, the literal utterance, that is, and, assuming this is possible, the nonmetonymic *utterance?* And this, even when the enunciation of it would be possible?

●

Wouldn't the utterance "I am dead," which he says is impossible, fall into the province of what he calls elsewhere—and calls on as—*utopic?* And doesn't this utopia impose itself in the place, if one can still say this, where metonymy is already at work on the *I* in its relation to itself, the *I* when it refers to nothing else but the one who is *presently* speaking? There would be something like a sentence of the *I*, and the time of this elliptical sentence would leave room for metonymic substitution. To give ourselves time, we would have to return here to that which implicitly links, in *Camera Lucida,* Time as a *punctum* to the metonymic force of the *punctum* . . .

•

"What must I do?" In *Camera Lucida* Barthes seems to approve of the one who places—of she who placed—"civil value" above "moral value" (*CL,* 67). In *Roland Barthes by Roland Barthes* he says that *morality* must be understood as "the precise opposite of ethics (it is the thinking of the body in a state of language)" (*RB,* 145).

•

Between the possibility and the impossibility of the "I am dead" there is the syntax of time and something like a category of imminence (that which points from the future and has reached the point of taking place). The imminence of death presents itself; it is always at the point—in presenting itself—of presenting itself no longer, so that death then stands between the metonymic eloquence of the "I am dead" and the instant when death ushers in absolute silence, allowing nothing more to be said (one point and that's it, period [*un point c'est tout*]). This punctual, punctuating singularity (and I understand "punctuating" here as an adjective but also as a type of verb, the enduring syntax of a sentence) irradiates the corpus from its place of imminence and allows one to breathe, in *Camera Lucida,* this "air" that becomes more and more dense, more and more haunted and peopled with ghosts. I use his words to speak of this: "emanation," "ecstasis," "madness," "magic."

•

It is inevitable [*fatal*], both just and unjust, that the most "autobiographical" books (those of the end, as I have heard said) begin at death to conceal all the other books. What is more, they begin with death. Were I myself to yield to this movement, I would no longer leave this *Roland Barthes by Roland Barthes,* which, on the whole, I never knew how to read. Between the photos and the graphics, all these texts I should have talked about, started with, or come closer to. . . . But didn't I do this without realizing it in the preceding fragments? For example, just a moment ago, almost by chance, under the titles "His Voice" ("inflection is the voice in so far as it is always past, silenced," "the voice is always *already* dead"), "Plural," "Difference,"

"Conflict," "What Is a Utopia For?" "Forgeries ('I Write Classic')," "The Circle of Fragments," "The Fragment as Illusion," "From the Fragment to the Journal," "Pause: Anamneses" ("The *biographeme* . . . is nothing but a factitious anamnesis: the one I lend to the author I love"), "Limpness of Important Words" ("History" and "Nature," for example), "Passing Bodies," "Foreseeable Discourse" (example: *Text of the Dead:* a litaneutical text, in which no word can be changed), "Relation to Psychoanalysis," "I Like/I Don't Like" (one line before the end, I try to understand how he could have written "*I don't like* . . . fidelity"; I know that he also said he liked it and that he was able to make a gift of this word; I suppose—it's a matter of tone, mode, inflection, and a certain way of saying quickly but incisively "I like, I don't like"—that in this case he did not like a certain pathos with which fidelity is so easily charged, and especially the word, the discourse on fidelity, which so quickly becomes tired, drab, listless, stale, forbidding, unfaithful), "Choosing Clothes," "Later . . ."

●

Contrapuntal theory or a procession of stigmata: a wound no doubt comes in (the) place of the point signed by singularity, in (the) place of its very instant (*stigmē*), at its point, its tip. But *in (the) place of* this event, place is given over, for the same wound, to substitution, which repeats itself there, retaining of the irreplaceable only a past desire.

●

I still cannot remember when I read or heard his name for the first time, and then how he became one for me. But anamnesis, even if it breaks off always too soon, promises itself each time to begin again: it remains to come.

CHAPTER 2

PAUL DE MAN

DECEMBER 6, 1919—DECEMBER 21, 1983

One of the most influential figures in American literary criticism and theory, Paul Adolph Michel de Man was born in Antwerp, Belgium, in 1919. He was raised by Magdalena de Brey and Jan Robert de Man in a well-to-do, liberal, nonreligious Flemish family. His grandfather, Jan van Beers, was a popular poet and his father a manufacturer of medical instruments and X-ray equipment. His uncle Hendrik de Man was at one time the Belgian minister of finance and the chairman of the Social Democratic Party. De Man attended high school at the Koninklijke Athenaeum in Antwerp, from which he graduated in 1937 magna cum laude. Two tragic events marked his early life: in 1936 his brother was killed in a bicycle accident at a railroad crossing, and the following year his mother committed suicide.

De Man entered the Ecole Polytechnique at the Free University of Brussels in 1937 to study engineering but transferred the following year to chemistry. He read widely in philosophy and literature during these years and attended weekly literary discussions at the university. In 1939 he joined the editorial boards of *Les cahiers du libre examen* (where he later became chief editor) and *Jeudi*.

De Man received a bachelor's degree with distinction in chemical science in 1940. In the same year, he met Ann Baraghian, a Romanian who had settled in Belgium, with whom he had a son, Hendrik. They married in 1944 and had two more sons, Robert, in 1945, and Marc, in 1946.

From December 1940 to November 1942 de Man contributed literary articles to the newspapers *Le soir* and *Het Vlaamsche Land*. Though he resigned his position at *Le soir* to protest the German editorial control of the paper, these articles were later to become the center of much controversy because of their anti-Semitic content. De Man then worked for the Agence Dechenne, a book distributor and publisher and, in 1945, cofounded a publishing firm of his own, Hermès, specializing in art books. The venture was short lived, however, when de Man's attempt to establish the firm in the United States proved unsuccessful. In 1945 he also published a Flemish translation of Melville's *Moby-Dick*.

After World War II de Man visited Paris, where he met such literary figures as Georges Bataille, Maurice Blanchot, and Henri Michaux. He went to the United States in 1948 and took a job as a clerk at the Doubleday bookstore in Grand Central Station in New York, before becoming an instructor of French at Bard College (1949–51). It was at Bard that de Man met his second wife, Patricia Woods. They were married in 1950 and had two children, Patricia and Michael. In 1951 de Man started teaching languages at the Berlitz School in Boston. He was admitted to Harvard's Comparative Literature program in 1952 and received his M.A. in 1954, becoming a member in that same year of Harvard's Society of Fellows. De Man earned money during these years translating articles for Henry Kissinger's journal *Confluence*. From 1955 to 1960 de Man taught courses in general education and comparative literature at Harvard in a non-tenure-track position. While working on his doctorate he spent six months in Ireland studying Yeats and a year in Paris, where he presented a paper at Jean Wahl's Collège philosophique. He received his doctorate in 1960 with a dissertation entitled "Mallarmé, Yeats, and the Post-Romantic Predicament."

From 1960 to 1967 de Man taught at Cornell, and from 1963 to 1970 he was an ordinarius in comparative literature at the University of Zurich, where he counted among his colleagues Emil Staiger and Georges Poulet. Between 1968 and 1970 de Man held the post of professor of humanities at Johns Hopkins, before moving to Yale in 1970. His presence at Yale, along with that of a number of other outstanding scholars, brought fame and prestige to what was considered the center of deconstructive theory in the United States in the late 1970s and early 1980s. This reputation was enhanced by the 1979 publication of *Deconstruction and Criticism*, which collected essays by de Man, Harold Bloom, Geoffrey Hartman, J. Hillis Miller, and Jacques Derrida.

De Man's first book, *Blindness and Insight,* written during the 1960s, was published in 1971. Although de Man's early essays had appeared in the 1950s in French, it was not until some of these essays were included as part of the second edition of *Blindness and Insight* that they began to be widely known. In 1972 de Man edited the French edition of Rilke's *Oeuvres* for Editions du Seuil in France. *Allegories of Reading,* a "rhetorical" reading of Rousseau, Nietzsche, Rilke, and Proust, was published in 1979. De Man remained at Yale for the rest of his academic career, where he became Sterling Professor and Chair of Comparative Literature and French in 1979.

Though a prominent teacher and significant voice in American literary criticism throughout the 1970s and early 1980s, de Man published a relatively small body of work during his lifetime. A number of important collections of essays have been published posthumously, most of which engage in a critique of "aesthetic ideology." *Rhetoric of Romanticism,* written over a twenty-seven-year period (1956–83), contains the bulk of de Man's writings on romanticism and includes essays on Keats, Yeats, Wordsworth, Shelley, and Hölderlin. *The Resistance to Theory,* which remained unfinished at the time of de Man's death, examines the work of theorists such as Michael Riffaterre, Hans Robert Jauss, Walter Benjamin, and Mikhail Bakhtin. *Critical Writings,* comprising twenty-five essays and reviews (most of which appeared before 1970), represents de Man's "critical" phase. *Romanticism and Contemporary Criticism* includes de Man's previously unpublished Gauss Seminar lectures given at Princeton in 1967. *Aesthetic Ideology,* de Man's major project at the time of his death, includes lectures given between 1977 and 1983 on Pascal, Kant, Hegel, and Schiller, among others.

De Man died of cancer in New Haven on December 21, 1983.

Forgive me for speaking in my own tongue. It's the only one I ever spoke with Paul de Man. It's also the one in which he often taught, wrote, and thought. What is more, I haven't the heart today to translate these few words, adding to them the suffering and distance, for you and for me, of a foreign accent. We are speaking today less in order to say something than to assure ourselves, with voice and with music, that we are together in the same thought. We know with what difficulty one finds right and decent words at such a moment when no recourse should be had to common usage since all conventions will seem either intolerable or vain.

If we have, as one says in French, "la mort dans l'âme," death in the soul, it is because from now on we are destined to speak *of* Paul de Man, instead of speaking *to* and *with* him, destined to speak of the teacher and of the friend who he remains for so many of us, whereas the most vivid desire and the one which, within us, has been most cruelly battered, the most forbidden desire from now on would be to speak, still, to Paul, to hear him and to respond to him. Not just within ourselves (we will continue, I will continue, to do that endlessly) but to speak to him and to hear him, himself, speaking to us. That's the impossible, and we can no longer even take the measure of this wound.

Speaking is impossible, but so too would be silence or absence or a refusal to share one's sadness. Let me simply ask you to forgive me if today finds me with the strength for only a few very simple words. At a later time, I will try to find better words, and more serene ones, for the friendship that ties me to Paul de Man (it was and remains unique), what I, like so many others, owe to his generosity, to his lucidity, to the ever so gentle force of his thought: since that morning in 1966 when I met him at a breakfast table in Baltimore, during a colloquium, where we spoke, among other things, of Rousseau and the *Essai sur l'origine des langues,* a text which was then seldom read in the university but which we had both been working on, each in his own way, without knowing it. From then on, nothing has ever come between us, not even a hint of

This homage was delivered January 18, 1984, at Yale University during a ceremony in memory of Paul de Man. Reprinted, with changes, from "In Memoriam: Of the Soul," translated by Kevin Newmark, in *Memoires for Paul de Man,* by Jacques Derrida (New York: Columbia University Press, 1989), xv–xx. © 1986 Columbia University Press. Reprinted by permission of the publisher. First published in *Yale French Studies,* no. 69 (New Haven: Yale University Press, 1985). First French publication, "In memoriam: De l'âme," in *Mémoires: Pour Paul de Man,* by Jacques Derrida (Paris: Galilée, 1988), 13–19.

disagreement. It was like the golden rule of an alliance, no doubt that of a trusting and unlimited friendship, but also the seal of a secret affirmation, a kind of shared faith in something that, still today, I wouldn't know how to circumscribe, to limit, to name (and that is as it should be). As you know, Paul was irony itself and, among all the vivid thoughts he leaves with us and leaves alive in us, there is as well an enigmatic reflection on irony and even, in the words of Schlegel which he had occasion to cite, an "irony of irony." At the heart of my attachment to him, there has also always been a certain beyond-of-irony which cast on his own a softening, generous light, reflecting a smiling compassion on everything he illuminated with his tireless vigilance. His lucidity was sometimes overpowering, making no concession to weakness, but it never gave in to that negative assurance with which the ironic consciousness is sometimes too easily satisfied.

At some later time, then, I will try to find better words for what his friendship brought to all of those who had the good fortune to be his friend, his colleague, his student; but also for his work and especially for the future of his work, undoubtedly one of the most influential of our time. His work, in other words, his teaching and his books, those already published and those soon to appear—because, to the very last and with an admirable strength, enthusiasm, and gaiety, he worked on ever new lectures and writing projects, enlarging and enriching still further the perspectives he had already opened up for us. As we know already, but as we shall also come to realize more and more, he transformed the field of literary theory, revitalizing all the channels that irrigate it both inside and outside the university, in the United States and in Europe. Besides a new style of interpretation, of reading, of teaching, he brought to bear the necessity of the polylogue and of a plurilinguistic refinement that was his genius—not only that of national languages (Flemish, French, German, English) but also of those idioms which are literature and philosophy, renewing as he did so the reading of Pascal as well as Rilke, of Descartes and Hölderlin, of Hegel and Keats, Rousseau and Shelley, Nietzsche and Kant, Locke and Diderot, Stendhal and Kierkegaard, Coleridge, Kleist, Wordsworth and Baudelaire, Proust, Mallarmé and Blanchot, Austin and Heidegger, Benjamin, Bakhtin, and so many others, contemporary or not. Never content merely to present new readings, he led one to think the very possibility of reading—and also sometimes the paradox of its impossibility. His commitment remains henceforth that of his friends and his students who owe it to him and to themselves to pursue what was begun by him and with him.

Beyond the manifest evidence of the published texts—his own as well as those that make reference to his—I, like many others, can attest to what is today the radiance of his thought and his words: in the United States, first of all, where so many universities are linked and enlivened by the large community of his disciples, the large family of his former students or colleagues who have remained his friends; but also in Europe at all the universities where I had, as I did here at Yale, the good fortune and the honor to work with him, often at his invitation. I think first of Zurich, where we came together so many times, with Patricia, with Hillis; and naturally I think of Paris, where he lived, published, and shared editorial or academic responsibilities (for example, for Johns Hopkins or Cornell—and again these were for us the occasion of so many encounters). I also know the impression his passage left on the universities of Constance, Berlin, and Stockholm. I will say nothing of Yale because you know this better than anyone and because today my memory is too given over to mourning for all that I have shared with him here during the last ten years, from the most simple day-to-dayness to the most intense moments in the work that allied us with each other and with others, the friends, students, and colleagues who grieve for him so close to me here.

I wanted only to *bear witness* as would befit the sort of admiring observer I have also been at his side in the American and European academic world. This is neither the time nor the place to give in to discreet revelations or too personal memories. I will refrain from speaking of such memories, therefore—I have too many of them, as do many of you, and they are so overwhelming that we prefer to be alone with them. But allow me to infringe this law of privacy long enough to evoke two memories, just two among so many others.

The last letter I received from Paul: I still don't know how to read the serenity or the cheerfulness which it displayed. I never knew to what extent he adopted this tone, in a gesture of noble and sovereign discretion, so as to console and spare his friends in their anxiety or their despair, or, on the contrary, to what extent he had succeeded in transfiguring what is still for us the worst. No doubt it was both. Among other things, he wrote what I am going to permit myself to read here because, rightly or wrongly, I received it as a message, confided to me, for his friends in distress. You'll hear a voice and a tone that are familiar to us: "All of this, as I was telling you [on the phone], seems prodigiously interesting to me and I'm enjoying myself a lot. I knew it all along but it is being borne out: death gains a great deal, as they say, when one gets to know it close up—that '*peu profond ruisseau calomnié la mort* [shallow stream calumniated as death].'" And after having cited this last line from Mallarmé's "Tombeau for Verlaine," he added: "Anyhow, I prefer that to the brutality of the word 'tumeur'"—which, in fact, is more terrible, more insinuating and menacing in French than in any other language [*tumeur/tu meurs:* you are dying].

I recall the second memory because it says something about music—and only music today seems to me bearable, consonant, able to give some measure of what unites us in the same thought. I had known for a long time, even though he spoke of it very rarely, that music occupied an important place in Paul's life and thought. On that particular night—it was 1979 and once again the occasion was a colloquium—we were driving through the streets of Chicago after a jazz concert. My older son, who had accompanied me, was talking with Paul about music, more precisely about musical instruments. This they were doing as the experts they both were, as technicians who know how to call things by their name. It was then I realized that Paul had never told me he was an experienced musician and that music had also been a practice with him. The word that let me know this was the word *âme* [soul] when, hearing Pierre, my son, and Paul speak with familiarity of the violin's or the bass's soul, I learned that the "soul" is the name one gives in French to the small and fragile piece of wood—always very exposed, very vulnerable—that is placed within the body of these instruments to support the bridge and assure the resonant communication of the two sounding boards. I didn't know why at that moment I was so strangely moved and unsettled in some dim recess by the conversation I was listening to: no doubt it was due to the word "soul," which always speaks to us at the same time of life and of death and makes us dream of immortality, like the argument of the lyre in the *Phaedo.*

And I will always regret, among so many other things, that I never again spoke of any of this with Paul. How was I to know that one day I would speak of that moment, that music and that soul, without him, before you who must forgive me for doing it just now so poorly, so painfully, when already everything is painful, so painful?

CHAPTER 3

MICHEL FOUCAULT

OCTOBER 15, 1926—JUNE 25, 1984

Born in Poitiers in 1926 to a conservative, Catholic family, Paul-Michel Foucault was the second of three children of Paul André Foucault, a well-known surgeon, and Anne Marie Malapert, herself the daughter of a surgeon. Foucault attended the Collège St. Stanislaus and then the Lycée Henri IV in Poitiers, passing the first part of the *baccalauréat classique* in 1942 and attending *hypokhâgne* the following year.[1] When he failed the competitive entrance exam to the Ecole Normale Supérieure, he was sent in 1945 for a year of studies at the namesake Lycée Henri IV in Paris, where he met Jean Hyppolite.

He passed the entrance exam to the Ecole Normale Supérieure with honors on his second attempt in

1. *Hypokhâgne* and *khâgne* are the two years "that some students continue with at high school after the *baccalauréat,* in preparation for entry into one of the Grandes Ecoles [such as the Ecole Normale Supérieure]. The level of work in these *classes préparatoires* is generally recognized to be more demanding than that of the first two years at University" (*Jacques Derrida,* by Geoffrey Bennington and Jacques Derrida, trans. Geoffrey Bennington [Chicago: University of Chicago Press, 1993], 328).

1946. He there met Pierre Bourdieu, Paul Veyne, and Maurice Pinguet. Among his professors was Louis Althusser, with whom he would develop a close friendship. For his thesis for the *diplôme d'études supérieures,* Foucault wrote on Hegel's *Phenomenology of Spirit* under the direction of Hyppolite.

Foucault obtained the *licence de philosophie* in 1948 and the *licence de psychologie* in 1949 at the Sorbonne, where Jean Wahl, Jean Beaufret, Jean Hyppolite, and Maurice Merleau-Ponty were leading figures. In July 1951 Foucault passed the *agrégation,* having failed the oral part of the exam the previous year.

In 1951 Foucault became *répétiteur* of psychology at the Ecole Normale Supérieure, where his course was attended by Gérard Genette, Paul Veyne, and Jacques Derrida, among others. He was exempted from military service during that same year for reasons of health. In June 1952 he passed his *diplôme de psychopathologie* at the Institute of Psychology of Paris and began teaching psychology at the University of Lille, as well as at the Ecole Normale. He was an avid reader of literature during these years, particularly writers such as Maurice Blanchot, Georges Bataille, and René Char. His interest in German psychiatry led him to visit Ludwig Binswanger in Switzerland in 1953 and to translate Binswanger's *Dream and Existence,* for which he also wrote a lengthy preface. In 1954 he attended Jacques Lacan's seminars at Sainte Anne and published *Maladie mentale et personnalité.* From 1955 to 1958 he taught at the University of Uppsala in Sweden, before moving to the Centre Français in Warsaw. In 1959, the year of his father's death, he took up a post at the Institut Français in Hamburg.

Foucault returned to France in 1960 to teach philosophy and psychology at the University of Clermont-Ferrand. There he met Gilles Deleuze and Daniel Defert, who was to become his companion from 1963 to the time of his death. In 1961 *Folie et déraison: Histoire de la folie à l'âge classique* and his complementary thesis, a translation of and introduction to Kant's *Anthropology,* were published. In May of the same year he defended his thesis, directed by Georges Canguilhem, and was awarded a *Doctorat ès lettres.* During the early 1960s Foucault wrote numerous texts on literary themes and figures, among them *Raymond Roussel.* He published *Birth of the Clinic* (1963) and joined the editorial committee of the journal *Critique.* He also developed a close friendship with the members of the *Tel Quel* group. Foucault participated in the famous Royaumont colloquium on Nietzsche organized by Deleuze in July 1964. Two years later he published *The Order of Things* and, with

Roger Laporte, edited a special issue of *Critique* devoted to Blanchot; his own essay, "The Thought of the Outside," constitutes a major contribution to Blanchot scholarship. From 1966 to 1968 Foucault resided in Sidi Bou Said, a small village in Tunisia, where he wrote *The Archaeology of Knowledge.*

Foucault returned to France in December 1968 to join the faculty of the experimental university at Vincennes, becoming a colleague and friend of Hélène Cixous. As a professor of philosophy entrusted with forming a new department, Foucault recruited Michel Serres, René Schérer, François Châtelet, Etienne Balibar, Alain Badiou, Jacques Rancière, and Gilles Deleuze to join him at Vincennes. In 1969 Foucault published his influential essay "What Is an Author?" The following year he was appointed, at the age of forty-three, to the chair of the history of systems of thought at the Collège de France. His inaugural lecture on December 2, 1970, was later published as *L'ordre du discours.* In 1972 Foucault published "My Heart, This Paper, This Fire," a critical and polemical response to Jacques Derrida's 1963 essay "Cogito and the History of Madness," which offered a reading and critique of Foucault's 1961 text on the history of madness. The two thinkers remained distant from one another until 1982, when Foucault circulated a letter on behalf of Derrida to protest his wrongful arrest in Prague.

The 1970s were a period of intense political activity for Foucault. He became involved in the movement for prison reform, helped create GIP (Groupe d'information sur les prisons), and published *Discipline and Punish* (1975), a major work on the history of the French penal system. During these years, Foucault lectured frequently in Brazil and North America, at places such as Berkeley, Irvine, Claremont, Stanford, Dartmouth, Princeton, and Columbia. With the publication of each new translation, interest in Foucault's work grew in the United States. The first volume of his *History of Sexuality,* published in 1976 (1978 in English), was to have an enormous influence on many academic disciplines. In 1981 Foucault participated in a major conference devoted to his work at the Davidson Center in Los Angeles.

In the early 1980s Foucault began to suffer symptoms of the AIDS virus—fatigue, weight loss, and pulmonary distress. Despite his condition, he continued his course at the Collège de France and, in 1984, corrected the proofs for further volumes in *The History of Sexuality.* In June 1984 he was hospitalized by his brother, Denys, at Saint Michel Hospital, before being transferred to the Salpetrière. He died on June 25 and was buried at Vendeuvre-du-Poitou.

"TO DO JUSTICE TO FREUD":
THE HISTORY OF MADNESS IN THE
AGE OF PSYCHOANALYSIS

When Elisabeth Roudinesco and René Major did me the honor and kindness of inviting me to a commemoration that would also be a reflection, to one of these genuine tributes where thought is conditioned by fidelity and fidelity honed by thought, I did not hesitate for one moment.

Above all, because I love memory. This is nothing original, of course, and yet, how else can one love? Indeed, thirty years ago the publication of this great book of Foucault was an event whose repercussions were so intense and multiple that I will not even try to identify them, much less measure them, deep inside me. Next, because I love friendship, and the trusting affection that Foucault showed me thirty years ago, which was to last for many years, was all the more precious in that, being shared, it corresponded to my professed admiration for him. Then, after 1972, what came to obscure this friendship, without, however, affecting my admiration, was not in fact alien to this book, and to a certain debate that ensued—or at least to its distant, delayed, and indirect effects. There was in all of this a sort of dramatic chain of events, a compulsive and repeated precipitation that I do not wish to describe here because I do not wish to be alone, to be the only one to speak of this after the death of Michel Foucault—except to say that this shadow that made us invisible to one another, that made us not associate with one another for nearly ten years (until January 1, 1982, when I returned from a Czech prison), is still part of a story that I love like life itself. It is part of a story or history that is related, and that by the same token relates me, to the book we are commemorating

This text was first delivered at the Sainte-Anne Hospital in Paris on November 23, 1991, at the Ninth Colloquium of the International Society for the History of Psychiatry and Psychoanalysis, which was devoted to Foucault's *Histoire de la folie* in order to mark the thirtieth anniversary of its publication. The colloquium was opened by Georges Canguilhem, to whose memory Derrida later dedicated the version of this text in *Résistances de la psychanalyse.* Reprinted, with changes, from "To Do Justice to Freud," translated by Pascale-Anne Brault and Michael Naas, *Critical Inquiry* 20, no. 2 (winter 1994): 227–66. Republished in *Resistances of Psychoanalysis,* by Jacques Derrida, translated by Peggy Kamuf, Pascale-Anne Brault, and Michael Naas (Stanford: Stanford University Press, 1998), 70–76, 113–18. First French publication, "'Etre juste avec Freud': L'histoire de la folie à l'âge de la psychanalyse," in *Penser la folie: Essais sur Michel Foucault,* proceedings of the Ninth Colloquium of the International Society for the History of Psychiatry and Psychoanalysis (Paris: Galilée, 1992), 141–95. Republished in *Résistances de la psychanalyse,* by Jacques Derrida (Paris: Galilée, 1996), 89–146. To follow the ambivalent role played by Freud in the work of Foucault, the interested reader will wish to look at the full text in *Resistances.*

here, to something like its postface, one of its postfaces, since the drama I just alluded to arose out of a certain postface, even out of a sort of postscript added by Foucault to a postface in 1972.

While accepting wholeheartedly this generous invitation, I nonetheless declined the accompanying suggestion that I return to the discussion that began some twenty-eight years ago. I declined for numerous reasons, the first being the one I just mentioned: one does not carry on a stormy discussion after the other has departed. Second, because this whole thing is more than overdetermined (so many difficult and intersecting texts—Descartes's, Foucault's—so many objections and responses, from me but also from all those, in France and elsewhere, who later came to act as arbiters), it has become too distant from me, and perhaps because of the drama just alluded to I no longer wished to return to it. In the end, the debate is archived and those who might be interested can analyze it as much as they want and decide for themselves. By rereading all the texts of this discussion, right up to the last word, and especially the last word, one will better be able to understand, I imagine, why I prefer not to give it a new impetus today. There is no privileged witness for such a situation—which, moreover, only ever has the chance of forming, and this from the very origin, with the possible disappearance of the witness. This is perhaps one of the meanings of any history of madness, one of the problems for any project or discourse concerning a history of madness, or even a history of sexuality: Is there any witnessing to madness? Who can witness? Does witnessing mean seeing? Is it to provide a reason [*rendre raison*]? Does it have an object? Is there any object? Is there a possible third that might provide a reason without objectifying, or even identifying, that is to say, without examining [*arraisoner*]?

Though I have decided not to return to what was debated close to thirty years ago, it would nevertheless be absurd, obsessional to the point of pathological, to say nothing of impossible, to give in to a sort of fetishistic denial and to think that I can protect myself from any contact with the place or meaning of this discussion. Although I intend to speak today of something else altogether, starting from a very recent rereading of *The History of Madness in the Classical Age,* I am not surprised, and you will probably not be either, to see the silhouette of certain questions reemerge: not their content, of course, to which I will in no way return, but their abstract type, the schema or specter of an analogous problematic. If I speak not of Descartes but of Freud, for example, if I thus avoid a figure who seems central to this book and who, because he is decisive as regards its center or centering of perspective, emerges right from the early pages on, right from the first border or approach, if I thus avoid this Cartesian reference in order to move toward another (psychoanalysis, Freudian or some other) that is evoked only on the edges of the book and is named only right near the end, or ends, on the other border, this will perhaps be once again in order to pose a question that will resemble the one that imposed itself upon me thirty years ago, namely, that of the very possibility of a history of madness.[1] The question will be, in the end, about the same, though it will be posed from another border, and it still imposes itself upon me as the first tribute owed such a book. If this book was possible, if it had from the beginning and retains today a certain monumental value, the presence and undeniable necessity of a *monument,* that is, of what imposes itself by recalling and cautioning, it must tell us, teach us, or ask us something about its own possibility.

About its own possibility *today:* yes, we are saying *today,* a certain today. Whatever else one may think of this book, whatever questions or reservations it might inspire in those who come at it from some other point of view, its pathbreaking force seems incontestable. Just as incontestable as the law according to which all pathbreaking opens the way only at a certain price, only, that is, by bolting shut other passages, by ligaturing, stitching up, or compressing, indeed repressing, at least provisionally, other veins. And so today, like yesterday, I mean in March of 1963, this question of the *today* is important to me, the question I tried to formulate yesterday. I ask you to pardon me this once, then, since I will not make a habit of it, for citing a few lines that then defined, in its general form, a task that seems to me still necessary, on the side of Freud this time rather than on the side of Descartes. By saying "on the side of Freud" rather than "on the side of Descartes," let us not give in too quickly to the naïveté that would precipitate us into believing that we are closer to a today with Freud than with Descartes, though this is the opinion of most historians.

Here, then, is the question of yesterday, of the today of yesterday, as I would translate it today, on the side of Freud, transporting it in this way into the today of today:

1.   See Michel Foucault, *Folie et déraison: Histoire de la folie à l'âge classique* (Paris: Plon, 1961), 53–57. A much-abridged version was published in 1964 and translated into English by Richard Howard under the title *Madness and Civilization: A History of Insanity in the Age of Reason* (New York: Pantheon, 1965). Since Derrida refers to the unabridged text of 1961 and works with the original title throughout, we have referred to this work as *The History of Madness* (or in some cases, *The History of Madness in the Classical Age*). For a more complete history of this text and of Foucault's debate with Derrida over it, see our note in Derrida's *Resistances of Psychoanalysis* (Stanford: Stanford University Press, 1998), 123 n. 1.—*Trans.*

Therefore, if Foucault's book, despite all the acknowledged im-
possibilities and difficulties [acknowledged by him, of course], was
capable of being written, we have the right to ask what, in the last
resort, supports this language without recourse or support ["without
recourse" and "without support" are expressions of Foucault that I
had just cited]: who enunciates the possibility of nonrecourse? Who
wrote and who is to understand, in what language and from what
historical situation of logos, who wrote and who is to understand
this history of madness? For it is not by chance that such a project
could take shape today. Without forgetting, *quite to the contrary,*
the audacity of Foucault's act in the *History of Madness,* we must
assume that a certain liberation of madness has gotten underway,
that psychiatry has opened itself up, however minimally [and, in the
end, I would be tempted simply to replace *psychiatry* with *psychoanalysis* in order to translate the today of yesterday into the today of
my question of today], and that the concept of madness as unreason,
if it ever had a unity, has been dislocated. And that a project such
as Foucault's can find its historical origin and passageway in the
opening produced by this dislocation.

  If Foucault, more than anyone else, is attentive and sensitive
to these kinds of questions, it nevertheless appears that he does not
acknowledge their quality of being prerequisite methodological or
philosophical considerations.[2]

If this type of question made any sense or had any legitimacy, if the
point was then to question that which, today, in this time that is ours, this
time in which Foucault's *History of Madness* was written, made possible
the event of such a discourse, it would have been more appropriate for me
to elaborate this problematic on the side of modernity, *a parte subjecti,* in
some sense, on the side where the book was written, thus on the side,
for example, of what must have happened to the modern psychiatry
mentioned in the passage I just read. To modern psychiatry or, indeed,
to psychoanalysis, or rather to psychoanalyses or psychoanalysts, since the
passage to the plural will be precisely what is at stake in this discussion.
It would have thus been more imperative to insist on modern psychiatry
or psychoanalysis than to direct the same question toward Descartes. To
study the place and role of psychoanalysis in the Foucaultian project of
a history of madness, as I am now going to try to do, might thus consist

---

2.   Jacques Derrida, "Cogito and the History of Madness," in *Writing and Difference,* trans.
Alan Bass (Chicago: University of Chicago Press, 1978), 38.

in correcting an oversight or in confronting more directly a problematic that I had left in a preliminary stage, as a general, programmatic frame, in the introduction to my lecture of 1963. That lecture made only one allusion to psychoanalysis. It is true, however, that it inscribed it from the very opening. In a protocol that laid out certain reading positions, I spoke of the way in which philosophical language is rooted in nonphilosophical language, and I recalled a rule of hermeneutical method that still seems to me valid for the historian of philosophy as well as for the psychoanalyst, namely, the necessity of first ascertaining a surface or manifest meaning and, thus, of speaking the language of the patient to whom one is listening: the necessity of gaining a good understanding, in a quasi-scholastic way, philologically and grammatically, by taking into account the dominant and stable conventions, of what Descartes *meant* on the already so difficult surface of his text, such as it is interpretable according to classical norms of reading; the necessity of gaining this understanding *before* submitting the first reading to a symptomatic and historical interpretation regulated by other axioms or protocols, *before and in order to* destabilize, wherever this is possible and if it is necessary, the authority of canonical interpretations. Whatever one ends up doing with it, one must begin by listening to the canon. It is in this context that I recalled Ferenczi's remark cited by Freud in *The Interpretation of Dreams* ("Every language has its own dream language") and Lagache's observations concerning polyglotism in analysis.[3]

In its general and historical form, my question concerned the *site* that *today* gives rise to a history of madness and thereby makes it possible. Such a question should have led me, it is true, toward the situation of psychiatry and psychoanalysis rather than toward a questioning of a reading of Descartes. This logic would have seemed more natural, and the consequence more immediate. But if, in so strictly delimiting the field, I substituted Descartes for Freud, it was perhaps not only because of the significant and strategic place that Foucault confers upon the Cartesian moment in the interpretation of the "Great Confinement" and of the "Classical Age," that is to say, in the layout of the very object of the book; it was already, at least implicitly, because of the role that the reference to a certain Descartes played in the thought of that time, in the early sixties, as close as possible to psychoanalysis, in the very element, in truth, of a certain psychoanalysis and Lacanian theory. This theory developed around the question of the subject and the subject of science. Whether it was a question of anticipated certainty and logical time (1945, in *Ecrits*) or, some years

3.   See n. 3 of Derrida, "Cogito and the History of Madness," 307–8.

later (1965–66), of the role of the cogito and—precisely—of the deceitful God in "La science et la vérité," Lacan returned time and again to a certain unsurpassability of Descartes.[4] In 1945, Lacan associated Descartes with Freud in his "Propos sur la causalité psychique" and concluded by saying that "neither Socrates nor Descartes nor Marx nor Freud can be 'surpassed,' insofar as they conducted their research with this passion for unveiling whose object is the truth."[5]

The title I have proposed for the few reflections I will risk today, "The History of Madness in the Age of Psychoanalysis," clearly indicates a change—a change in time, in tense, mood, and voice. It is no longer a question of the age *described* by a *History of Madness*. It is no longer a question of an epoch or period, such as the classical age, that would, inasmuch as it is its very object, stand before the history of madness as Foucault writes it. It is a question today of the age to which the book itself belongs, the age out of which it takes place, the age that provides its situation: it is a question of the age that is *describing* rather than the age that is *described*. In my title, "the history of madness" ought to be in quotation marks since the title designates the age of the book, "The History (*historia rerum gestarum*) of Madness"—as a book—in the age of psychoanalysis and not the history (*res gestae*) of madness, of madness itself, in the age of psychoanalysis, even though, as we will see, Foucault regularly attempts to objectify psychoanalysis and to reduce it to that of which he speaks rather than to that out of which he speaks. What will interest me will thus be the time and historical conditions in which the book is rooted, those that it takes as its point of departure, and not so much the time or historical conditions that it recounts and tries in a certain sense to objectify. Were one to trust too readily in the opposition between subject and object, as well as in the category of objectification (something that I here believe to be neither possible nor just, and hardly faithful to Foucault's own intention), one would say for the sake of convenience that it is a question of considering the history of madness *a parte subjecti,* that is, from the side where it is written or inscribed and not from the side of what it describes.

Now, from the side where this history is written, there is, of course, a certain state of psychiatry—as well as psychoanalysis. Would Foucault's project have been possible without psychoanalysis, with which it

---

4. See Jacques Lacan, "Propos sur la causalité psychique" and "La science et la vérité," in *Ecrits* (Paris: Seuil, 1966), 209, 219–44. The latter was translated by Bruce Fink under the title "Science and Truth," *Newsletter of the Freudian Field* 3, nos. 1–2 (1989): 4–29.

5. Lacan, "Propos sur la causalité psychique," 193.

is contemporary and of which it speaks little and in such an equivocal or ambivalent manner in the book? Does the project owe psychoanalysis anything? What? Would the debt, if it had been contracted, be essential? Or would it, on the contrary, define the very thing from which the project had to detach itself, in a critical fashion, in order to take shape? In a word, what is the situation of psychoanalysis at the moment of, and with respect to, Foucault's book? And how does this book situate its project with respect not only to psychoanalysis in general but to a particular psychoanalysis, at a particular phase of its history, in one or another of its figures? [. . .]

The question that I would have liked to formulate would thus aim neither to protect psychoanalysis against some new attack nor to cast the slightest doubt upon the importance, necessity, and legitimacy of Foucault's extremely interesting project concerning this great history of sexuality. My question would only seek—and this would be, in sum, a sort of modest contribution—to complicate somewhat an axiomatic and, on the basis of this, perhaps, certain discursive or conceptual procedures, particularly regarding the way in which this axiomatic is inscribed in its age, in the historical field that serves as a point of departure, and in its reference to psychoanalysis. In a word, without compromising in the least the necessity of reinscribing almost "all" psychoanalysis (assuming one could seriously say such a thing, which I do not believe one can: psychoanalysis *itself, all* psychoanalysis, *the whole truth about all* psychoanalysis) into a history that precedes and exceeds it, it would be a question of becoming interested in certain gestures, in certain works, in certain moments of certain works of psychoanalysis, Freudian and post-Freudian (for one cannot, especially in France, seriously treat this subject by limiting oneself to a strictly Freudian discourse and apparatus), in certain traits of a consequently nonglobalizable psychoanalysis, one that is divided and multiple (like the powers that Foucault ceaselessly reminds us are essentially dispersed). It would then be a question of admitting that these necessarily fragmentary or disjointed movements say and do, provide resources for saying and doing, what *The History of Sexuality* (*The Will to Knowledge*) wishes to say, what it *means* [*veut dire*], and what it wishes to do (to know and to make known) with regard to psychoanalysis. In other words, if one still wanted to speak in terms of age—something that I would only ever do in the form of citation—at this point, here on this line, concerning some trait that is on the side out of which the history of sexuality is written rather than on the side of what it describes or objectifies, one would have to say that Foucault's project in its possibility belongs too much to "the age of psychoanalysis" for it, when claiming to thematize psychoanalysis, to do anything other than let psychoanalysis continue to speak obliquely of itself and to mark one of its folds in a scene that I will not call self-referential or specular and whose structural complication I will not even try to describe (I have tried to do this elsewhere). This is not only because of what withdraws this history from the regime of representation (because of what already inscribes the possibility of this history in and after the age of Freud and Heidegger—to use these names as mere indications for the sake of convenience). It is also for a reason that interests us here more directly: what Foucault announces and denounces about the relation between pleasure and power, in what he calls the "double impetus: pleasure and power,"[6] would find, already in Freud, to say nothing of those who followed, discussed, transformed, and displaced him, the very resources for the objection leveled against the "good genius," the so very bad "good genius," of the father of psychoanalysis. I will situate this with just a word in order to conclude.

Foucault clearly cautioned us: this history of sexuality was not to be a historian's history. A "genealogy of desiring man" was to be neither a history of representations nor a history of behaviors or sexual practices. This would lead one to think that sexuality cannot become an object of history without seriously affecting the historian's practice and the concept of history. Moreover, Foucault puts quotation marks around the word "sexuality": "the quotation marks have a certain importance," he adds.[7] We are thus also dealing here with the history of a word, with its uses starting in the nineteenth century and the reformulation of the vocabulary in relation to a large number of other phenomena, from biological mechanisms to traditional and new norms, to the institutions that support these, be they religious, juridical, pedagogical, or medical (for example, psychoanalytic).

This history of the uses of a word is neither nominalist nor essentialist. It concerns procedures and, more precisely, zones of "problematization." It is a "history of truth" as a history of *problematizations,* and even as an "archeology of problematizations," "through which being offers itself as something that can and must be thought."[8] The point is to analyze not simply behaviors, ideas, or ideologies but, above all, the *problematizations* in which a thought of being intersects "practices" and "practices of the self," a "genealogy of practices of the self" through which these problematizations are formed. With its reflexive vigilance and care in thinking itself in its

6. Michel Foucault, *The History of Sexuality,* vol. 1, *An Introduction,* trans. Robert Hurley (New York: Vintage Books, 1980), 45.

7. Michel Foucault, *The History of Sexuality,* vol. 2, *The Use of Pleasure,* trans. Robert Hurley (New York: Pantheon Books, 1985), 3.

8. Foucault, *The Use of Pleasure,* 11–13.

rigorous specificity, such an analysis thus calls for the *problematization of its own problematization*. And this must *itself* also question itself, with the same archeological and genealogical care, the same care that it itself methodically prescribes.

When confronted with a historical problematization of such scope and thematic richness, one should not be satisfied either with a mere survey or with asking in just a few minutes an overarching question so as to insure some sort of synoptic mastery. What we can and must try to do in such a situation is to pay tribute to a work this great and this uncertain by means of a question that it itself raises, by means of a question that it carries within itself, that it keeps in reserve in its unlimited potential, one of the questions that can thus be deciphered within it, a question that keeps it in suspense, holding its breath [*tient . . . en haleine*]—and, thus, keeps it alive.

For me, one such question would be the one I tried to formulate a few years ago during a conference honoring Foucault at New York University.[9] It was developed by means of a problematization of the concept of power and of the theme of what Foucault calls the *spiral* in the duality power/pleasure. Leaving aside the huge question of the concept of power and of what gives it its alleged unity under the essential dispersion rightly recalled by Foucault himself, I will pull out only a thread: it would lead to that which, in a certain Freud and at the center of a certain French heritage of Freud, would not only never let itself be objectified by the Foucaultian problematization but would actually contribute to it in the most determinate and efficient way, thereby deserving to be inscribed on the thematizing rather than on the thematized border of this history of sexuality. I wonder what Foucault would have said, in this perspective and were he to have taken this into account, not of "Freud" or of psychoanalysis "itself" *in general*—which does not exist any more than power does as one big central and homogeneous corpus—but, for example, since this is only one example, about an undertaking like *Beyond the Pleasure Principle,* about something in its lineage or between its filial connections—along with everything that has been inherited, repeated, or discussed from it since then. In following one of these threads or filial connections, one of the most discreet, in following the abyssal, unassignable, and unmasterable strategy of this text, a strategy that is finally without strategy, one begins to see that this text not only opens up the horizon of a beyond of the

9.   The following analysis intersects a much longer treatment of the subject in an unpublished paper entitled "Beyond the Power Principle," which I presented at a conference honoring Foucault organized at New York University by Thomas Bishop in April 1986.

pleasure principle (the hypothesis of such a beyond never really seeming to be of interest to Foucault) against which the whole economy of pleasure needs to be rethought, complicated, pursued in its most unrecognizable ruses and detours. By means of one of these filiations—another one unwinding the spool of the *fort/da* that continues to interest us—this text also problematizes, in its greatest radicality, the agency of power and mastery. In a discreet and difficult passage, an original drive for power or drive for mastery (*Bemächtigungstrieb*) is mentioned. It is very difficult to know if this drive for power is still dependent upon the pleasure principle, indeed, upon sexuality as such, upon the austere monarchy of sex that Foucault denounces on the last page of his book.

How would Foucault have situated this drive for mastery in his discourse on power or on irreducibly plural powers? How would he have read this drive, had he read it, in this extremely enigmatic text of Freud? How would he have interpreted the recurring references to the demonic from someone who then makes himself, according to his own terms, the "devil's advocate" and who becomes interested in the hypothesis of a late or derived appearance of sex and sexual pleasure? In the whole problematization whose history he describes, how would Foucault have inscribed this passage from *Beyond the Pleasure Principle,* and this concept and these questions (with all the debates to which this book of Freud either directly or indirectly gave rise, in a sort of overdetermining capitalization, particularly in the France of our age, beginning with everything in Lacan that takes its point of departure in the repetition compulsion [*Wiederholungszwang*])? Would he have inscribed this problematic matrix *within* the whole whose history he describes? Or would he have put it on the other side, on the side of what allows one, on the contrary, to delimit the whole, indeed, to problematize it? And thus on a side that no longer belongs to the whole, nor, I would be tempted to think, to any whole, such that the very idea of a gathering of problematization or procedure [*dispositif*], to say nothing any longer of age, *episteme,* paradigm, or epoch, would make for so many problematic names, just as problematic as the very idea of problematization?

This is one of the questions that I would have liked to ask him. I am trying, since this is, unfortunately, the only recourse left us in the solitude of questioning, to imagine the principle of the reply. It would perhaps be something like this: what one must stop believing in is principality or principleness, in the problematic of the principle, in the principled unity of pleasure and power, or of some drive that is thought to be more originary than the other. The theme of the *spiral* would be that of a drive duality (power/pleasure) that is *without principle.*

Is not what Freud was looking for, under the names "death drive" and "repetition compulsion," that which, coming "before" the principle (of pleasure or reality), would remain forever heterogeneous to the principle of principle?

It is *the spirit of this spiral* that keeps one in suspense, holding one's breath—and, thus, keeps one alive.

The question would thus once again be given a new impetus: is not the duality in question, this spiraled duality, precisely what Freud tried to oppose to all monisms by speaking of a dual drive and of a death drive, of a death drive that was no doubt not alien to the drive for mastery? And, thus, to what is most alive in life, to its very living on [*survivance*]?

I am still trying to imagine Foucault's response. I can't quite do it. I would have so much liked for him to take it on himself.

But in this place where no one now can answer for him, in the absolute silence where we remain nonetheless turned toward him, I would venture to wager that, in a sentence that I will not construct for him, he would have associated and yet also dissociated, he would have placed back to back, mastery and death, that is, the same—death *and* the master, death *as* the master.

CHAPTER 4

MAX LOREAU

JUNE 7, 1928—JANUARY 7, 1990

Belgian poet, writer, aesthete, and philosopher Max Loreau was born in Brussels in 1928 and spent most of his childhood and adolescence in Wemmel, on the outskirts of Brussels. He attended schools in Laeken and Koekelberg before studying classical philology and philosophy at the Free University in Brussels. Roger Goosens, writer, poet, professor of Greek, and reader of Nietzsche, was Loreau's most influential teacher during this period. Although most of Loreau's own work focuses on contemporary poets, painters and writers, he always felt an affinity for classical authors such as Homer, Lucretius, Virgil, and Dante, whom he studied at the university.

In the early 1950s Loreau married and helped raise a family of three children. From 1951 to 1955 he performed his military service, taught briefly in a high school, and continued his philosophical studies at the Free University in Brussels. He there earned his doctorate in philosophy in 1961 with a thesis entitled "L'humanisme rhétorique de Lorenzo Valla et la formation de la pensée bourgeoise en Italie." His doctoral research led him to Florence, a city that would later inspire his book of poems *Florence portée aux nues* (1986).

After his university studies, Loreau became a member of Le Fonds National de la Recherche Scientifique (the Belgian equivalent of France's Centre National de la Recherche Scientifique) and later a professor of modern philosophy and aesthetics at the Free University (1964–69). He was married a second time, in 1967, to Francine Loreau. Active in student gatherings at the Free University in Brussels in 1968, Loreau abandoned his academic career the following year to devote himself entirely to writing.

Throughout the 1950s and 1960s Loreau pursued his interests in art, photography, and poetry writing. In 1963 he met the painter Jean Dubuffet, with whom he would develop a close friendship and to whom he would devote numerous studies, including *Dubuffet et le voyage au centre de la perception* (1966), the philosophical commentary "Art, Culture et Subversion," published in May 1968 and later collected in *La peinture à l'oeuvre et l'énigme du corps* (1980). Loreau also edited the first twenty-eight volumes of Dubuffet's *Catalogue des travaux.*

Loreau's interest in Henri Michaux's "mescaline drawings" led him to make the acquaintance of the poet in 1964. His first work of poetry, *Cerceaux 'sorcellent,* illustrated by Dubuffet, appeared in 1967. In 1973 he published *Cri: Eclat et phases*—his *livre-clef*—a book in which philosophy and poetic writing are intimately woven together. Loreau also began a long correspondence during this period with Christian Dotrement, the founder of the avant-garde group Cobra, to whom Loreau devoted a text entitled *Les logogrammes de Christian Dotrement* (1975). In the late 1970s Loreau experimented with short stories (*Nouvelles des êtres et des pas,* 1976) and published *Chants de perpétuelle venue* (1978). He became a frequent contributor to the journal *Po&sie* and later joined its editorial board; his book on the poet Michel Deguy was a result of this association.

La peinture à l'oeuvre, a collection of Loreau's essays on art, poetry, painting, and language, was published in 1980. The text, centred around "the secret of the body," staged a confrontation between poetic language and pictorial form. Throughout the 1980s Loreau continued to publish critical studies on contemporary art, on such artists as Pierre Alechinsky, Karel Appel, Willem de Kooning, Dubuffet, Dotrement, and René Magritte.

In 1987 Loreau published *En quête d'un autre commencement,* a major collection of essays on philosophy (including two lengthy studies of Hegel dating from 1969–70), art (Picasso), poetry and literature (Saint-John Perse, Louis-René des Forêts). *L'attrait du commencement,* which appeared the following year, was published in conjunction with an exhibition of paintings organized by Loreau at the Centre Culturel de la Communauté Française in Brussels on the occasion of his sixtieth birthday. Like all of Loreau's work on art, this book is concerned with the "inexhaustible enigma of painting." The poetic work "Dans l'éclat du moment—Le matin d'Orphée," written in collaboration with Gérard Garcin, who had on several occasions put Loreau's poems to music, was performed and recorded by the Nouvel Orchestre Philharmonique in September 1988 for Radio France.

In 1988 Loreau fell ill with cancer and underwent surgery and chemotherapy. He spent eight months in the hospital recovering from the loss of speech and memory that had resulted from the surgery and medications. These experiences are described in *L'épreuve,* Loreau's last work, published shortly before his death. In 1989 the monumental *La genèse du phénomène,* a study of Plato, Kant, and Heidegger, was published. In this text Loreau gave a philosophical shape to his abiding interest in the birth and genesis of phenomena and the notion of creation in art, philosophy, and poetry.

Loreau lost his struggle with cancer on January 7, 1990. In May of that year the Collège International de Philosophie devoted a special session to his work.

Ris Orangis, July 15, 1991

Dear Francine,

[. . .]

It is also in order to call you to witness that I turn to you today. In the end I wasn't able to write what I had wanted to dedicate to the memory of Max, something that would be worthy of him, that would show the extent of my admiration for the singular force of his thought, that would do justice to the intractable intensity of his bodily struggle with language, *in language,* already in language's own struggle with itself, something that would resemble what he has left living in me, in us, that would also be worthy of the friendship he offered me, a friendship of which I have no doubt shown myself, for a long time now, to be unworthy.

But already, you see (and I prefer addressing you first, Francine, for you have been the closest witness to what I no doubt will not be able to say here), this language linking "force" to guilt would probably not have pleased Max. I do not like it either, but what is the use of not acknowledging guilt when it remains infinite despite every claim to the contrary? Already with these first words so tentatively ventured, I feel I am being unjust, with an injustice without limit.

Why do just the right words escape me here?

Having tried time and again to write, having failed over and over, I had to admit to myself that something else was preventing me from writing beyond all the "mitigating circumstances": fatigue, false emergencies, frantic running around, doing too many things at once, living at an absurd pace—I remember Max once accusing me of all this, as we were parting on a train platform in Brussels, during what turned out to be our last meeting. He seemed to reproach me for these things as though they were a kind of distraction, diversion, or means of escape, far from that intense interiority to which one might retreat or fold in upon, to which he knew how to bend or give in, if only better to think space and reopen the outside, each time as if for the first time. He let me hear his objection with what seemed to me a friendly and deserved severity, though also with a smile that perhaps feigned incomprehension. Beyond every "circumstance," then, some other thing puts me at a loss for just the right words. What other thing?

This being at a loss says something, of course, about mourning and about its truth, the impossible mourning that nonetheless remains at work,

Translated by Pascale-Anne Brault and Michael Naas for this volume. First French publication, "Lettre à Francine Loreau," in *Max Loreau* (Brussels: Lebeer-Hossmann, 1991), 95–105.

endlessly hollowing out the depths of our memories, beneath their great beaches and beneath each grain of sand, beneath the phenomenal or public scope of our destiny and behind the fleeting, inapparent moments, those without archive and without words (a meeting in a café, a letter eagerly torn open, a burst of laughter revealing the teeth, a tone of the voice, an intonation on the phone, a style of handwriting in a letter, a parting in a train station, and each time we say that we do not know, that we do not know if and when and where we will meet again). This being at a loss also has to do with a duty: to let the friend speak, to turn speech over to him, his speech, and especially not to take it from him, not to take it in his place—no offense seems worse at the death of a friend (and I already feel that I have fallen prey to it)—to allow him to speak, to occupy his silence or to take up speech oneself only in order, if this is possible, to give it back to him.

I have often felt this loss, for I have already lost too many friends (and the discourse of mourning is more threatened than others, though it should be less, by the generality of the genre, and silence would here be the only rigorous response to such a fateful necessity). I have already lost too many friends and I lack the strength to speak publicly and to recall each time another end of the world, the same end, another, and each time it is nothing less than an origin of the world, each time the sole world, the unique world, which, in its end, appears to us as it was at the origin—sole and unique—and shows us what it owes to the origin, that is to say, what it will have been, beyond every future anterior. And you know that the origin of this appearing without any present thing, without presence even, this presence without phenomenon, this phenomenon with no other beginning than the rending cry that separates language from itself at its birth, on the verge of articulation, in the very first spacing of the proper body, was, as you know, beyond every Thing, the theme, task, and unrelenting desire of Max: to try to the very end to turn, to make fold, or rather to let fold of itself, to turn inside out, to operate through this operation of writing and voice, through the initialing of the work, this turn that converts both body and thought to the reengendering of this origin of the world, and to recapture the becoming apparent of the appearing rather than what has appeared. Every instant of Max's writing bears witness to this, on the very edge, on the fold of this originary rending, on the fold that marks in advance or else keeps the trace of this rending, the fold that genesis makes with death.[1]

1.   Derrida works throughout this text with the themes and titles of many of Loreau's works: *La genèse du phénomène* (Paris: Minuit, 1989), *Nouvelles des êtres et des pas*

No, I sense that what is at stake in this loss, in the depths of my affection for Max, is some thing other, an even more singular thing. (I dare not say the Thing, for fear of being seized, submerged, reengulfed right here by his *Cry,* for he gave us already long ago the poem of the Thing. I quote, almost at random: "and the Cry having stopped, the Thing is there, radiant, bare, discovered, as if detached," as if the Thing were the end of the cry, at once the beginning and the end of language in "the equal, indifferent Thing, detached at present,"[2] or "something that is stable—and that is nothing, empty and limitless space—a mass that remains the same, invariable, that does not evolve when the view changes, when it expends itself in evolutions, when the head or body changes place; hence something that remains unchanged—the Thing—in relation to force—the view— that gives of itself unsparingly and goes" [C, 166], as if the Thing were the figure of both death and the immobilized monument, the two faces or two silences of the same forgetting, the two faces of memory that we do not wish to see, that our mourning endures but cannot possibly want.)

Some thing—which was everything but the Thing, everything and nothing so as to avoid the Thing—something happened that separated us, but in friendship, I believe, as if midway along a path. Separating us, then, without separating us, without, as far as I am concerned, either my friendship or my admiring attention being put into question. But little by little, toward the end of the seventies, after a good ten years of meetings, letters, exchanges, as I'm sure you remember, a silence settled in, and then invisibility, a communication no doubt more and more indirect—silent in any case. I suffered from this and suffer even more today since I feel responsible for it, and once again beyond all those "circumstances" that— unfortunately, for this experience is all too common—often lead to such situations (distance, the infrequency of meetings, and then, gaining ground day by day, gaining on the day itself, invisibility, the unbearable and yet endured certainty that in the days that are left us we can count on one hand the promised or probable meetings with those whom we love and of whom our life is, as we say, made up).

I don't know how Max would have felt and interpreted this separa- tion (and to remain silent about it today would be an indecent lie and the worst of betrayals). It remains a secret, for me one of the absolute secrets of this life, and of what is best in this life. I say "best in this life" because this

---

(Paris: Gallimard, 1978), *Chants de perpétuelle venue* (Paris: Gallimard, 1978), and *Vue d'intérieur (Le drame de la naissance du globe)* (Montmorency: Carte Blanche, 1986), to name a few.—*Trans.*

2.   Max Loreau, *Cri: Eclat et phases* (Paris: Gallimard, 1973), 37 (hereafter abbreviated as *C*).

very separation never stopped making me think, or giving me to think, and I would like to have received it today as a gift from Max, whether he knew it or not. He knew, to be sure, that what separates—divides and cleaves— by the same token also *gives,* and that it is not necessary to know, indeed that it is necessary not to know, and thus recognize, restitute, or identify; he knew that the *without return* is necessary in order to give. Earlier, I said that our separation was "silent" [*muette*], and I quoted from his *Cry* the words "gives unsparingly" (Max's language was itself unsparing, it gave unsparingly): "force—the view—that gives of itself unsparingly and goes." A few years later, here is what his *Seagull* [*Mouette*], yes, *gave* to be heard, accomplishing it and by the same token *giving* it in its flight—"for nothing but to see" [*rien que pour voir*]. (It would be necessary to ponder ad infinitum the extraordinary syntax of this "for nothing but to see"; beyond negation and position—nothing [*rien*] is the no (step) [*pas*]—it speaks the just withdrawal of the Thing (*res*), just to see and *give* or bring to the light of day, according to the voice, before the voice, after it, in what relates rhythm to the cry and the cry to flight):

> as far as the eye can't see
> the voice you see, silences
> THIS VOICE, SO OUT OF ITS SENSES
> SO OUT OF ITS SENSES AND SO CONTAINED
> THAT IT CLAMORS FOR NOTHING BUT TO SEE
> . . . .
> cleave(s)
> and cleaving cleans away
> and leaning cleaves and sees, a way
> cleaving to have clearing room
> and seeing to it to cleave it all
> indefinitely divides
> and gives and gives
> and gives unsparingly
> yields the endless day[3]

You no doubt know more about this separation between us than I do, dear Francine, this separation in life before that other one, but the secret will remain. No one will ever know anything essential about it. No one

---

3.   À vue perdue / voix tue / SI EPERDUE SA VOIX / SI EPERDUE ET SI CONTENUE / QU'ELLE CLAME RIEN QUE POUR VOIR . . . fend / et fendant épanche / et 'panchant fende et voie / fendant à franche percée / et voyant à tout fendre / indéfiniment tranche / et donne et donne / prodigue / dispense le jour sans fin.

will ever be able to testify to it, not even those of us who were closest, and especially not me. But I am nonetheless tempted to think that the silence of separation (like the secret that bears it) perhaps came, or at least I would like to hope—better than long-winded or philosophical explanations could have—*to say* by enigma, to say in silence and in secret, what happened to us and what must be able to be felt in the published texts, I mean in the things of the "endless day."

Because this is in principle readable in the things of the day, readable for those who might be interested in it; because I would like to believe that it comes close, through certain irregular movements, without any cartography, to what I will venture to call here, for lack of a better word, *thought* or *language* or, in their bodily struggle, the *idiom* or the *cry;* because these movements are undoubtably not decisions; because they remain, though just barely, displacements for which one cannot answer or be responsible; because it should not be measured against some continuous narrative or interpretation; because this cannot be summed up or gathered into a whole, especially for whoever remains alone, after Max's death; because I do not want to be the only one to speak about what concerns the two of us, and, a frightful hypothesis, claim to have the last word on what took place between us, I will say nothing, nothing other than the separation or loss that I have not stopped talking about, though these are, of course, negative translations of what, in truth, I received or will have been given since Max and I first crossed by one another.

Forgive me then, Francine, for continuing on like this for just a bit longer, but I would like to sketch out just one of the figures that has imposed itself upon me for some time now (and it is precisely the figure of what remains unfigurable): here, traces of no's and of steps [*traces de pas*], of "beings and of (no) steps [*d'êtres et de pas*]," on a beach or in the desert, attest that two were destined *to cross right by one another* [*se croiser*]. I use these words, evoking the crossing or crossroads, to speak neither of the cross, the point at the center of which two trajectories come in effect, in fact, to traverse one another, or one the other, thus assuring us that the meeting indeed took place, nor, more literally or to the letter, of the chi or the chiasm, the point of chiasm beyond which two lines become distant from or lose one another to infinity, nor even of the indubitable point of tangency and contact assured by a crossing of paths. No, I am speaking rather of "crossing right by one another," in passing, from afar, without any assured contact, without any assurance, "crossing right by one another" in an improbable "meeting," that is to say, without proof, forever intangible, intangent, and intact, without witness, the time of an interminable greeting to which each one alone and the others alone (all of them alone and each alone and without witnesses) will think they can bear witness, the "crossing right by one another" of two at once finite and "perpetual" arrivals [*venues "perpétuelles"*], perpetually finite, having come from who knows where and from a distance that remains unascribable by anyone. It is this arrival that I nonetheless had the good fortune to be given (I am here to attest to it, I am here only to the extent that I can still attest to it), a good fortune that still leaves life in me. In this proximity, I hesitate to say at the instant but at the point of crossing of such a "crossing right by one another," or, better, at the point when this crossing is so imminent that one never knows whether it is taking place, whether it will have taken place or not, and no one will ever know this, the trace itself, which was already there, imprints onto the two vestiges the form of an ellipsis, a way of being silent from which two movements take up or pursue one another "to death." That is, pursue one another toward their most common destination, their most commonly shared experience, without anyone being able to count the paths, whether there was one, one that was *one,* or two or more, without anyone being able to account for this, and to know whether the distancing, once again, between the traces of (no) steps, in the trace and in the (no) step, doesn't amount to the same thing. Can one figure the figure of these beings or steps or not(s)? I try to sketch out this trajectory but I never get there; I get lost because I am still engaged in it for a time, but I would not be there, I will no longer be there, without Max.

I am rereading him right now in wonder, better no doubt than ever before. I would like to quote everything, read or reread everything aloud. Everyone can—everyone should—do this. I was thinking, for example, that words beginning in *int,* the letters *i.n.t.* suit him well, like a signature, precisely because they are absent from his name. They do indeed seem to sign the high tension that was his, and that could be felt when you saw, heard, or read him. These letters came to me too when I wanted to speak about him. (Already earlier, "po*int,*" [and what in French is not pronounced in these letters], or "*int*ense," "*int*ractable," "*int*erior," and just an instant ago, "tension"; I could have also said "*int*ransigent," "*int*erior" or "*int*imate"—for even his insistence on the outside, breaking open, space, and the opening, was held taut in a sort of restraint or reserve, folded up or gathered together toward a *point de dedans* [toward no inside, toward a point inside]—and like the *pas* [the no, the step], like the *rien que* [nothing but], the *point* remains suspended between the indefiniteness of negation and the power of affirmation.) I can see on each page that these are indeed *his* words, and this vocabulary gathers and sometimes condenses, intensifies, so to speak, its density in the course of a single page.

Thus, in *Cry,* though I could multiply the examples endlessly:

> (no) central point that it projects at the extreme point of the gaze
> around a landmark point it has planted in them, where it has
> become implanted and thanks to which, while remaining at a
> distance from them by the full length of its axis, thus keeping them
> at a distance, pushing them away, holding back their surge with
> all the strength of this sunken point, this intense point, holding at
> a distance their violences around this point and protecting itself
> from them with all the pressure of the gaze taut like a piercing
> trait or dart . . . (through the point of the gaze, it is both within and
> without them) . . . the body, losing sight, losing its view, at the same
> time loses its axis, and thus its outsides (for it is sight—or the cry
> burst open into sight—that separates it from its outsides and keeps
> them from its insides. (*C,* 110)

I am also rereading some of his letters, so numerous and so beautiful.
I hesitate to quote from them, out of discretion, though it would be hard
to determine whether it is mine or his; and yet I want to let him have the
last word here. How to let him have the last word and yet speak of him, of
him alone? In order not to draw from what everyone can read out there
of the public thing, I will select a few sentences written by his hand, ones
that speak precisely of him, very early on of his work, and much better
than I could. Limiting myself to the oldest ones, the initial ones, those
that followed our first meetings, I cite them not in order to withdraw or
to let him speak alone of himself, but because I like, in transcribing, to
underwrite and listen to his voice, and to look at his writing, I mean the
way he forms his letters, his manner, his hand.

July 30, 1966 (we had only recently met; he was talking about a
community of solitary beings and of ashes without witness):

> It will thus probably be necessary to go on to other, more perilous,
> exercises of an aphilosophical nature. For, after all, what we seek
> is the (no) point where what has come to be settled gets unsettled,
> where what is getting ready to greet you gets thrown off course.
> But so that there may be life and health and fluid thought, it is
> indispensable that there be, at times, here and there, some signs
> of a community—so that a new disruption might be undertaken.
> Without such signs we are thrown into madness, into an acceler-
> ating thought that is nothing but immobility: speed destroys itself
> by stalling in place and the appearing is there but the form of the
> appeared . . . a desire for other activities in which the representation

of the necessity of abolishing representation is abolished for the
sake of the apparition that is nothing but itself and leaves behind
itself no ashes. To make the ashes disappear (like burnt nylon or
Styrofoam)—that is what is most difficult, that is the task.

August 9, 1966 (he was talking about Artaud and about some
"definitive things" that are, he said, "dangerous to live and to apply,"
and toward which it is "especially dangerous to *throw oneself* abruptly"):

> These things must be taken on progressively, with caution; oth-
> erwise, beware of suicide. In the end it is a matter of returning to
> animal life without renouncing thought, of reintroducing phos-
> phorescent life into thought: it is difficult not to slip at one point or
> another. And all it takes is for one to indulge in these practices in
> solitude—every theatrical dimension being suspended—and very
> quickly one no longer understands the others. The task is to be able
> to keep company with both madness and the others. And madness
> is so tempting for us who have learnt only to keep company with
> others. . . . So tempting and so frightening.

One year later, in a letter of August 23, 1967 (in the course of a
discussion about metaphysics and the necessity of writing "hybrid" texts
in which "each of two positions"—that of a writing that has broken with
metaphysics and that of, so to speak, the professional philosopher, the one
he no longer wanted to be—"is in some way contaminated by the other
and seen from the other"):

> It is a matter of finding the way that allows one to escape these
> positions from within. I think I have found it in the hyperbolic
> systematization of metaphysical oppositions. What bothers me, in
> the end, in traditional metaphysics, is not so much the oppositions
> but the fact that their terms have not been sufficiently op-posed,
> that they are not kept at a sufficient distance from one another
> and are not left face to face long enough. It is in this sustained op-
> position and distancing that a way for us to escape metaphysics
> is called for and indicated. But this way can only be traced from
> within metaphysics: it is necessary to begin looking at it from a
> metaphysical point of view in order to discover conceptually and
> metaphysically that it calls for nonmetaphysics and the nonconcept.
> The text "the work of art as creation" tries to be a marker along
> this path. . . . When I speak of art, I can only consider it within
> the system of culture. In this system, there is a privileged meaning:
> it carries within itself the memory of something that precedes

culture . . . it carries into the heart of culture the necessity of the noncultural, and into the heart of representation the necessity of nonpresence.

October 3, 1967, in a postscript:

I want to be done with our language of vision. Our language is a language of cops, a language of reports. We spend our time reporting others, directing traffic. But I don't want to be a cop. Vision is founded on speech, not the contrary. Speech is the emission of space (spacing . . .). We must find a way to leave in words only the residue of vision that is indispensable to their being "received."

February 12, 1968:

I intend to write a new "sequel." Up until now I was profoundly disturbed because I could see only bits and pieces of movements, without any links. It now seems that these fragments of trajectories have succeeded in forming a longer, more continuous gesture. I can thus say that things are "gesturing," even "gestating." It should be something like my *Aeneid* (complete with its own little descent into Hell). I feel like sleeping—that's about all the effect it has on me.

November 24, 1973 (concerning *Cri: Eclat et phases,* which was due to appear shortly):

It is a sort of philosophical litany or incantation, a disjointed and nightmarish mathematics—in short, a [and then there's an underlined word that I have never been able to make out, something like "black" or "drunk"] philosophy. It is at once rigorous and rigorously impossible (as with everything that is rigorously rigorous). As you can see, I don't quite know what it is and I am afraid that others will know even less. . . . It seems to me, when you have it right before your eyes, to be a kind of philosophical poem, composed by a Presocratic Lucretius who is beginning to lose it.

[. . .]
Yes, an intense desire to begin again now, to begin, in truth, to read him today, and I will do so, as if I could still hope to surprise, on the other side, on this other side of a cry or of a song of perpetual coming, the share of darkness in a voice that I know, that I can still hear very distinctly, as if I were finally going to *see* this voice on the side from which it is coming to this immense poem, from the *other side,* the side of the body, deep down in the throat where it is engorged (and I even hear in this expression the

name of the gorge cut into a mountainside, not far from some spring or source, but also the fall: the fall, and then the torrent, the dam, high tension, danger of death). [. . .]

Francine, I was happy to see you the other day at the Collège International de Philosophie, in the company of friends who found just the right words to speak about Max.

You remain in my thoughts, the two of you, faithfully.

Jacques D.

P.S. (September 10, 1991).

I had not yet read *Florence portée aux nues,* or *L'épreuve.* I receive them and am reading them today as a present gift—that is to say, for one who knows how to wait. And in order to prolong the *gift* [*don*] (a word that no doubt orients an impossible and thus necessary thought, the most absent and most urgent of our present time, that of the unthinkable but irrecusable sharing out), I will cite, following the "and gives and gives" cited earlier, "Give" [*Donne*], in *Florence portée aux nues,* where the verb is a noun, a name, and the act a call—which says it all and beyond the all:

GIVE
Light of giving
of fecundity,
spontaneous light
as exorbitant
in its self-forgetting
as the first circle opening[4]

And since I could feel something in *int* breaking through in these texts, around the *int*imate, the *int*erior, and the po*int,* here in *Florence . . .* —as in *L'épreuve,* where something "intimate but very far away" is recalled—we read:

Memory
without knowing it opens
. . . .
so that the intimate might break through[5]

and elsewhere, "a heart timid to intimacy."[6]

---

4.   DONNE / Lumière de donne / de fécondité, / lumière spontanée / aussi exorbitante / en son oubli de soi / que le premier cercle s'ouvrant.

5.   Mémoire / sans le savoir s'ouvre / . . . pour que puisse poindre de l'intime.

6.   Coeur à l'intime farouche.

CHAPTER 5

JEAN-MARIE BENOIST

APRIL 4, 1942—AUGUST 1, 1990

Author, educator, journalist, and philosopher Jean-Marie Benoist was born in Paris, the son of Jean Benoist, an engineer, and Suzanne Guesde. His great grandfather, Jules Guesde, was the founder of the French Workers' Party and a minister in the Third Republic (1914–16). Benoist studied at the Lycée Malherbe in Caen, and subsequently at the Lycées Henri IV and Louis-le-Grand in Paris, before entering the Ecole Normale Supérieure in Paris in 1963. In the same year he received two B.A.'s, one in philosophy and another in literature. He passed his *agrégation* in philosophy in 1966.

In October 1964 Benoist married painter-engraver Nathalie Isabelle Bréaud, with whom he had three children, Fabrice, Aliénor, and Sylvain. He took the post of professor of philosophy at the Lycée Français in London (1966–70) before becoming the cultural attaché at the French embassy (1970–74). In 1970 he published *Marx est mort* as a provocation and response to the events of May 1968 in France. Upon his return to France in 1974 he was appointed *maître-assistant* at the Collège de France, becoming a colleague of Claude Lévi-Srauss. The following year Benoist published *The Structural Revolution,* which took a critical stance toward the structuralist movement, and *Tyrannie du logos,* a study of the relation between Plato, the Sophists, and the birth of metaphysics.

During the 1970s Benoist was considered a member of the group of *nouveaux philosophes* who garnered much media attention in France. (Benoist engaged Gilles Deleuze in a heated public debate concerning the movement of the *nouveaux philosophes* in the columns of *Le Monde.*) In 1978 Benoist ran as a candidate for the right-leaning party Union pour la démocratie française (UDF) against communist candidate Georges Marchais in the legislative elections. Two pamphlets outlining his ideas against the left (*Un singulier programme* and *Les nouveaux primaires*) were published that year. In September of 1978 Benoist was married a second time, to Catherine Cécile Dewavrin, with whom he had two children, Olivier and Alexis. In 1980 he took part in the nationwide discussion regarding the French educational system, publishing *La génération sacrifiée* as his contribution to the debate.

In the early 1980s Benoist was a professor at New York University in France and lectured at l'Ecole Nationale des Ponts et Chaussées. He also held the chair of history of modern civilization at the Collège de France, from 1981 to 1990, where he became a friend and colleague of Roland Barthes. Throughout his career Benoist taught periodically in the United States, as a visiting professor at Harvard, the University of Pennsylvania, New York University, and Georgetown.

As a result of his growing interest in politics and foreign policy, Benoist founded the European Center for International Relations and Strategy (CERIS) in 1984 and joined the national advisory board to the right-wing political party Rassemblement pour la République (RPR) in 1985. During the 1980s he was a regular contributor to *Le Monde* and *Le Figaro* (for which he wrote articles on democracy and liberalism) as well as to *Le Quotidien de Paris.* Benoist also authored a number of prefaces for exhibition catalog; notable among them is a text devoted to Claude Garache. The last book he authored, *Les outils de la liberté,* advocated a return to Rousseau and Montesquieu.

Benoist died of cancer on August 1, 1990, at the age of forty-eight in the city of Megève in the Haute-Savoie region of France.

The Taste of Tears

> For the god of writing is also the god of death. He will punish the imprudent who, in their quest for unlimited knowledge, end up *drinking the dissolved book*. . . . To drink the tear and wonder about the strangeness of its taste compared to one's own . . .
>
> Jean-Marie Benoist, *The Geometry of the Metaphysical Poets*

To have a friend: to keep him. To follow him with your eyes. Still to see him when he is no longer there and to try to know, listen to, or read him when you know that you will see him no longer—and that is to cry.

To have a friend, to look at him, to follow him with your eyes, to admire him in friendship, is to know in a more intense way, already injured, always insistent, and more and more unforgettable, that one of the two of you will inevitably see the other die. One of us, each says to himself, the day will come when one of the two of us will see himself no longer seeing the other and so will carry the other within him a while longer, his eyes following without seeing, the world suspended by some unique tear, each time unique, through which everything from then on, through which the world itself—and this day will come—will come to be reflected quivering, reflecting disappearance itself: the world, the whole world, the world itself, for death takes from us not only some particular life within the world, some moment that belongs to us, but, each time, without limit, someone through whom the world, and first of all our own world, will have opened up in a both finite and infinite—mortally infinite—way. That is the blurred and transparent testimony borne by this tear, this small, infinitely small, tear, which the mourning of friends passes through and endures even before death, and always singularly so, always irreplaceably. Jean-Marie Benoist, with whom I shared, among so many other things, a veneration for John Donne, will have spoken so well of what he called, twenty years ago, "the geometry of the metaphysical poets," and of this tear of the world, of world, this world-tear in *A Valediction: Of Weeping:*

> A globe, yea world, by that impression grow,
> Till thy tears mix'd with mine do overflow
> This world, by waters sent from thee, my heavens dissolvèd so.

Translated by Pascale-Anne Brault and Michael Naas for this volume. First French publication, "Le goût des larmes," in *Jean-Marie Benoist: Hommages* (Imprimerie Lancry Graphic, 1993), 13–17. *The Geometry of the Metaphysical Poets,* cited in the epigraph, is the proposed title of a book that was never published.

Then there comes a time, in the course of a generation, the gravity of which becomes for some, myself among them today, more and more palpable, when you reach an age, if you will, where more and more friends leave you, oftentimes younger than you, sometimes as young as a son or daughter. My admiration, as well as my affection, for Jean-Marie has in fact resembled, for close to a quarter of a century now, that of an older brother who finds himself astonished, and more and more so, though always in a somewhat tender way, by the audacity of thought, the growing force, the justified self-confidence of someone whom he first knew, precisely, with the still tender traits of a very young thinker, but one already sharp, rigorous, ironic, iconoclastic, unsubmissive, covetous above all else of his freedom, his audacity, and his daring. During our first encounters at the Ecole Normale in 1964, I remember having felt some perplexity, along with a sort of irritated concern. But a certain complicity brought us closer together very quickly through our work and our reading, a joyful and confident complicity to which I owe a great deal: it reassured me at a time when I needed it, and it was to do so for years with a constancy for which I will always be grateful, the sort of warm fidelity without which things have little meaning. I like to say "complicity" because often, in the beginning, between 1968 and 1975, a deep agreement (I mean in our philosophical thought and interests) sometimes took on the air of an alliance in a symbolical conspiracy in the midst of the culture of the time. And I liked a lot, indeed I never stopped liking, the mischievous eye, the devilish grin in the middle of that somewhat childlike face, the sometimes biting irony, the polemical verve of Jean-Marie.

I will not speak here of his work, or, I should also say, of his action, of all that is most readily accessible, public, and known: always intelligent and courageous, this work in action was a constant engagement with the philosophical, political, and religious debates of the times. A provocative engagement, sometimes ahead of the times, the conviction of an enlightened avant-gardist, of someone sent out ahead to enlighten us—and I mean this in the sense of the Enlightenment and of his dear Montesquieu. (It was particularly that beacon entitled *Marx est mort*—in 1970!—that, in spite of my agreement with the essence of the "theses," an agreement that he invoked in advance, caused me to have some reservations, which I still have today—why conceal it?—concerning the effects sought after, the strategy, the connotations, or, so to speak, the "pragmatics" of the judgment, and these reservations, to which he was sensitive and which he judged, I think, with some severity, had silently begun to separate us, though even when they became more pronounced they never compromised the friendship I have mentioned.) He had an acute sense of the tremors that transform the landscape of history and the ground of thought. (I am thinking here of his very first articles, which announced an entire trajectory, "Towards an International Social Contract," and "Marcuse, an Aufklärer against Enlightenment," and then of the two beautiful books that followed in 1975, *Tyrannie du logos* and *The Structural Revolution,* which we must read again and again; you will notice, as I have, how well they have held up over time, resisting the various fashions of the day.)

I wish instead to turn today to the "golden years," those I quietly lament and that are less visibly public: the numerous visits in London at the French Institute or in Oxford when I would come for lectures, the wonderful hospitality of Jean-Marie and Nathalie, everything that happens between friends around an ambassador of culture who is open, intelligent, joyous, inventive, incisive (Jean-Marie Benoist was exemplary in these ways as well), the meetings, the discussions, the "parties," the nighttime jaunts through the city.

I am presently rereading all the letters from that period, and there are many of them (several spoke of his work in progress, of great books promised on *The proper of man* and the English metaphysical poets— promised and given through other books and under other titles), and since that time I've always kept on one of my shelves a strange and precious object, something more than precious, in truth, a priceless sign signed by his hand (his large and beautiful black handwriting, high, angular, quick, at once impatient and perfect): a white box on the bottom of which is written "This is not a pipe," and then, right below, the word "is" under erasure with an *x* through it: "this is a pipe." One day (and this is part of a long story) I had confided to Jean-Marie what a certain gift meant to me, a square pipe given to me by my father shortly before his death. This pipe, which stood upright on its bowl when I put it down on the table to write, had been lost many times, found again, broken, repaired—and one day forgotten in London, in the Benoists' living room. Having repatriated it after receiving my telegram, Jean-Marie himself in turn forgot to bring it when he came to visit me on the rue d'Ulm, so he then sent it to me through the mail, recalling, at the bottom of the box, that no, really, between us, and how right he was, this given thing, though it was also one, would not have been a pipe.

I can feel that by writing with a certain tone, and by privileging some memories rather than others, I am letting myself be invaded tonight, at this hour, by English signs: *English* because I was so happy during our meetings in London (probably more than in Paris, which I blame in the end—blaming myself first of all, of course—when I think that it was things still much too "Parisian," that is, too provincial, what might appear to be ideologico-political divisions but are, in fact, little more than petty infighting, things that did not concern us, that should not have concerned either him or me, parochial tempests, that ended up "clouding" our relationship; I blame myself for this more than ever today, and for having taken these things much more seriously than they deserved to be, as if death were not keeping watch, as if we were not supposed to see it coming; but I always knew—and I blame myself today for not having told him this—that these clouds left intact in me what they seemed to conceal of my friendship; and even when we had, as we say, lost sight of one another, I remained fascinated at a distance by the grand gestures of this hell of a man, even if I sometimes mumbled to myself); *English* too because I felt how much England had marked his thinking, about politics in particular; *English,* finally, because of certain literary passions, as I have said, that I shared with him, and that probably went beyond literature, toward what he called, once again in *The Geometry of the Metaphysical Poets,* "proper names in shreds," or "the discourse on shadows," and, particularly, "anamorphosis and the tear."

Yes, we must read and reread what Jean-Marie Benoist has left us. I will do so again, but for the moment, between confiding and thinking, which are never totally foreign to one another, I am trying to discern what he will have let us glimpse about tears: through tears.

He does not teach us that we must not cry; he reminds us that we must not *taste* a tear: "The act of tasting the tear is a desire to reannex the other"; one must not "drink the tear and wonder about the strangeness of its taste compared to one's own."

Therefore: not to cry over oneself. (But does one ever do this? Does one ever do anything but this? That is the question that quivers in every tear, deploration or imploration itself.)

One should not develop a taste for mourning, and yet mourn we *must.*

We *must,* but we must not like it—mourning, that is, mourning *itself,* if such a thing exists: not to like or love through one's own tear but only through the other, and every tear is from the other, the friend, the living, as long as we ourselves are living, reminding us, in holding life, to hold on to it.

CHAPTER 6

LOUIS ALTHUSSER

OCTOBER 16, 1918—OCTOBER 22, 1990

Considered to be one of the most influential Western thinkers on Marxism, Louis Althusser was born in 1918 in the city of Birmandreis, near Algiers, to Charles-Joseph Althusser and Lucienne Marthe Berger. Born into a *pied-noir* family, Althusser lived in Algeria until 1930, when his father was sent to Marseilles as a senior bank executive. After six years in Marseilles, where Althusser attended the Lycée Saint Charles, the family moved to Lyon. Althusser there attended the Lycée du Parc, studying under Jean Guitton, and prepared for the entrance exam to the Ecole Normale Supérieure. Though admitted to the school in 1939, his educational plans had to be delayed when he was called up to military service and dispatched to the Training Center for Reserve Cadet Officers in Issoire. In June 1940 he was captured by the Germans and spent more than four years in a prisoner-of-war camp in Schleswig-Holstein. Althusser's memoirs and correspondence detailing his internment have been published as *Journal de captivité: Stalag XA/1940–1945.*

At the end of the war, Althusser was finally able to pursue his studies at the Ecole Normale Supérieure. In 1946 he met Hélène Rytmann-Legotien, who would become his lifetime companion and whom he would eventually marry in 1976. Hélène was a militant in Lyon in the 1930s and had taken part in Resistance activities during the war.

Soon after the war, Althusser began suffering from depression and was admitted to a psychiatric hospital. While convalescing in a small town in the French Alps, he wrote his *diplôme d'études supérieures,* "On Content in the Thought of G. W. F. Hegel." He had started to read Hegel seriously in 1946 under the influence of his close friend Jacques Martin. Both Althusser and Martin successfully defended theses on Hegel with Gaston Bachelard.

At the Ecole Normale, Althusser came to know Jean-Toussaint Desanti and the Vietnamese Marxist philosopher and phenomenologist Tran Duc Thao. He played an active role in the Catholic "Tala Circle" as well as in the students' union, which was fighting for official recognition. Althusser passed his *agrégation* exam in 1948, scoring first in the written examination and second in the oral.

In 1948 Althusser was appointed philosophy tutor or *répétiteur* (a *caïman* in the school's slang) at the Ecole Normale Supérieure, a position that endeared him to the students he coached for the *agrégation* exam. He held this post (officially as *maître-assistant* and *secrétaire de l'Ecole littéraire* of the Ecole Normale Supérieure) until the end of his career in November 1980. Althusser defended his *doctorat d'état* at the University of Picardy in Amiens in 1975 on the basis of published work.

His first book, *Montesquieu: La politique et l'histoire,* appeared in 1959. In 1960 he edited and translated a number of Feuerbach's writings, collected under the title *Manifestes philosophiques.* His seminal text *For Marx* (1965), followed by *Reading Capital,* written with Etienne Balibar and others (1965), *Lenin and Philosophy and Other Essays* (1969), and *Philosophy and the Spontaneous Philosophy of the Scientists and Other Essays* (1974), constituted a fundamental renewal of Marxist thought. Long considered the leading intellectual in the French Communist Party, which he had joined in 1948, Althusser engaged in a bitter struggle during the 1970s against the party and publicly criticized it in 1978 in *Ce qui ne peut plus durer dans le parti communiste.*

From the 1950s onward Althusser was under constant medical supervision and endured many years of hospitalization, electroconvulsive treatment, narcotherapy, and analysis for manic depression. He was also deeply affected by the suicide in August 1963 of his friend Jacques Martin, to whom *For Marx* is dedicated.

Althusser's life took a dramatic turn in November 1980 when he was arrested for the strangulation murder of his wife. He was ultimately declared unfit to plead (*non-lieu* under the French penal code) and was confined to the Sainte-Anne psychiatric hospital. For the next several years he lived in various public and private clinics in the Paris area. Althusser explains his actions and his state of great mental confusion at the time of this event in his posthumously published autobiography, *The Future Lasts Forever.*

Althusser died in 1990 of cardiac arrest at the Denis Forestier Geriatric Center. A number of very significant works have been published since his death, including two volumes of autobiographical writings, one volume of correspondence, two volumes of psychoanalytic writings, and four volumes of philosophical and political writings.

Text Read at Louis Althusser's Funeral

I knew in advance that I would be unable to speak today, unable, as they say, to find the words.

Forgive me, then, for reading, and for reading not what I believe I should say—does anyone ever know what to say at such times?—but just enough to prevent silence from completely taking over, a few shreds of what I was able to tear away from the silence within which I, like you, no doubt, might be tempted to take refuge at this moment.

I learned of Louis's death less than twenty-four hours ago upon my return from Prague—and the very name of that city already strikes me as so violent, almost unpronounceable. I knew that upon returning from Prague I had to call him: I promised him I would.

Someone who is here today and who was with Louis when I spoke to him last on the phone probably remembers: when I promised to call him and go visit him after my trip, his last words, the last words I would hear from Louis, were, "If I'm still alive, yes, give me a call and come over, and hurry." I answered him somewhat playfully and in an offhanded way, in order to conceal my anxiety and my sadness, "Okay, I'll give you a call and come over."

Louis, there's no more time left, and I no longer have the strength to call you, or even to speak—not to you (you are at once too absent and too close: in me, inside me), and, even less, to others about you, even if they are, as is here the case, your friends, our friends.

I don't have the heart to relate stories or to deliver a eulogy: there would be too much to say and this is not the right time. Our friends, your friends who are here today, know why it is almost indecent to speak right now—and to continue to address our words to you. But silence too is unbearable. I cannot bear the thought of silence, as if you in me could not bear the thought.

Upon the death of a loved one or a friend, when you have shared so much with them (and this has been my good fortune, for my life has been linked in so many strange ways to that of Louis Althusser for some thirty-eight years now, beginning in 1952, when the *caïman* received in his office the young student I then was, and then again later when, in the same place, I worked at his side for almost twenty years), when you

Translated by Pascale-Anne Brault and Michael Naas for this volume. First French publication, "Louis Althusser," *Les lettres françaises* 4 (December 1990): 25–26.

recall not only the light moments and the carefree laughter of day-to-day life but the intense moments of work, teaching, and thinking, of the philosophical and political *polemos,* or all the wounds and the worst heartbreaks, the moments of drama and of mourning, there is always, as we know, upon the death of a friend, that culpable tendency—egotistical, to be sure, narcissistic as well, but irrepressible—that consists in bemoaning and taking pity, that is, taking pity on oneself, by saying, as I myself do, because these conventional words nonetheless manage to convey a certain truth about this compassion: "A whole part of my life, a long, rich, and intense stretch of my living self has been interrupted today, comes to an end and thus dies with Louis in order to continue to accompany him, as in the past, but this time without return and into the depths of absolute darkness." What is coming to an end, what Louis is taking away with him, is not only something or other that we would have shared at some point or another, in one place or another, but the world itself, a certain origin of the world—his origin, no doubt, but also that of the world in which I lived, in which we lived a unique story. It is a story that is, in any case, irreplaceable, and it will have had one meaning or another for the two of us, even if this meaning could not have been the same, and not even the same just for him. It is a world that is for us the whole world, the only world, and it sinks into an abyss from which no memory—even if we keep the memory, and we will keep it—can save it.

Although I find a certain intolerable violence in this movement that consists in bemoaning one's own death upon the death of a friend, I have no desire to abstain completely from it: it is the only way left to keep Louis in me, to keep myself by keeping him in me, just as, I am sure, you are all doing, each with his or her own memory (which actually becomes memory only through this movement of mourning), each with his or her own little torn-off piece of history. And this was such a rich, tormented, and singular history, a murderous and still unthinkable tragedy, inseparable as well from the history of our time, so laden with the entire philosophical, political, geopolitical history of our time—a history that each of us still apprehends with his or her own images. And there were so many images, the most beautiful and the most terrible, though all forever indissociable from the unique adventure that bears the name Louis Althusser. Our belonging to this time—and I think I can speak for everyone here—was indelibly marked by him, by what he sought, experimented with, and risked at the highest of costs; it was marked by all the movements of his passion, whether determined or suspended, at once authoritarian and hesitant, contradictory, consequential, or convulsive, all the movements of that extraordinary passion that left him no respite, since it spared him nothing, with its theatrical rhythms, its great voids, its long stretches of silence, its vertiginous retreats, all those impressive interruptions themselves interrupted by demonstrations, forceful offensives, and powerful eruptions of which each of his books preserves the burning trace, having first transformed the landscape around the volcano.

Louis Althusser traversed so many lives—ours, first of all—so many personal, historical, philosophical, and political adventures; he marked, inflected, and influenced so many discourses, actions, and existences through the radiating and provocative force of his thought, of his ways of being, speaking, teaching, that the most diverse and contradictory testimonies will never succeed in exhausting their source. The fact that each of us had a different relationship with Louis Althusser (and I am not speaking just about philosophy or politics), the fact that each of us knows that, through this singular prism, we caught but a glimpse of a secret, an inexhaustible secret for us, no doubt, but also, though in a completely different way, fathomless for him as well, the fact that Louis was other for others, for other people, at one time or another, within academia and without, at the rue d'Ulm or elsewhere in France, within the Communist Party, within parties and outside them, in Europe and beyond, the fact that each of us loved a different Louis Althusser, at some time or another, in some decade or another, or, as it was my good fortune, right up until the very end—this generous multiplicity, this very overabundance makes it incumbent upon us not to totalize or simplify, not to immobilize him or fix a trajectory, not to seek some advantage, not to cancel things out or try to get even, and especially not to calculate, not to appropriate or reappropriate (even if it be through that paradoxical form of manipulating or calculating reappropriation called rejection), not to take hold of what was inappropriable and must remain so. Each of us no doubt has a thousand faces, but those who knew Louis Althusser know that this law found in him a shining, striking, and hyperbolic example. His work is great, first of all, by what it attests to and by what it risks, by what it traversed with that multiple, fractured, and often interrupted flash, by the enormous risks taken and all that was endured: his adventure is singular, it belongs to no one.

I have little trouble speaking here (as I feel I must) about what might have separated us, or indeed opposed us (implicitly or not, sometimes harshly, over both small and important matters), because none of this ever compromised in the least the foundation of our friendship, which was in fact all the more dear to me on account of these things. For at no time was I able to consider what was happening to him or through him, in these places that I still inhabit with him, as anything other than a string of upheavals, earthquakes, or awakenings of volcanoes, the singular or

collective tragedies of our time—of the time that I, like you, will have
shared with him. Never, in spite of everything that might have separated
us or distanced us from one another, was I able or did I wish to observe, that
is, with the neutrality of a spectator, what was happening to him or through
him. For everything that, thanks to him or through him, has occupied my
entire adult life, including those devastating trials of which we are all
thinking, I will always remain, from the bottom of my heart, grateful.
Grateful for what is irreplaceable. And what remains most present in my
eyes, most alive today, closest and most precious, is, of course, his face,
Louis's so very handsome face, that high forehead, his smile, everything
that, in him, during the moments of peace—and there were moments of
peace, as many of you here know—radiated kindness, the need for love
and the giving of love in return, displaying an incomparable attentiveness
to the youth of what is coming, curiously on the lookout from daybreak on
for the signs of things still waiting to be understood, everything that upsets
order, programs, facile connections, and predictability. What remains for
me most alive today is what in the light of that face bespoke a lucidity
at once implacable and understanding, by turns resigned or triumphant,
not unlike the verve of certain of his declarations. What I love most in
him, no doubt because it was him, what fascinated me in what others no
doubt knew better than I, and from much closer up than I, was his sense
of and taste for grandeur, for a certain grandeur, for the great theater of
political tragedy where what is larger than life comes to occupy, mislead,
or pitilessly break the private body of its actors.

Whenever public discourse about Althusser drops proper names like
so many signposts or trails upon a territory to be occupied, the names that
can be heard are, for example, those of Montesquieu or Rousseau, Marx or
Lenin. Yet those who came close to Althusser, whether behind the great
curtains of that political theater or by his bedside in the hospital, know they
owe it to the truth to name others, Pascal, for example, and Dostoyevsky,
and Nietzsche—and Artaud.

At bottom, I know that Louis doesn't hear me; he hears me only
inside me, inside us (though we are only ever *ourselves* from that place
within us where the other, the mortal other, resonates). And I know well
that his voice within me is insisting that I not pretend to speak to him.
And I also know that I have nothing to teach you who are here, *since* you
are here.

But beyond this grave and above your heads, I dream of addressing
those who will come after him, or already after us, those who, as can be
seen by more than one sign, unfortunately, are too much in a hurry to
understand, interpret, classify, fix, reduce, simplify, close off, and judge—

and thus are certain to misunderstand, whether we are talking about this most singular destiny or about the trials of existence, thought, and politics, which can never be separated. I would ask them to stop for a moment, to take the time to listen to our time (for we had no other), to decipher as patiently as possible everything in our time that was marked and promised in the life, work, and name of Louis Althusser. Not only because the scale of this destiny should command respect (as well as a respect for the time—our time—from which these other generations come) but also because the still open wounds, the scars or hopes that were ours and that they will recognize in this time, are sure to teach them something essential of what remains to be heard, read, thought, and done. As long as I live, that is, as long as I retain the memory of what Louis Althusser gave me to live with him, close to him, this is what I would like to recall to those who will not have been of his time or who will not have taken the time to turn toward him. And this is what I hope to say better one day, without bidding adieu, for Louis Althusser.

I wish now to turn it over to him, to let him speak. For another last word, once again his. Rereading some of his work late into last night, the following passage imposed itself on me rather than I reading it or electing it to be reread here. It is from one of his first texts, "Bertolazzi and Brecht" (1962):

> Yes, we are first united by an institution—the performance—but, more deeply, by the same myths, the same themes, that govern us without our consent, by the same spontaneously lived ideology. Yes, even if it is the ideology of the poor *par excellence,* as in *El Nost Milan,* we eat of the same bread, we have the same rages, the same rebellions, the same madness (at least in memory, where this ever-imminent possibility haunts us), if not the same prostration before a time unmoved by any History. Yes, like Mother Courage, we have the same war at our gates, and a handsbreadth from us, if not in us, the same horrible blindness, the same dust in our eyes, the same earth in our mouths. We even have the same dawn and night, we skirt the same abysses: our unconsciousness. We even share the same history—and that is how it all started.[1]

---

1.   Louis Althusser, "The 'Piccolo Teatro': Bertolazzi and Brecht," in *For Marx,* trans. Ben Brewster (New York: Verso, 1996), 151.

CHAPTER 7

EDMOND JABÈS

APRIL 16, 1912—JANUARY 2, 1991

Edmond Jabès was born in Cairo on April 16, 1912, though his father inadvertently registered him as being born on the fourteenth of that month. Jabès often made mention in his work of this original difference; in *Elya* (1969), he asks: "Is it to this error in calculation that I unconsciously owe the feeling that I have always been separated from my life by forty-eight hours? The two days added to mine could be lived only in death."

Jabès's family belonged to Cairo's high Jewish bourgeoisie. Though his family retained their Italian nationality, they remained French in culture. Jabès thus received a French education in Cairo, first at the Collège Saint-Jean-Baptiste-de-la-Salle (1917–24) and then at the Lycée Français (1924–29). From 1930 to 1934 he worked toward a *licence de lettres* at the Sorbonne. He then abandoned his studies to dedicate himself to writing, supporting himself, like his father, as a stockbroker.

Jabès's mother was a small, self-effacing woman who withdrew into herself upon the death of her daughter, Marcelle, in 1924. Innumerable traces of this traumatic loss of his older sister from tuberculosis can be found in Jabès's writings. Jabès once compared this loss to a "second birth." He said in an interview: "My sister died practically in my arms. I was alone at her deathbed. I remember having told her something like: 'You can't die. It's not possible.' To which she replied with exactly these words: 'Don't think about death. Don't cry. One cannot escape one's destiny.' That day I understood that there is a language for death, just as there is a language for life."[1]

During the 1930s and early 1940s, Jabès worked with several organizations to help combat anti-Semitism and fascism. He founded the League of Youth against Antisemitism in Cairo and was one of the organizers of the Groupe antifasciste italien and the Groupement des amitiés françaises. It was during these years that Jabès published his first poems and met such notable figures as Roger Caillois, Paul Eluard, André Gide, Henri Michaux, and Philippe Soupault. Jabès's long correspondence with Max Jacob also dates back to this period. In 1935 he married Arlette Cohen, with whom he had two daughters, Viviane and Nemat.

The discovery of the extermination camps in 1945 proved to be a defining event in Jabès's life and work. It led to a long meditation on the meaning of history and the possibility of writing about such an unthinkable event. In the late 1940s and 1950s Jabès contributed regularly to *La part du sable,* a surrealist journal founded in Cairo, as well as to numerous other literary magazines in France and elsewhere. In 1957, Jabès left an Egypt that had become unbearable for Jews and settled definitively in Paris with his family, taking French nationality in 1967. This unchosen exile marked a new point of departure in an unforeseeable adventure that would lead him, in his words, "from the desert to the book." Jabès's first major collection of poems, *I Build My Dwelling* (poems written between 1943 and 1957), was published in 1959. The 1950s were also marked by friendships with Maurice Blanchot, René Char, Michel Leiris, and Maurice Nadeau, as well as Gabriel Bounoure, who would become the first important critic to write on his work.

In the 1960s Jabès published the first volumes of his *Book of Questions,* a work that would garner him much praise and critical attention. (During most of these years Jabès was working for a film production company in Neuilly, near Paris, and so did much of his writing on the metro to and from work.) These books, like many that were to follow, constitute an open work that brings together poetry and narrative, tales and dialogues, thoughts and meditations, combining the most classical language with the most inventive "writing of the book." Using the language and themes of

1.   Edmond Jabès, *Du désert au livre: Entretiens avec Marcel Cohen* (Paris: Pierre Belfond, 1981), 23.

philosophy, psychoanalysis, politics, and the arts, it confronts some of the most pressing issues of our time, from the question of Jewish identity to the Shoah to apartheid.

Jabès insists throughout his writing on the relationship between his own destiny as an exile and the discovery of a Judaism he had barely suspected. The general orientation of his writing is perhaps best reflected in the exergue of *The Book of Questions:* "You are the one who writes and the one who is written." In their simplicity, these words indicate the movement of a search, a quest by and for a self that cannot take refuge or find comfort in the security of some presupposed identity. As he wrote in a very early poem, already announcing this sort of autobiography of the other man, this "other subject": "I am searching for a man I do not know, who has never been more myself than since I have been looking for him."

Throughout *The Book of Questions* (1963–73), *The Book of Resemblances* (1976–80), *The Book of Margins* (1975–84), *The Book of Limits* (1982–87), and *The Book of Hospitality* (1991), Jabès continued to investigate the privileged role of the stranger in the experience of the book and the unique relationship between life and writing. When he wrote, "I am. I become. I write," he was seeking to describe not only his relationship to the book but the very nature of his freedom.

Jabès was the recipient of many prestigious awards, among them the Prix des Critiques (1970), the Prix des Arts, des Lettres et des Sciences de la Fondation du Judaisme Français (1982), the Prix Pasolini (1983), the Citadella Prize (1987), and the Grand Prix National de Poésie (1987).

As if by design, the story of Jabès's mistaken birth date had an unexpected sequel at the other end of his life. When Gallimard republished in 1991 Jabès's *Book of Resemblances,* the short biographical notice gave as the date of Jabès's death January 4, 1991, when he had in fact died in Paris on January 2, exactly forty-eight hours earlier.

LETTER TO DIDIER CAHEN

Nice-Prague, February 29—March 1 [1992]

Dear Didier,

From the other side of the world, where I will be on the 16th of April, I shall join you heart and soul in this great and fitting homage to Edmond Jabès. I would have been—thus I am—among you, and I am pleased that this commemoration is taking place at the Collège International de Philosophie; no place seems to me more appropriate, better suited, named, called, destined. From the very beginning we wished it to be a place that would welcome and encourage poetic thinking, and it is in precisely these terms that you have chosen to mark this anniversary.

At the moment when Edmond Jabès, according to his own account, is reaching eighty years of age (for I remember him confiding in me one day certain doubts he had about his exact date of birth and the way it had been officially registered, as if the difference of a day or two made his birth just as unlocatable, just as unthinkable, as death itself), I think both fervently and melancholically of our first meetings some thirty years ago. I had just discovered *The Book of Questions,* by chance, in a little newsstand in the suburbs, and I recall having heard resonate within it, from places at once immemorial and at that time so little explored, so difficult to make out, a voice that I felt would no longer leave us, even if one day he, Edmond Jabès, whom I did not yet know, of whom I knew nothing, not even whether or where he was still living, would one day be silenced, leaving us alone with his books. There was already in this first reading a certain experience of apophatic silence, of absence, the desert, paths opened up off all the beaten tracks, deported memory—in short, mourning, every impossible mourning.[1]

Friendship had thus already come to be reflected in mourning, in the eyes of the poem, even before friendship—I mean before the friendship that later brought us together, when we were neighbors, between the rue de l'Epée de Bois and the rue d'Ulm, on one occasion with Celan, on another

Derrida's letter is addressed to Didier Cahen, author of *Edmond Jabès* (Paris: Belfond, 1991) and organizer of the homage to Jabès, who died January 2, 1991. The event was held at the Collège International de Philosophie in Paris on April 16, 1992, the eightieth anniversary of Jabès's birth. Translated by Pascale-Anne Brault and Michael Naas for this volume. Previously unpublished.

1. Derrida devoted two essays to Jabès in the 1960s, "Edmond Jabès and the Question of the Book," first published in 1964 in *Critique* (20, 201), 99–115, and then republished in 1967 in *Writing and Difference,* trans. Alan Bass (Chicago: University of Chicago Press, 1978), 64–78, and "Ellipsis," the last essay in *Writing and Difference* (294–300).—*Trans.*

with Gabriel Bounoure (a great friendship for which I have Edmond Jabès to thank).[2]

When friendship begins before friendship, it touches upon death, indeed, it is born in mourning. But it is also doubly affirmed, twice sealed; this recognition, this gratitude before all knowledge, is, I believe, destined to survive. And already from its birth: in all the books of questions, those that bear and those that keep their name silent, beyond books and their titles, beyond blind words. Edmond Jabès knew that books are here to no avail, no more than questions are, not to mention answers.

If I have the desire, if it is, in truth, so easy for me to feel so close to you this April 16, all the way from the Pacific Coast, it is not only because the readers, admirers, and friends of Edmond Jabès are gathered in a place that is so close and dear to me. It is also because the best witnesses of this invisible sharing-out wherein thought and the poem intersect remain, for me, other friends, Michel Deguy, and especially you yourself, dear Didier, along with those whom you've allowed me to address in this way. Please express my enduring affection and fidelity to Arlette Jabès.

Your friend, affectionately,

Jacques

---

2.   Gabriel Bounoure was an important literary critic both before and after the war and a close friend of Jabès. Derrida dedicated his essay "Ellipsis" to him.—*Trans.*

CHAPTER 8

JOSEPH N. RIDDEL

SEPTEMBER 11, 1931 — SEPTEMBER 7, 1991

Distinguished American literary critic and theorist Joseph Riddel was born in Grantsville, West Virginia, in 1931. He attended Glenville College, where he received his B.A. in 1953. After serving in the U.S. Army from 1953 to 1955, he went on to the University of Wisconsin, receiving an M.S. in 1956 and a Ph.D. in English in 1960. He took up a position in the fall of 1960 as an assistant professor of English at Duke University. In April 1963 he married Virginia Lee Johnson, with whom he had three children, Kevin, Valerie, and Vanessa. Riddel taught at Duke until 1965, when he moved to the State University of New York at Buffalo, where he remained until 1972. First a visiting professor at the University of California, Los Angeles, in 1971, Riddel joined that university permanently as a professor of English in 1973.

Riddel's first book, *The Clairvoyant Eye,* published in 1965, is a reading of Wallace Stevens's poems and theory of imagination. His second book, *C. Day Lewis* (1971), examines the poetry and thought of England's poet laureate. In 1974 he published *The Inverted Bell,* by most accounts the first significant full-length work of American "deconstructive criticism." This book, a radical reinterpretation of William Carlos Williams's poetics, is an exploration of the question of origins, a question that would occupy Riddel for most of his life. Throughout the mid-1970s Riddel contributed important articles, many published in journals such as *Diacritics* and *boundary 2,* to the debate surrounding the influence of Continental philosophy (especially Nietzsche, Heidegger, and Derrida) on American literary criticism. In 1979 he joined the editorial board of *boundary 2.* From the late 1970s onward Riddel turned his attention to the relationship between philosophy and literature, in particular to the problem of defining a uniquely "American" literature and idiom.

Much of Riddel's work in the 1980s was devoted to a sustained study of the relationship between French thought, especially deconstruction, and nineteenth- and twentieth-century American letters (Emerson, Poe, Melville, Hawthorne, James, Pound, Olson). Many of these essays were collected and published posthumously in *Purloined Letters. The Turning Word,* published in 1996, contains essays chosen for publication by Riddel himself before his death. This book pairs a number of writers and thinkers (Hilda Doolittle and Freud, Hart Crane and Hegel, Gertrude Stein and Bergson) in a rigorous analysis of the nature of poetic performance and the function of metaphor in philosophical language.

Riddel became director of the Center for Critical Studies and the Human Sciences at UCLA in 1988. He held visiting professorships at the Universities of Rhode Island and California at Riverside and at the Center for Twentieth Century Studies at the University of Wisconsin–Milwaukee. In 1990 he was Longstreet Professor at Emory University.

Riddel died from complications of pulmonary disease on September 7, 1991.

I would have so much wished to be there today, here that is, among you, friends (colleagues, students) of Joe Riddel. Allow me to say that to you as simply as possible. In Los Angeles and at his university, where, with the generosity that we all knew, he more than once welcomed me, helped and guided me. I would have liked to be able myself to express, here and now, both my sadness and how much I loved and admired Joe. And also to tell you why I will do so forever, why it is a great friend to whom I bid farewell, and why I will still need him in the future, why to me he is irreplaceable.

Everything happened too quickly: like a race to death that left us only enough time to pass and wave to each other, from one automobile to another, before the fatal accident. Our meetings were rare, too rare I had begun to think, and all were dedicated to that unbelieving hope that haunts just our most intense friendships: the promise that we would see each other more often later on, that in the end we would speak without end and be together, interminably. This promise now interrupted, broken all of a sudden, and yet still indestructible, I take to be infinitely renewed by death itself. And I will remain turned toward him, toward the so vibrant memory of him that I have, turned toward the glimpse that I was granted of him so rapidly, too rapidly, and turned toward what he leaves us with, to read and to think.

Never has this desperate but radiant certainty been more alive in me: what we call "being together," what we call "getting together" with those whom we love—the physical proximity, the shared joys of the day (a dinner with Joe and other friends in Los Angeles or in Irvine, for example, a complicitous burst of laughter in the middle of a colloquium, right here, less than two years ago, a walk one summer evening in Paris)—we know that the unforgettable singularity of such moments will never be replaced by anything else, not even by that which they promise or keep in reserve. They are irreplaceable, and that is precisely the reason for despairing. But we also know that they would be nothing, or not very much, without the rich intensity of this very reserve. Blessed were the moments that I lived in Joe's vicinity, in Irvine, Los Angeles, Paris, in the university and

Composed October 17, 1991, and delivered on behalf of the author October 24, 1991, at a memorial service held at UCLA. Reprinted, with changes, from "A demi-mot," French text with English translation by Samuel Weber, in *America's Modernisms: Revaluing the Cannon: Essays in Honor of Joseph N. Riddel,* edited by Kathryne V. Lindberg and Joseph G. Kronick (Baton Rouge: Louisiana State University Press, 1996), 26–38. Copyright © 1995 by Louisiana State University Press. Reprinted with permission.

outside the university. Yet I know that if such moments had the force and depth that they still retain in my heart, it is because, as brief as they were, alas, and as rare, they were inhabited and traversed, in a manner that was both silent and verbose, by the poets and philosophers whom we read, in a certain way, *together,* and who gave friendship—for they were there, I remain convinced, only to serve friendship—its meaning, its rhythm, its breath, I would even say its inspiration, even if they weren't always the same philosophers, the same poets, the same works that we approached, nor the same places, the same titles, and the same names, at the same time and in the same manner.

In the haste of what I called the "race to death," these moments, these places, these names, and these names of places, which we had to recognize and which also recognized us in advance—all were as though pre-occupied by the power (both the potentiality and the force, the *dynamis*) of the writers of the past, or of the ghosts to come who spoke to each other through us, in turn provoking us to speak, to make or let them live in us, taking us as witnesses to each curve in the race, through the questions, the debates, the deliberations without end, through risky thoughts, accelerating or slamming on the brakes, through the roads or the aporias of writing into which they cast us, led us, and predicted our encounters, down to the very manner that we had in common, despite the difference of languages and histories, of orienting ourselves in this heritage while understanding each other very quickly, with scarcely a word, *à demi-mot* as we say in French. *Demi-mort,* half-dead, is what I should say because death, we also knew from a gay science (strange, that gaiety of Joe's, in which I felt the worry, the wound, but in which I also sensed the gamble, the challenge, and the provocation)—because death, in short, lay waiting at every turn, announcing itself between the lines and predestining each name.

And Joe taught me to find my way about—I would almost say to drive—not only in a certain American literature (Poe, Melville, Pound and Stein, Stevens and Williams), an American literature of which he is, I believe, one of the very great readers of this century, one of those—very rare when you think of it—who have known how to put the gravest and most inventive stakes of the philosophy or theory of the time to the test of your literature in its greatest singularity. But Joe, author of "Reading America/American Readers," also helped me to orient myself, quite simply and nothing less, in American culture.[1] Little by little I understood that where American culture was concerned, and in particular the academic

---

1.   Joseph Riddel, "Reading America/American Readers," *Modern Language Notes* 99 (1984): 903–27.

institution, his judgments on ideas and on persons, on writings and on discourses, his positions and commitments, had that solitary lucidity— yes, quite solitary, I believe, in its rigor, incisiveness, courage, irony, and serenity—upon which it is preferable, I am convinced, always to rely. And I had confidence in him, in his solitude itself, a certain intellectual solitude; I had confidence in the choice he made of a small number, of a certain scarcity let us say, in particular places in the university, on the least traveled roads, on the least-easy routes, the least-normalized avenues of thought, of reading and writing. I had confidence in him, and the confidence that he in turn demonstrated in me was always one of the encouragements that counted the most for me in this country. In the shocks and struggles that, particularly in the last decade or two, have tormented our historical, political, or academic landscape, I often found myself implicitly getting my bearings, especially where things American were concerned, from Joe's judgment and positions. Without literally asking his advice (I said that we saw each other and spoke relatively little), I drew reassurance from reading him, looking for bright signals in his own movements, evaluations, choices, in his manner of conducting himself—of driving, if you will— which always seemed to me to be one of the most necessary courses of conduct, even if, or precisely because, it was full of risks: in short, it seemed to me more apt and equitable to be on his side, *at his side,* even if at times it seemed to be the side of the road that was least safe, the least comfortable side of solitude or of the precarious edge.

I never came back to California, in the spring, without hoping to see Joe, and when I return in the future there will be a shadow. I will have to act as though—but how can I believe it?—our friendship did not require getting together any more, as though it had always been destined to breathe through the apparatus of books and dead letters, as it did for several years, at the very beginning. Permit me to recall a story that Joe liked to tell publicly each time he welcomed me to this university. I hear him even now, I see his smile, and I have the impression that what I am about to say is spoken through him; I would even like to tell you this story in his own voice, through his mouth, just as one can have the desire to eat from the mouth of a dead friend—and I also loved the sensual way Joe loved to eat, and I loved to share that joy with him. It was in 1975, I believe—we didn't know each other yet. From Buffalo, Joe, at the suggestion of Hillis Miller or Eugenio Donato, had sent me *The Inverted Bell.* Already this book, which opened up so many new avenues, played gravely and powerfully with the proper name, which is to say, with death, and it is one of the things, among others, that impressed me immediately. For of what, of whom, to whom are we speaking, here, now, in his absolute absence, if not of the name, in and to the name, of Joe Riddel? Even during the course of life, of our lifetime as of Joe's lifetime, we know this and knew it already: the name signs death and marks life with a fold [*ride*] to be deciphered. The name races toward death even more quickly than we do, we who naively believe that we bear it. It bears us with infinite speed toward the end. It is in advance the name of a dead person. And of a premature death that comes to us in it, through it, without ever being properly our own. Without waiting, Joe followed in Williams, as he often did elsewhere, the fatal passage of his own name. One letter passing the other along the way, the permutation of two letters sufficed to play with everything that encrypted itself already, joyously and tragically, in the cipher of his name, R.I.D.D.E.L., a name that had become common enough (as noun) for others, including myself, to have found *literally,* and I mean down to the very letter, in their own patronyms, something essential to share: a sort of irresistible competition in the race to death. I remember well certain pages in "Poem and City: The Sarcophagus of Time." For example, to introduce a Williams citation, Joe wrote the following, which announced what he would later entitle "The Hermeneutical Self—Notes Toward an 'American' Practice" (*boundary 2* [1984]): "The world is a 'riddle' for the Puritan, a riddle only partly decoded by an original Word or Text, the Bible. Even man in a state of grace is condemned to interpretation. Characteristically, Williams concludes the Mather section with the following remark: 'Unriddle these Things.'"[2]

Since we are speaking of the survival of the name, which in announcing our death thereby effaces itself, de-nominates or de-nominates itself in the common name (or noun), carrying away in advance the person who bears it properly—*Unriddling these Things* reminds me also of something Joe described elsewhere, and what I would call a certain *unnaming effect* of nomination itself. In this Joe saw quite simply the privilege of poetry. I will say that what is involved here, once again, is patronymics. In "Juda Becomes New Haven," in 1980, concerning *The Auroras of Autumn* by Wallace Stevens, he wrote: "The naming that erases, that unnames, is reserved, however, for poetry, a privilege it putatively claims only by undermining the status of ephebe or son."[3]

Some time after having read *The Inverted Bell* then, in 1975, in order to let him know of my admiring recognition and gratitude, I sent Joe a letter. To his Buffalo address. He wasn't there any longer, something I didn't yet know. Already he wasn't there any more. This letter might

2.   Joseph Riddel, *The Inverted Bell: Modernism and the Counterpoetics of William Carlos Williams* (Baton Rouge: Louisiana State University Press, 1974), 157.
3.   Joseph Riddel, "Juda Becomes New Haven," *Diacritics* 10 (summer 1980): 29.

easily never have reached him, the race thus never coming to an end or else being condemned to the fate of those "dead letters" wherein is buried the enigma of all the Bartlebys of the world, our impossible brothers ("On errands of life, these letters speed to death. Ah Bartleby! Ah Humanity!"). Months later, perhaps more than a year later—I don't remember any more all the stages, or how many detours or universities it passed through, or how many friendly hands—finally my letter reached Joe there, or rather, here, in California, where I for my part had not yet set foot. Joe often told this story, in this very place. I frequently thought of it, later, above all while reading what he had written, always with the same verve, cruel and grave, on "The Purloined Letter," concerning proper names and place-names, in his marvelous text of 1980, "The 'Crypt' of Edgar Poe," a crypt he compares to the center of the pyramid in Melville's *Pierre; or, The Ambiguities* ("By vast pains we mine into the pyramid; by horrible gropings we come to the central room; with joy we espy the sarcophagus; but we lift the lid— and no body is there!—"). This pyramid or this cenotaph, is it not also a "memorial"—and this place here, whose emptiness today sucks us in rather than our breathing it?

Thus, at our first meeting, several years later, I had already read much of him; we had in advance gone a long way together, literally, by letters, without meeting each other; we were ahead of ourselves and had already done much racing together; a strange familiarity already brought us closer, something I loved right away and which was never contradicted between us by distance, absence, modest discretion, silence, even ignorance of what our lives might be like on the other side, that other side of our lives, the most invisible and most exposed, the most dangerous part of our respective races. As if we didn't know, as if we knew without knowing, and most enigmatically, as though we didn't need to know what we didn't know about each other. As if we knew too much to need to know any more—and this is why the enigma will never be separated from the sieve [*crible*], a riddle from a riddle, if you like, and interpretation from selection. As though in the acceleration of this very brief race, we knew in advance that we would never have time to see and know everything about each other. We had to drive very fast, faster and faster.

Why name here the race with such insistence, why so many car races and racing cars? Because of speed, to be sure, and the cruelty of time that is lacking, but also because of accidents and of death, which await us at each curve in the road. And then also because I am obsessed by another memory of Joe, close to my heart. It was a fleeting instant, a furtive exchange of looks, a slight incident at the end of a California day. For years this memory has haunted me and I would like to share it with you. It was shortly after the death of Eugenio Donato, our dear and old common friend, at whose place, moreover, we first met, and who cultivated a scholarly and sophisticated taste for cars of great distinction, for those machines that are as nervous as racehorses, those you drive, if I may say so, by hand, without automatic transmission. Less than one year after Eugenio's death, then, I saw Joe again, in April of 1984, at Irvine. I had just evoked, in a lecture, the memory of Paul de Man and of Eugenio Donato, who had died a few months apart. In leaving the university, I accompanied Joe to the parking lot and he asked me, with a smile of complicity, pointing toward his car and eyeing my reaction: "Take a look. What do you think of it? Does it remind you of anything?" I immediately recognized Eugenio's car. Joe had done what had to be done; he had undoubtedly bought it to keep after the death of our friend, to live in, to drive, so that it could go on racing until the very end—and I am certain that at that moment, in April 1984, there were three of us at least, friends, who were crazy enough to love this gesture. A gesture, signed "Riddel," which played faithfully with life and death as with the mystery of a shift in gears, as with the letter of a poem on the road or in the city.

To conclude, I would like to leave or give back the word to Joe—his words. With the awareness of sacrificing, I detach once more, hastily, this, from "Poem and City: The Sarcophagus of Time" (*The Inverted Bell*, 158):

> As Williams puts it in *Paterson,* a "riddle (in the Joycean mode—
> . . .)" which holds the enigma of death at its center:
>
> What end but love, that stares death in the eye?
> . . . .
> Sing me a song to make death tolerable, a song
> of a man and a woman: the riddle of a man
> and a woman.

CHAPTER 9

MICHEL SERVIÈRE

SEPTEMBER 21, 1941 — OCTOBER 7, 1991

Michel Servière was born on September 21, 1941, at Royat, Puy-de-Dôme. His father, like his grandfather, was a traveling merchant in the neighboring mountains. His mother, a great lover of poetry, was the first to instill in him an interest in aesthetics and the arts. He attended the lycée in Clermont-Ferrand, where he befriended Eric Blondel and took philosophy classes with Jean Granier. It was in the classes of Granier that Servière was first introduced to the works of Nietzsche, which were to have a decisive influence on his own thought and work.

After studies in Lyon and Paris, Servière passed his *agrégation* in philosophy and began teaching in Montluçon in 1968. He was then appointed to a position in the French lycée in Tunis. He eventually returned to France to teach at the lycée of Grenoble, where he was instrumental in bringing together artists, poets, and philosophers to discuss their work. These meetings quickly became indispensable to him, in terms of both the friendships he formed through them and the influence they had on his work, which began to focus more and more on the relationship between philosophy and the arts, as well as on the visual aspects of writing.

Servière later joined Jean Granier as his assistant at the University of Rouen. His dissertation research on Nietzsche and his interest in the stylistic forms of philosophy led him during this time to the works of Jacques Derrida. (In 1989 Servière contributed an article on Derrida to the *Encyclopédie philosophique universelle.*) Servière eventually completed his dissertation on Nietzsche under the direction of Roland Barthes. This work, still unpublished, argues that Nietzsche's early writings can be read only by following the reinscription of eristics and protreptics—subjects usually excluded from the philosophical tradition—within an apparently neutral discursive form.

While *maître de conférences* in aesthetics at the University of Rouen, Servière founded and directed, together with painter Denis Godefroy, the art gallery Déclinaisons. He organized a number of contemporary art exhibits and published collections of poetry during the late 1970s. He was also involved in the preparatory work leading to the opening of the Orsay Museum in Paris. Beginning in 1984 Servière taught at the Collège International de Philosophie and organized and contributed to numerous national and international colloquia and exhibits. His reflections during the late 1980s revolved around the subject of art and the indissociable relation between works and their signature.

Servière died suddenly on October 7, 1991, from a cerebral aneurism. The conference he had organized under the title "Art after Philosophy . . . Art and Concept," at which Jacques Derrida had agreed to participate, was held in his absence and in his memory in November of that year.

As If There Were an Art
of the Signature

You can imagine how difficult it is, how hard and how painful, how much I am pained and saddened, at having to speak now in order to respond to Michel Servière himself, when it is, in truth, him without him whom we have just heard.

I want to do it, however; we owe it to him, and we must also do it for him. Not to respond for him but to respond to him: to him alive in order to keep him alive in us, there where he never stopped speaking and writing, addressing us as we have just heard once again by way of a friendly voice that received his own, inhabiting it or letting itself be inhabited by it.

The first time I heard the voice of Michel Servière—and I had already tried at that time, with great difficulty, to respond to him—was just about twenty years ago, in July 1972, during a conference at Cerisy on Nietzsche. At the end of a lecture that I had begun with a date, "In seventy two (*The Birth of Tragedy*)," Michel asked me, on this occasion, a difficult question concerning, precisely, *the occasion,* concerning what he occasionally referred to that day as the "occasion."

He had used the name "occasion" to refer to a mythological figure, that of a certain castration. The one in which woman does not believe— and of which I had just spoken. I asked him what he meant by "occasion." He described a woman, as if he were seeing her in a painting. He analyzed a sort of tableau, a surrealist allegory, another silhouette of poetic inspiration. He sketched out a figure at once threatening and threatened—an allegory of death: a razor in one hand and a veil unfurling in the wind.

I was struck without really understanding, but I still remember this with an emotion whose intensity is easily rekindled.

I haven't stopped thinking since Michel's death about these frightful occasions, this occasion of the occasion itself, these strange appointments we make with death, and sometimes, as is here the case, with dead friends, as if a cruel timepiece, more clever than us, had calculated the fall, the accident, the case, the cadence, and the occasion, the days of misfortune and of reckoning, such that we might find ourselves *today,* at this moment, *la mort dans l'âme,* as we say, with death in the soul, gathered together now

Translated by Pascale-Anne Brault and Michael Naas for this volume. First French publication, "Comme s'il y avait un art de la signature," preface to *Le sujet de l'art,* by Michel Servière (Paris: L'Harmattan, 1997), 5–8.

by Michel Servière, by him himself, by his own hand, by the organizer, the master of ceremonies, the host and the spirit of this meeting, this seance, by him around him as around his absence, but in the presence of a beautiful, intense text, which, with the refinement of kings, he was able to bring to a close before coming to an end.

For he had signed before leaving.

And we know that a signature not only signs but speaks to us always of death.

Before anything else, even before the name, a signature bespeaks the possible death of the one who bears the name; it offers assurances of this beyond the death that it recalls just as soon, the death that is promised, given, or received, the death that thus always comes before coming—and so, alas, comes always before its time. There where to expect it always means not to be expecting it.

Today, I would wish to relate—and with the same agitation that overtook me then—that enigmatic question concerning the occasion that he asked me twenty years ago and the first words of the last letter he wrote me at the beginning of this year. I have that letter here in front of me. It's dated January 29 (1991). In his beautiful, elegant and flowing handwriting, he began: "The year has begun so badly that I hesitate to send you my usual wishes for the new year."

Yes, the year had begun badly. I assume, without knowing for certain, since this is all I have to go on, that he was referring to the war (the so-called Gulf War) and to the dead who were then roaming about their occasion.

The year is ending badly, we know this only too well now. And the same letter set the occasion; it prepared a place for the fateful so as to announce the unforeseeable.

Speaking of this conference and inviting me to participate in it, Michel wrote: "You could either give a presentation of some sort or else participate in an open discussion with me on the theme: 'Art, Concept, Signature.'" Yes, the signature always has the knack or art of speaking to us of death; that is its secret, it seals everything that is said with this monumental epitaph. It gives the concept, the concept of death and all other concepts insofar as they bear death. But it withdraws—as and in the same stroke—and effaces itself from the concept. If it were beautiful, and this sometimes happens, it would be because it is *without concept,* like a finality or ending without end. If there were an art of the signature . . .

I accepted his invitation wholeheartedly, of course, first of all because I wished to speak with him, to hear him, to tell him once again, and publicly, how much I admire his work. Particularly all he has done on the portrait and the self-portrait, which became a text of reference for me when I myself last year ventured in that direction—and what was at issue were tears and a certain mourning of the gaze in the art of the portrait. But I also admire his work on the signature and, more generally, on everything that comes from painting to provoke the philosopher. And Michel never missed the occasion for such provocations.

We will not have spoken together enough, Michel Servière and I. I blame myself for having taken advantage of his discretion and for having let certain things be said in silence, too much silence, the things of friendship and of thought, which in the end cannot be separated.

But today, for him, for us, for those close to him, for those who love and admire him, I thought it necessary to continue to speak, for the love of life, and precisely because this love is wounded. To speak to Michel Servière, to hear him and to try to respond to him, in whatever way we live or interpret the strange time of this response, and what within this time defies the serenity of all our representations of the present, the past, and the future anterior.

Please be understanding, then, and forgive me for doing it all too poorly, with such pain and difficulty.[1]

1. The conference organized by Michel Servière, "Art after Philosophy . . . Art and Concept," took place on November 18–20, 1991, despite his sudden death. Jacques Derrida later agreed to have the text he read on that occasion published as a preface to Michel Servière's *Le sujet de l'art.—Editor's note to* Le sujet de l'art.

CHAPTER 10

LOUIS MARIN

MAY 22, 1931—OCTOBER 29, 1992

For many years director of studies at the Ecole des Hautes Etudes en Sciences Sociales in Paris, Louis Marin was a noted semiotician, philosopher, and historian of art and a renowned expert in seventeenth-century studies in France. Born in 1931 in Grenoble, Marin attended the Lycée Grenoble (1940–47) and then the Lycées le Parc in Lyon and Louis-le-Grand in Paris. He studied at the Ecole Normale Supérieure from 1950 to 1954, where he passed the *agrégation* (placing second in the national exam) and was awarded a *docteur ès lettres*. At the beginning of his career, he was *attaché de recherches* at the Centre National de la Recherche Scientifique (1954–55) and taught at the Lycées Saint Quentin and Hoche of Versailles (1957–58). Marin spent the next six years abroad, as the French cultural counselor in Turkey and at the Institut Français in London.

From 1967 to 1972 Marin held various posts at the Universities of Paris I, Nanterre, and the Sorbonne, as well as at the Ecole Normale Supérieure and the Ecole Pratique des Hautes Etudes. From 1972 to 1978 Marin spent much of his time in the United States, holding posts at the University of California at San Diego and then at

Johns Hopkins University and Columbia. He obtained his long-term position as *directeur d'études* in "Systems of Representation—Arts and Language" at the Ecole des Hautes Etudes in 1978. Marin remained throughout his career a regular visitor to the United States, teaching at the University of California at Irvine, the State University of New York at Buffalo (as Jones Professor), Cornell, Princeton, and the University of Chicago. He became a permanent fellow of the Humanities Center at Johns Hopkins in 1983. He was also on the editorial board of many journals, including *Critique, Traverses, Glyph, Word and Image,* and *Modern Language Notes.*

Marin's early work was devoted to an analysis of the proper name and its relation to the pictorial figure. In *The Semiotics of the Passion Narratives* (1971), Marin conducted a "toponymic" study of the Eucharist in relation to signs and language, broaching topics such as force, narrative, and the body that would be taken up in several subsequent works. *Utopics* (1973) continued his analysis of proper names and "the neutral" through an examination of utopic places and practices. The book revolves around a close reading of Thomas More's *Utopia* but also includes discussions of Disneyland as a utopic space and Iannis Xenakis's writings as a poetic practice of "utopia." In *La voix excommuniée* (1979) Marin examines the idea of autobiography, reading texts by Stendhal, Rousseau, and Perrault in an attempt to understand the paradoxes encountered when one tries to write about oneself.

Throughout his career Marin devoted a major portion of his work to Pascal. He was the editor of Pascal's *Pensées* (published by Didier in 1969) and wrote the introduction to the *Logic of Port-Royal* (1970); his *La critique du discours* (1975) is a semiotic analysis of this logic. In *The Portrait of the King* (1981), Marin pursued Pascal's insights regarding representation and power in an analysis of the portrait of the king as the real presence of the king. *Pascal et Port-Royal,* a collection of essays written on related topics, was published posthumously in 1997.

Marin's other great love was art, and some of his most penetrating studies, such as *To Destroy Painting, Jean-Charles Blais, Opacité de la peinture, Des pouvoirs de l'image, De la représentation, Philippe de Champaigne,* and *Sublime Poussin,* explore the relationship between painting and discourse. Moving across an extraordinary range of genres, Marin undertook a rigorous analysis of modern representation in relation to such notions as the portrait, the powers of the image, force, autobiography, memory, and narrative. His stated aim in these studies was to "transform painting into discourse and divert images into language." *To Destroy Painting* (1977) is an exploration of sixteenth- and seventeenth-century European painting, particularly the works of Poussin and Caravaggio. *Opacité de la peinture* (1989) is a collection devoted to the works of Italian Renaissance painters in which Marin analyzes the theory of representation and of signs in these works.

A number of significant texts have been published posthumously. *Des pouvoirs de l'image* (1993) interrogates the "being of the image" through a reading of La Fontaine, Rousseau, Diderot, Corneille, Shakespeare, Pascal, Vasari, and Nietzsche. *De la représentation,* a collection of articles selected from among some three hundred papers published by Marin between 1960 and 1992, appeared in 1994. The articles chosen exemplify the wide variety of Marin's interests, ranging from topics in epistemology to aesthetics and theology. *Philippe de Champaigne* (1995) is a major study of the work of this seventeenth-century Belgian painter, situating it in relation to the theological and mystical texts of Augustine, Antoine Arnauld, and Pascal. The book extends Marin's lifelong exploration of the Age of Representation. Though Marin was unable to write his proposed book on Nicolas Poussin, the intended companion piece to his work on Philippe de Champaigne, ten major essays were collected in 1995 and published under the title *Sublime Poussin. De l'entretien* (1997) is a short book of interviews with Marin presenting his later works on art.

Marin passed away in Paris on October 29, 1992, at the age of sixty-one. He was survived by his wife, Françoise Marin, and three children. An homage was organized in his honor at the Pompidou Center in Paris on January 28, 1993.

By Force of Mourning

Who could ever speak of the work of Louis Marin?

Who would already know how to speak of the works of Louis Marin and of all the work that bore them, a work without measure?

Work: that which makes for a work, for an *oeuvre,* indeed that which works—and works to open: *opus* and *opening, oeuvre* and *overture:* the work or labor of the *oeuvre* insofar as it engenders, produces, and brings to light, but also labor or travail as suffering, as the enduring of force, as the pain of the one who gives. Of the one who gives birth, who brings to the light of day and gives something to be seen, who enables or empowers, who gives the force to know and to be able to see—and all these are powers of the image, the pain of what is given and of the one who takes the pains to help us see, read, and think.

Who could ever speak of all the work and works of Louis Marin?

As for this work—but what does one do when one works?

When one works *on* work, on the work of mourning, when one works at the work of mourning, one is already, yes, already, *doing* such work, enduring this work of mourning from the very start, letting it work within oneself, and thus authorizing oneself to do it, according it to oneself, according it within oneself, and giving oneself this liberty of finitude, the most worthy and the freest possible.

One cannot hold a discourse *on* the "work of mourning" without taking part in it, without announcing or partaking in [*se faire part de*] death, and first of all in one's own death. In the announcement of one's own death, which says, in short, "I am dead," "I died"—such as this book lets it be heard—one should be able to say, and I have tried to say this in the past, that all work is also the work of mourning. All work in general works *at mourning.* In and of itself. Even when it has the power to give birth,

This text is the transcription of a talk given January 28, 1993, at the Pompidou Center in Paris during a conference honoring Louis Marin and acknowledging the forthcoming publication of *Des pouvoirs de l'image: Gloses* (Paris: Seuil, 1993). Reprinted, with changes, from "By Force of Mourning," translated by Pascale-Anne Brault and Michael Naas, *Critical Inquiry* 22, no. 2 (winter 1996): 171–92. No French publication.

even and especially when it plans to bring something to light and let it be seen. The work of mourning is not one kind of work among other possible kinds; an activity of the kind "work" is by no means a specific figure for production in general.

There is thus no metalanguage for the language in which a work of mourning is at work. This is also why one should not be able to say anything about the work of mourning, anything about this subject, since it cannot become a theme, only another experience of mourning that comes to work over the one who intends to speak. To speak of mourning or of anything else. And that is why whoever thus works *at* the work of mourning learns the impossible—and that mourning is interminable. Inconsolable. Irreconcilable. Right up until death—that is what whoever works at mourning knows, working at mourning as both their object and their resource, working *at mourning* as one would speak of a painter working *at a painting* but also of a machine working *at such and such an energy level,* the theme of work thus becoming their very force, and their term, a principle.

What might be this principle of mourning? And what was its force? What is, what will have been, what will still be tomorrow, the energy of Louis Marin?

Let us begin by letting him speak. Here are a few words, his words, that say something difficult to understand. They advance a truth, advance toward a singular aporia that Louis Marin states or rather announces precisely on the subject of "mourning."

It says, and for the moment I cite just part of a sentence, as if it were all of a sudden suspended, an interruption coming to take its breath away: "the modalities of a work of mourning of the absolute of 'force.'"[1]

This fragment of a long sentence by Louis Marin names—and we thus repeat it—"the modalities of a work of mourning of the absolute of 'force.'"

Five nouns linked together, which can be read as the scanned filiation of a single genitive in the preface of his last book. And never before had I paid attention to the terrible ambiguity of this expression "the last book" of Louis Marin. It makes it impossible to decide between the final book and simply the most recent one, the last one to have come out. For there will be others. This one will simply be the last to have come out, though we know that those that will come out later will have been completed before this

---

1.   Louis Marin, *Des pouvoirs de l'image: Gloses* (Paris: Seuil, 1993), 16–17 (hereafter abbreviated as *P*).

one, which will thus remain in the end, and forever, the last one. Forever. From now on the final one.

The preface to *Des pouvoirs de l'image: Gloses* thus announces and pronounces that it will address the "modalities of a work of mourning of the absolute of 'force.'" The slow and cautious procession, the vigilant theory of these complements of the noun leave no determination exempt from analysis. If the word "force" is here in quotation marks, it is for a good reason; it is because the mourning in question and the so-called work of mourning are not self-evident; they go beyond understanding in some way, they go past the usual understanding of this word "force," indeed, they just don't quite go. It is a question, in truth, of the impossible itself. And that is why I took the risk of speaking a moment ago of an aporia. You will also understand, for this is the law, the law of mourning, and the law of the law, always in mourning, that it would have to fail in order to succeed. In order to succeed, it would well have to *fail,* to fail *well.* It would well have to fail, for this is what has to be so, in failing *well.* That is what would have to be. And while it is always promised, it will never be assured.

In the era of psychoanalysis, we all of course speak, and we can always go on speaking, about the "successful" work of mourning—or, inversely, as if it were precisely the contrary, about a "melancholia" that would signal the failure of such work. But if we are to follow Louis Marin, here comes a work without force, a work that would have to work at renouncing force, its own force, a work that would have to work at failure, and thus at mourning and getting over force, a work working at its own unproductivity, absolutely, working to absolve or to absolve itself of whatever might be absolute about "force," and thus of something like "force" itself: "a work of mourning of the absolute of 'force,'" says Louis Marin, keeping the word "force" between quotation marks that just won't let go. It is a question of the absolute renunciation of the absolute of force, of the absolute of force in its impossibility and unavoidability; both at once, as inaccessible as it is ineluctable.

What then is force, absolutely? But also: what is this "without force," this state of being drained, without any force, where death, where the death of a friend, leaves us, when we also have to work at mourning force? Is the "without force," the mourning of force, possible? In the end this is the question Marin leaves us. It is with this question that he leaves us, like rich and powerless heirs, that is, both provided for and at a loss, given over to being forlorn and distraught, full of and fortified by him, responsible and voiceless.

Though he leaves us with this question, at least he will have refor-
mulated it in a new and singular way, indicating another path, another
way to engage or to be engaged with it, with this proliferating thought
that buzzes like a hive. (What is force—force itself, absolute force, if there
is any? Where does it come from? How does one recognize it? How does
one measure it? What is the greatest force—the invulnerable force? And
if this infallible force were the place of the greatest weakness, for example,
the place of the "defenselessness" of death, of the dead's "defenselessness,"
of their helplessness, of their "without force," and of the "defenselessness"
and thus the "without-force of the survivors faced with death"? What is
meant by "force," in quotation marks? What is that?)

Let us look for another way to engage this aporetic question to which
there are however so many different points of entry. They all come down to
asking in the end what *is* this thing called "force." In the quotation marks
that suspend even the assurance of a term of reference, the question would
seem to mark out a strange path. Which one? Force itself—by preceding
and thus violating in advance, in some sense, the possibility of a question
concerning it—force itself would trouble, disturb, dislocate the very form
of the question "what is?" the imperturbable "what is?" the authority of
what is called the ontological question.

For the powers of the image lead back perhaps in the last resort to
this power, to the force of an image that must be protected from every
ontology. It would have to be protected from such ontologies because it
itself, in truth, protects itself from them; it begins, and this is precisely the
force of its force, by tearing itself away from an ontological tradition of the
question "what is?" Marin recalls already in the introduction to his book
that this tradition itself tended to consider the image as a lesser being, that
is, as a being without power, or as a weaker and inferior being, a being
of little power, of little force. To submit the image to the question "what
is?" would thus already be to miss the image and its force, the image in
its force, which has to do perhaps not with what it is or is not, with the
fact that it is not or does not have much being, but with the fact that its
logic or rather its dynamic, its *dynamis,* the dynasty of its force, will not
submit to an onto-logic: its dynamo-logic would no longer be, would have
never been, a logic of being, an ontology. Or rather, to come at it from the
other direction, which actually makes more sense: the ontological order
(that is, philosophy) would have been constituted as such for not knowing
the powers of the image: *for* not knowing or denying them, in the double
sense of this "for," that is, *because* it did not take them into account, but
also *for* mistaking them, *with a view to* doing so, so as to oppose them, in
this most veiled and clandestine war, to the unavowed counterpower of

a denial intended to assure an ontological power *over* the image, over the power of the image, over its *dynamis.*

Dynamis: the word seems indispensable. If I emphasize it so forcefully, while Louis Marin uses it only once in his preface as an apposition to the words "force" and "virtue," *virtù* ("the force in the image and of the image, the *virtù,* the virtue, the *dynamis* that 'propels' it to vision" [*P,* 18]), it is because this concept plays, it seems to me, a decisive role as soon as it is protected or withdrawn from the traditional ontology that generally dominates it. We will later see that this *dynamis* here links in a most original way both the ideas it has always associated—namely, force, power, and *virtù*—and the ideas of the possible or the virtual *as such,* that is to say, a virtual that has no vocation to go into action, or rather, whose going into action or whose enactment does not destroy its virtual power.

With what does this have to do (if one can say this, since the logic of the act and of acting, of doing, is precisely what is at stake here)? It would have to do with a possible that is in potential of being only on the condition of remaining possible as possible, and of marking within itself—the scar of a wound and the potentialization of force—the interruption of this going into action, this enactment, an absolute interruption that bears no other seal here than that of death: whence a thought of the *virtual work,* one might also say of a virtual space, of an *opus,* an *opus operatum,* that would accomplish the possible *as such* without effacing it or even enacting it in reality. The thought of a spectral power of the virtual work. One that envelops or develops within itself a thought of death. Only death, which is not, or rather mourning, which takes its place in advance, can open up this space of absolute *dynamis:* force, virtue, the possible as such, without which one understands nothing of the power of the image. And this "understands nothing," this ontological denial, would be nothing other than philosophy itself, which thus cannot be considered to be one conjuring practice among others. For trying to reduce, weaken, and wear out a power of the image so as to subject it to itself, this philosophical exorcism of such powerful scope would—and this would be my hypothesis—in some way *regard* death.

It would regard that which should not be seen, and so denied, namely death. This clandestine war of denial would thus be waged in the shadows, in that twilight space of what is called mourning: the mourning that follows death but also the mourning that is prepared and that we expect from the very beginning to follow upon the death of those we love. Love or friendship would be nothing other than the passion, the endurance, and the patience of this work.

Whence this paradox: when Marin puts a question mark after the being of the image ("The being of the image?" [*P,* 10]) and later answers:

"The being of the image, in a word, would be its force: but how are we to think this 'force'?" and when he once again puts the word force into quotation marks—this would amount to substituting force for being. But the logic of this substitution—and this is the reason for the conditional ("*would be* its force")—itself calls for the quotation marks. *For this force owes it to itself not to be.* It owes it to itself not to be a being. It must thus now be on intimate terms with what is not force, with its opposite, with the "without-force," a domestic and paradoxically necessary commerce being established between them. The greatest force is to be seen in the infinite renunciation of force, in the absolute interruption of force by the without-force. Death, or rather mourning, the mourning of the absolute of force: that is the name, or one of the names, of this affect that unites force to the without-force, thereby relating the manifestation of force, as image, to the being without force of *that which* it manifests or lets be seen, right before our very eyes and according to our mourning.

For what appears most striking from the very opening of this last book, *Des pouvoirs de l'image,* is that it brings about in an irresistible way a double conversion, I dare not say a double reversal. There is first of all the turn or move by which Marin protects the question of the image from the authority of ontology, and this is already a question of force and of power. Then there is the other turn or move whereby this first move finds its truth or its law in—if we can now put it in a nonontological way—what I would be tempted to call, using a code that would have precisely nothing Heideggerian about it, the being-toward-death of the image. Or, let us say to avoid ambiguity, the *being-to-death* of an image that *has* the force, that *is nothing other than* the force, *to resist, to consist, and to exist* in death, precisely there where it does not insist in being or in the presence of being. This *being-to-death* would oblige us to think the image not as the weakened reproduction of what it would imitate, not as a *mimēme,* a simple image, idol, or icon, at least as they are conventionally understood (for it is a question of moving away from this convention), but as the increase of power, the origin, in truth, of authority, the image itself becoming the author, the author and the augmentation of the *auctoritas* insofar as it finds its paradigm, which is also its *enargeia,* in the image of the dead.

In other words, we would not have *images,* a *typology of images* among which a particular class representing the dead or death might be identified. For it would be from death, from what might be called the *point of view of death,* or more precisely, of the dead, the dead man or woman, or more precisely still, from the point of view of the *face* of the dead in their portraiture, that an image would give seeing, that is, not only would give *itself* to be seen but would give insofar as it sees, as if it were seeing as much as seen.

A displacement of the point of view, therefore, which quite obviously inscribes all the essays of this book into the ongoing tradition of work undertaken by Marin for many years concerning that which founds the foundation and institutes the institution of power in a certain logic of representation. And this work, as we all know, allowed him in the course of so many innovative, fertile, and brilliant analyses to articulate a thought of the theologico-political and a certain icono-semiological theory of representation.

Yet it seems to me (and this is a reading hypothesis that regards, if I may say this, only me, and indicates only a moment of my mournful reading) that in these important developments of earlier research an inflection or break comes to inscribe a paradox. This paradox complicates and in turn illuminates, it seems to me, the earlier trajectory. It concerns the mourning of force or the force of mourning, that is to say, a law according to which the greatest force does not consist in continually expanding ad infinitum but develops its maximal intensity, so to speak, only at the mad moment of decision, at the point of its absolute interruption, there where *dynamis* remains virtuality, namely, a virtual work as such. A moment of infinite renunciation as the potentialization of the virtual work. But the virtual work is not one category of work or image among others; it is the essence of the work, a nonessential essence, since it is an essence that remains possible *as such*. And this is death (or at least that's what this word here signifies—and there where there is no death in itself that would ever be possible as such there is only the experience of mourning without death: mourning is the phenomenon of death and it is the only phenomenon behind which there is nothing; the *phainesthai* of this phenomenon is the only possible access to an original thought of the image, and so on). Here is death, then, there where the image annuls its representative presence, there where, more precisely, the non-re-productive intensity of the *re-* of representation gains in power what the present that it represents loses in presence. And this point, which also punctuates an entire way of thinking the temporalization of time, is evidently the point, not of death itself, but of mourning, and of the mourning of the absolute of force.

If, therefore, the first examples Marin proposes in order to make this power of the image visible and energetic, in order to *illustrate* it, are images of the dead, one should not see here a simply fortuitous occurrence. It is in the re-presentation of the dead that the power of the image is exemplary. When Marin asks about this *re-* of representation, about the substitutive value that this *re-* indicates at the moment when that which was present is

no longer present and comes to be re-presented, and when he then takes
the example of the disappearance of the present as death, it is in order not
only to track a re-presentation or an absolute substitution of representation
for presence, but also to detect within it an increase, a re-gaining of force
or a supplement of intensity in presence, and thus a sort of potency or
potentialization of power for which the schema of substitutive value, of
mere replacement, can give no account. Representation is here no longer
a simple reproductive re-presentation; it is such a regaining of presence,
such a recrudescence or resurgence of presence thereby intensified, that it
allows lack to be thought, the default of presence or the mourning that
had hollowed out in advance the so-called primitive or originary presence,
the presence that is represented, the so-called living presence.

Here, in a word, is the question of the image, the image put into
question, not the question "What is the image?" but "image?" Let us read
Marin (*P,* 11):

> The prefix *re-* brings into this term the value of substitution. Some-
> thing that *was* present and *is* no longer is *now* represented. In
> place of something that is present *elsewhere,* there is here a present,
> a *given.*

I emphasize "elsewhere" here, though we are going to see in a moment that
the radical example of death makes of this "elsewhere," which refers to a
Gospel, the metonymy of a possible "nowhere," or at least of an elsewhere
without locality, without a home in presentable space, in the given space
of presentation.

> . . . there is here a present, a *given:* image?

This single-word question—"image?"—is going to come up more than
once. But is it really a question of an image? Can one still speak of an
image when representation seems to do more than represent, when it
actually gains in intensity and force, when it seems to have even more
power than that of which it is said to be the image or the imitation?
Marin's response will necessarily be double, *no and yes: no,* it is not simply
an image if we are to accept the ontological concept of the image as the
mimetic and weakened double of the thing itself; *yes,* for it is the very
essence, the proper power, the *dynamis* of the image, if one thinks the
image on the basis of death, that is, in truth, on the basis of the mourning
that will confer upon it its power and an increase in intensive force. Let us
continue this reading.

> . . . image? Instead of representation, then, there is an absence in
> time or space, or rather an other.

The replacement of "absence" by "other" here no doubt indicates that the substitutive value is no longer operative in the couple "absence/presence" but in the couple "same/other" that introduces the dimension of mourning.

> . . . an other, and a substitution takes place from an other to this
> other, in its place. Thus, in this primitive (or originary) scene of
> the Christian West, the angel at the tomb on the morning of the
> Resurrection—"he is not here, he is elsewhere, in Galilee, as he
> had said"—which substitutes a message for this thing, for this
> dead body and its inertia, which makes appear the "force" [again in
> quotation marks, and we will later see why] of an utterance whose
> content is, nonetheless, limited to remarking upon an absence, "he
> is not here . . . ," the absence of the "same" in the heterogeneity of
> another semiotic potential, language.

Let us pause for a moment at this allusion to "the heterogeneity of another semiotic potential, language" in the presentation of the image. It explains and justifies in advance the very form of Marin's book, namely, the necessity of a textual weaving of words and images, the imbrication of glosses sewn upon the iconic tissue: glosses upon glosses that are, in truth, just as originary as the image, as an image that language will have made possible, and glosses of glosses that we here can only gloss in turn, on one side or the other of the image. Marin immediately goes on to repeat this question in a word ("image?"). He links it this time to the theme of resurrection and transfiguration:

> Here—look here, listen here—in place of a cadaver, removed from
> the agency of signification, from the ritual gesturality of the funeral
> unction, a message: this exchange between the cadaver and lan-
> guage, the gap of this exchange, is precisely the resurrection of the
> body, and the traversing of this gap, the ontological transfiguration
> of the body: image?

The question is repeated: "image?" This elliptical question without verb or copula suggests that the image is more than an image, stronger or *more forceful* than the image defined and weakened by ontology. The same ellipsis also lets something else be thought: outside the evangelical, doctrinal, or dogmatic space of the Resurrection, before it, more originary than it, but in an originarity of which Christianity makes an event, there would be the very possibility, the power, the force of resurrection and of transfiguration that will be treated so magnificently in gloss 8 of the book, to which I will return in a moment; this force would here stem from the semiotic heterogeneity, from the power of language, and from the power of alterity that works over the being-to-death of every image.

> Between dead cadaver [a strange redundancy, "dead cadaver,"
> which leaves no chance for illusion or hallucination] and enunciated
> message, the enunciation so *powerful* of/by an absence [*puissante*
> *d'une absence*]—

I emphasize "powerful," the key word in this expression "the enunciation so powerful of/by an absence," because the adjective "powerful" matters more than both the subject, "enunciation," and the complement of the noun, "of/by an absence."

> —and it is in this that its pragmatic and historical force resides, its
> foundational efficacity—the absence of the founding body.

The logic of these propositions is dictated by a thought of the foundation itself as the power of the image: the body is not first founding and then, once dead or absent, confirmed in its founding power. No, this power comes to it from the imaginal transfiguration. This founding power advenes thanks to and as the result of the imaginal transfiguration. The foundation is first of all imaginal; it is from the very start fantastic or phantasmic: under certain conditions, of course, and this is the central problem of the pragmatic conditions of such efficacity; all of history is at issue here, and, first of all, the enigma of all the examples taken in such an exemplary way, that is, at once invariant and (yet) indifferent, open to variation, from the Gospels. In any case, it will be said that this founding power of the image or of the portrait (of the king, for example), with all the political dimensions that Marin never ceased to analyze, did not exist before death. This power comes to it from this imaginal representation, from "the exchange between the cadaver and language," from the "ontological transfiguration of the body."

But what might this mean? Why did the founding power of the image not exist before death? What might it mean in general for something not to exist before death, when the anticipation of death comes so indisputably to hollow out the living present that precedes it, and when mourning is at work, as we know, before death?

It means perhaps that the power of the image as the power of death does not wait for death, but is marked out in everything—and for everything—that awaits death: the death of the king gets its efficacity from the portrait made before the death of the king, and every image enacts its efficacity only by signifying the death from which it draws all its power.

> It is this ("the absence of the founding body") that will constantly require throughout the ages that the body be covered over, buried, and in a way monumentalized by and in its representations. Such would be the first effect of representation *in general.*

I emphasize "in general." Such generality affects the Christian example with the sign of a possible imaginary variation, as if the privilege of Christian culture were, in a sort of phenomenological eidetic reduction, but the imaginary basis for an intuition of a general essence concerning the nature of representation or imagination in general, beyond the Christic space. When Marin here names the "first effect," he is not pointing out a simple consequence, something that would follow upon the operation of the image: interested, as always—as the great Pascalian that he was—in the logic of the effect, in the reason of effects, he knows that the image is nothing, that it does not exist before or outside the effect, the word "effect" designating at once the change brought about and that which *has an effect,* namely, the energy of the aspect, of the manifestation, of visibility, of *phainesthai.* The reason of effects thus comes not so much from the principle of reason or causality as from the fact that it reveals the power of representation, an essence of representation that effectuates more than its so-called ontological essence. If I gloss things in my own way, all the while trying not to be unfaithful to Marin's intention, if I oppose the "reason of effects," which Marin does not invoke directly here, to the "principle of reason" and, implicitly, to the interpretation of it given by Heidegger, whom Marin, it seems to me, if I am not speaking too hastily here, never evokes in this work (except indirectly, in a note concerning a reference by Panofsky to Heidegger [*P,* 205]), it is to try to make sense of the underlying reason for this silence and to try implicitly or obliquely to justify it, assuming that a silence can ever be justified. For Heidegger always associates the predominance and the closure of a certain accentuation of the Principle of reason (that is, of the *Satz vom Grund* as principle of causality or of final causality, the *Grund* or the foundation here being the cause), especially since the seventeenth century, with a certain authority of representation. In so doing he perhaps misses out on understanding how the authority or power, and particularly the theologico-political power of representation, even if aesthetic, might come to it, in its very founding agency, precisely from its lack or absence of *Grund,* from the *Abgrund* on the basis of which it founds: for it founds precisely there where the founding body, the founding agency or existence, comes to disappear in death, to act as the one who has disappeared or passed away. All these are problems or dimensions of the foundation, and first of all of the political foundation—in and through representation—that, as such, never interested Heidegger, if I am not mistaken, at least not in *The Principle of Reason,* which is *also,* however, a meditation upon that which happens to representation, and through representation, in the seventeenth century.

> Such would be the "primitive" of representation as effect: to pre-
> sentify, to make the absent present, as if that which returned were
> the same.

There is here, then, an acute thought of mourning and of the phantom that returns, of haunting and spectrality: beyond the alternative between presence and absence, beyond negative or positive perception even, the effect of the image would stem from the fantastic force of the specter, and from a supplement of force; and the increase becomes fantastic at the very heart of lack, for Marin immediately raises the stakes, capitalizes the stakes with regard to a capital surplus value of the image, with regard, in sum, to the *interest* of the image and the desire for the image:

> Such would be the "primitive" of representation as effect: to pre-
> sentify, to make the absent present, as if that which returned were
> the same and sometimes better, *more* intense, *more* forceful than if it
> were the same. (My emphasis)

The "more" here seems affected by an "as if" ("as if it were the same"), but the more intensity or force, far from being lessened or attenuated by the fiction of the "as if," draws from it, on the contrary, all its *dynamis,* at once its power and its increase of potential being, of being in potential. There is also here, I would be tempted to say, a theory of the capital and of the capitalization of energy, there where capital is represented from its heraldic depths [*abîme*], both in the chief or head (of state, for example) and in the capital portrait. For this is also a book on the decapitation of the king (look at entreglose 8 entitled "The Severed Head" on Corneille's *Death of Pompey*) and on the fate of this form of capital punishment that turns regicide into an event whose possibility is inscribed right on the effect called "portrait of the king."

To reinforce this demonstration of force and of what links power to death, Marin goes on to cite an extraordinary text by Alberti. In book II of his treatise *On Painting,* Alberti speaks of death and of friendship. I could not help but recall a certain moment during a seminar we taught together three years ago when we asked about what links friendship to the testamentary experience, particularly in a certain text of Montaigne, of whom Marin was also a marvelous reader. What does Alberti say here? If painting has within itself a force that is absolutely divine (*vim divinam*) it is because it makes the absent present: "as friendship is said to do," Alberti then adds, thinking perhaps of a certain text of Aristotle, the very one that Montaigne evokes and that we had discussed in this seminar.[2] Alberti then moves on—right to the limit of death. Death is not one example of absence among others; it speaks to us of absence itself by naming the most absent of absences, the one that is given by death. Henceforth death, which is expressed, in sum, by all the other absences as absences, is what gives painting its greatest force, for "divine force" also means "the greatest force." But because it bears death, so to speak, this greatest force is also the "without-force," the mourning of the absolute of "force." For to suggest, as I have just done, that "divine force" means "the greatest force" is not simply to call divine that which is the greatest, that in relation to which nothing greater can be thought, as St. Anselm would say, or to think it according to a schema of ordinary meaning that would unite the idea of God to the superlative; it is also to approach the divinity of the divine on the basis of death, or rather as the mourning-bearing power that makes the greatest force equal to the without-force, to the mourning of the absolute of "force." Under these conditions, the schemas of the eucharistic transubstantiation, of the transfiguration or the resurrection, even if taken outside the context of pure Christian dogmatism, retain an exemplary value for Marin's works, in the most enigmatic sense of this Christian exemplarity. This exemplarity does not suggest one occurrence among others but the occurrence of the unique and irreplaceable historical advent that allows one to give an account of all the effects of the "portrait of the king." By allowing them to take place, by giving them their proper place, it determines Marin's so necessary and so rigorous analyses on this subject—be it in the book that bears this title (*Portrait of the King*)[3] or in the second part of this last book, "The Genealogical and Political Powers of the Image."

What do all these analyses, each one emanating beauty and truth, show? To put it all too poorly in a word, they demonstrate and display what, in the course of history, allows one to say, following Pascal, that "the portrait of the king is the king" and that it is the "'portrait effect,' the mimetic effect, the effect of representation, that *makes* the king" (*P,* 187).

2.   Leon Battista Alberti, *On Painting,* trans. John R. Spencer (New Haven: Yale University Press, 1956), 63.

3.   Louis Marin, *Portrait of the King,* trans. Martha M. Houle (Minneapolis: University of Minnesota Press, 1988).

This logic presupposes that a sort of death of the king comes *in advance* to divide the king's body in two: the individual or real body on the one hand; the fictive—ideal or representative—body of dignity on the other. (The politico-juridical history of the two bodies of the king in Christian Europe, such as it is analyzed by Ernst Kantorowicz, plays an organizing role in these texts of Marin; it runs through them, as we know, as the continuous thread of an axiomatic—so indispensable and obvious that Kantorowicz hardly has to be mentioned.) Now, as we know, this dividing or this redoubling of the king's body, this functional death of the physical body in the body of dignity, what Marin elsewhere calls the "caesura of the royal body,"[4] could be written into the rights of absolute and hereditary monarchy only on the basis of a Christian doctrine. I'll cite just one sentence, at the end of gloss 6 ("The Portrait of the King, Shipwrecked"), which would here have to be read extremely closely: "The king in his portrait, the king as image, the king-representation, is thus in the 'parable' a parody of the eucharistic mystery of the mystic body and of real presence" (*P*, 194).

One could readily show, in fact, that this logic remains at work wherever there is a monarchy in a Christian country, even in a Christian democracy, I mean in a democratic regime with a Christian culture, as soon as the unity or the independence of the nation-state is represented in the body of a monarch or president, no matter what the length of the term or the forms of inheritance by election (filiation or succession), indeed, no matter what the mode of election.

But let's return to Alberti: "Painting," he writes, "contains an absolutely divine force [*in se vim admodum divinam habet*] that not only makes absent men present, as friendship is said to do, but shows the dead to the living so that even after many centuries [*defunctus long post saecula viventibus exhibeat*] they may be recognized by them with great pleasure and with great admiration for the painter" (quoted in *P*, 11). In Alberti's description we see pleasure and admiration becoming inextricably linked to mourning, the force of the three affects increasing from their combination.

Yet it is necessary here to underscore an obvious fact. It could easily be forgotten because it is so obvious, like the nose in the middle of one's face. It is that the image and representation are treated by Alberti—and by Marin citing Alberti—*on the basis of the portrait*. The portrait is not just any painting. It thus has to be recalled why it is the history of the image *as portrait* that must be investigated in order to analyze power, particularly the theologico-political power of representation. The portrait

---

4. See Marin, *Lectures traversières* (Paris: Albin Michel, 1992), 179–93.

is not one fiction or figure, one face of the figure, among others. Not only because it represents *at once* the gaze that gazes at us *and* the head that governs the body *and* the chief or head who governs the social body. (In his political analyses Marx is always interested just as much in the head of those who govern as in the logic of capital.) But especially because, like the photographic portrait, its relation to the referent appears (and it is this appearance that counts even if one must not trust it) irreducible. This fiction of the figure, of the face, is given as essentially nonfictive, and it claims to give us—and Barthes relied a good deal, perhaps a bit too much, on this claim—what once was and could not not have been present before the gaze or before the lens. What the portrait says, the *title* "portrait" (and it is because a title is of the order of discourse that we are here in a gloss), is that what is shown, portraitured, is what was (supposed to have been) real, really present. This is obviously not the case of every other pictorial figure or fiction, which do not then strictly speaking deserve the name of representation, or even, in the end, that of image. The portrait is here the capital representation insofar as it represents the capital element in a power of the image. Forcing things only a bit, one could say that, *at least* from the point of view of the theologico-political power guaranteed by the portrait of the king, and based on Marin's analysis, there is no difference between painting and photography, for the photographic portrait continues to guarantee, and sometimes even accentuates, the function of the painted portrait. The photographic technique fulfills even more powerfully the pictorial vocation, namely, to seize the dead and transfigure them—to resuscitate as *having been* the one who (singularly, he or she) will have been. The presidential portraits that can be seen today in all places of public authority (government agencies, town halls, departmental and municipal buildings, police stations) express the origin, identity, and place of the capital gathering of legitimate power insofar as it holds us in its gaze and looks at us looking at it by recalling us to what looks at and regards us, that is, to our responsibility before it and in its eyes. It is also true that photography at the same time goes against the very vocation it fulfills or continues since it makes the portrait available to everyone. Through this technical democratization, photography tends to destroy the aura and rarity of painting that restrict the commissioning of the painted portrait, which sometimes turns out to be a masterpiece, to certain privileged places, of which the court is at the very least the metonymic figure. In any case, one should not be surprised to see Marin, just after having spoken of what is "most intense" and "most forceful" about the effect of representation, and just before citing Alberti, make reference in a single sentence to photography, and more precisely to the photograph of someone who, as we say, has disappeared or "passed away," the photograph, like the portrait, having the virtue of making appear the one who has disappeared, of making them reappear with greater clarity or *enargeia*. Before citing Alberti, Marin acts as if he were giving an example merely in passing, a few words of pedagogic illustration: "Thus the photograph of someone who has passed away displayed on the mantel" (*P,* 11).

I am going to have to break this off, for there is not enough time; but before saying in a few words in what direction I would have liked to share with you the reading of this great book, I would especially like to convey to you, trying not to take advantage of the emotion, how difficult and painful it is for me to speak here of this book. This difficulty or pain has nothing to do with the time we do or do not have this evening; we and, alas, we alone, will later have more time. A bit more time.

Such difficulty or pain has to do with the strange time of reading that the time of the writing of this book will have, as if in advance, imprinted in us, the friends of Louis.

I imagine him writing these lines, citing and glossing Alberti in his preface not long before his death, working on a book he knew he might not see, that is, might not, while still living, see come out. The book, as *you* will see, multiplies these analyses, these examples, these images of what I would call the survival effect, the effect of living on. Louis not only saw death coming, as we all see it coming without seeing it, as we all expect it without expecting it. He approached death, which approached him, more and more quickly; he approached it in preceding it, and anticipated it with these images and glosses, for which the grammar of the future anterior no doubt does not suffice to convey their force and time, their tense. The future anterior is still a simplistic modalization of a fundamental present or representation; simplistic because still too simple to be able to translate the strange temporality that here gives its force to the mourning affect of which we are speaking. It would likewise be too simple, though true in an oblique way, to say that Louis Marin, citing Alberti and speaking of the portrait of others, of death and of friendship, painted himself in advance, painting at the same time his grieving friends, pointing us out to ourselves in advance with a finger, and signing the extraordinary utterance, which he comments upon elsewhere, that allows one to say "I died" (this incredible grammar, this impossible time or tense that he analyzes in *La voix excommuniée*).[5]

To say "I died," "I am dead," is not simply a future anterior. It is the strange time of his writing, the strange time of reading that looks

5. See Marin, *La voix excommuniée: Essais de mémoire* (Paris: Galilée, 1981), 64.

at and regards us in advance this evening, that will have regarded us, that will regard us long after us. The "I died" is not a phenomenologico-grammatical monstrosity, a scandal of common sense or an impossible sentence with no meaning. It is the time or tense, the graphological time, the implicit tempo of all writing, all painting, of every trace, and even of the presumed present of every *cogito ergo sum*. (For this phrase, as I tried to show a long time ago elsewhere, necessarily implies an "I am dead." In Descartes one cannot separate these words and the system of their enunciation from what is considered to be one of Descartes's minor discourses, namely, what he says of the Eucharist when he dares, more or less clandestinely, to enter into the debate among theologians on this subject. I later tried to show this again in a seminar where I referred, of course, to the works of Marin on the Eucharist and added to them this Cartesian gloss.)

During the past few weeks spent admiring *Des pouvoirs de l'image* I kept saying to myself that I have never known such an emotion in reading a book. It was not only the emotion of mourning that we all know and recognize, even if it hits us each time in a new and singular way, like the end of the world, an emotion that overwhelms us each time we come across the surviving testimonies of the lost friend, across all the "images" that the one who has "passed away" has left or passed on to us.

There was, this time, something more, something else as well. There was another emotion that came to overwhelm this first mourning, this common mourning, coming to make it turn upon itself, I would almost want to say to reflect it to the point of vertigo, another emotion, another quality and intensity of emotion, at once too painful and strangely peaceful, which had to do, I believe, with a certain time of reading.

Without even trying to say something more, however minimal, about this magnificent book and about the strange time of reading by which I was overwhelmed, I would like to venture a few words on the subject of mourning, and on the time of an interminable mourning, so as not to rush ahead—something I would deem intolerable—to speak this evening of the last book of Marin as I might have spoken in another time and in more conventional circumstances of his most recent book. In returning regularly to common places, I mean to the places that were common to us, sitting in the office I shared with him for so long on boulevard Raspail, walking around the Maison des Sciences de l'Homme, taking part just recently in a discussion during the seminar he led for many years with certain among you whom I see in this room, I have said to myself that, ever since psychoanalysis came to mark this discourse, the image commonly used to characterize mourning is that of an interiorization (an idealizing incorporation, introjection, consumption of the other, in effect, an experience that would have received one of its essential aspects from the Eucharist, which was, for Louis, the great Thing, the great mourning-object, both his object and the object of his mourning, to which he will have devoted a work so original and all-consuming, a work that relentlessly pursues the eucharistic body from every side—exegetical, philosophical, historical, logical, linguistic—as if it were necessary before dying to come to know what mourning is, to know how to come to terms with death, and how to transfigure the work of death into a work that gives and gives something to be seen). Now, if the modes of interiorization or of subjectification that psychoanalysis talks about are in some respects undeniable in the work of mourning where the death of the friend leaves us, that is, leaves us alone, I told myself the following, which is certainly not original but which I feel with a singular acuteness and, indeed, an increased intensity: if this interiorization is not possible, if it must not—and this is the unbearable paradox of fidelity—be possible and completed, it would not be because of a limit, because of a border that cannot be crossed, because of a frontier that comes to enclose a given space, organizing finitude into an inside and an outside that would be, in effect, homogeneous with one another, symmetrical and commensurable on each side of an indivisible line. It would be, rather, because of another organization of space and of visibility, of the gazing and the gazed upon. Whatever the truth, alas, of this inevitable interiorization (the friend can no longer be but *in us,* and whatever we may believe about the afterlife, about living-on, according to all the possible forms of faith, it is *in us* that these movements might appear), this being-in-us reveals a truth *to and at death,* at the moment of death, and even before death, by everything in us that prepares itself for and awaits death, that is, in the undeniable anticipation of mourning that constitutes friendship. It reveals the truth of its topology and tropology. When we say "in us," when we speak so easily and so painfully of inside and outside, we are naming space, we are speaking of a visibility of the body, a geometry of gazes, an orientation of perspectives. *We are speaking of images.* What is only *in us* seems to be reducible to images, which might be memories or monuments, but which are reducible in any case to a memory that consists of *visible* scenes that are no longer anything but *images,* since the other of whom they are the images appears only as the one who has disappeared or passed away, as the one who, having passed away, leaves "in us" only images. He is no more, he whom we see in images or in recollection, he of whom we speak, whom we cite, whom we try to let speak—he is no more, he is no longer here, no longer there. And nothing can begin to dissipate the terrifying and chilling light of this certainty. As if respect for this certainty were still a debt, the last one, owed to the friend.

What this rhetoric of space, this topology and this tropology, miss, what this description of lack lacks, is that the force of the image has to do less with the fact that one sees something in it than with the fact that one is seen there in it. The image sees more than it is seen. The image looks at us. (Indeed, some of you here this evening, Hubert Damisch in particular, work on this inversion of the gaze that comes from painting and on the dissymmetry and demastering brought about by such an inversion, and everything Marin tells us of the portrait has to do, in the end, with this inversion of dissymmetry that can be interiorized only by exceeding, fracturing, wounding, injuring, traumatizing the interiority that it inhabits or that welcomes it through hospitality, love, or friendship. This dissymmetry also inscribes—unless it actually depends on it—an essential anachrony in our being exposed to the other; it dislocates all contemporaneity at the very heart of what we have our sights on at the same time.)

Louis Marin is outside and he is looking at me, he himself, and I am an image for him. At this very moment. There where I can say *cogito, sum,* I know that I am an image for the other and am looked at by the other, even and especially by the mortal other. I move right before his eyes, and the force of this image is irreversible (because of the reversion, the conversion, of force into weakness and vice versa). Louis Marin is looking at me, and it is for this, for him, that I am here this evening. He is my law, the law, and I appear before him, before his word and his gaze. In my relationship to myself, he is here in me before me, stronger or more forceful than I. It might be said that I came because other witnesses asked me to, because I appear also before those close to him, Françoise, Anne, Frédérique, and Judith, before his friends and the friends we had in common. This is surely true, but I would not have felt this imperative before them had I not known that what unites us is at once common and outside us, and that we are all looked at (each one of us singularly) by the one who, with each page, will have providentially deciphered and prescribed, arranged in advance, a reading of what is happening here, of what makes the present scene possible, foreseeing and watching over it with the benevolent regard (since it is he who watches out to watch over us) and with all the love of someone who can say, at the moment of dying, even if he is not Christ or even Christian, *hoc est meum corpus, which is given for you. Do this in remembrance of me* (Luke 22.19).

We are all looked at, I said, and each one singularly, by Louis Marin. He looks at us. *In us.* He looks in us. This witness sees in us. And from now on more than ever. But what might this indicate beyond a mere rhetorical commonplace? It would indicate an *absolute* excess and dissymmetry in the space of what relates us to ourselves and constitutes the "being-in-us," the "being-us," in something completely other than a mere subjective interiority: in a place open to an infinite transcendence. The one who looks at us in us—and *for whom* we are—is no longer; he is completely other, infinitely other, as he has always been, and death has more than ever entrusted him, given him over, distanced him, in this infinite alterity. However narcissistic it may be, our subjective speculation can no longer seize and appropriate this gaze before which we appear at the moment when, bearing it in us, bearing it along with every movement of our bearing or comportment, we can get over our mourning *of him* only by getting over *our* mourning, by getting over, by ourselves, the mourning of ourselves, I mean the mourning of our autonomy, of everything that would make us the measure of ourselves. That is the excess and the dissymmetry: we bear *in ourselves* the gaze that Louis Marin bears *on us.* Powers of the image. This gaze is his, and it will always remain his, infinitely; it comes from him singularly, from him alone, alone as always, more alone than ever, over there, outside, far away. Far away in us. In us, there where this power of the image comes to open the being-far-away. This excess also brings about the limitless enlargement of the image. Its power of dilation gives it its greatest force in the mourning of the absolute of "force."

It was, in the end, the experience of this time of reading that I discovered. Louis Marin described this scene on each page of his book, all the while mobilizing a corpus at once extremely diverse and singularly rich. I was thus read, I said to myself, and staged by what I read; I found myself caught up in the time of his time, inscribed, situated by this other present that was still his this summer. And my sadness, while trying to distinguish itself from his, could never really dissociate itself from it. It still resonates in the very scope and score of his time. He remained the master of it, as one would say of a subject or a disciple.

It would be necessary to accede or do justice to this torsion of the time of reading. At once painful and fascinated, it calls or recalls in advance a sort of living present, or what is assumed to be so, that is, our own living present, toward the present of Louis Marin, toward the other fractured present of the one who, having written this book in a more or less continuous fashion over several years, developing still further premises elaborated for more than twenty years, wrote or reviewed a few months ago, I imagine, the preface, and reread—the ultimate test or proof—as the editors tell us, almost all the proofs, almost, or just about, the final proofs, the final test.

In doing this, he will have brought to term, that is, right up to the final interruption, the ordeal or the putting to the test of this default of force wherein is marked the "mourning of the absolute of 'force.'"

For, in the end, what does this book tell us, in its at once paradoxical and prudent thesis, I would even say in its fantastic aporia, or, if you prefer, its ontological fiction? That this power whose effects it analyzes does not exist. It never attains existence, that is, the presence of the present. *There is* power, there are *effects* of power, but power does not exist. It is nothing. It *is attached to death,* which is not. There is only "force," the quotation marks reminding us that the effect of force is attached to the representative fiction. This fiction counts only on the death of the one who is thought to hold power, from whom it then withdraws power by feigning to confer it upon him in the portrait. The trait of the portrait, its infinite attraction, is that it subtracts or withdraws: it withdraws or takes back all the power that it confers, because it requires already in advance the death of the subject, the death of the king as subject and of the subject of the subject in question, that is, of everything related to its reference:

> In the representation that is power, in the power that is representation, the real—provided one understands by "real" the always deferred fulfillment of this desire—is nothing other than the fantastic image in which the subject would contemplate itself as absolute.
>
> If it is of the essence of all forces to tend toward the absolute, it is part of the "reality" of its subject never to be content with not being so. The representation-effects that constitute powers and that powers in turn permit and authorize would be the modalities (historical, anthropological, sociological . . .) of a work—though infinite in space and time—of the mourning of the absolute of 'force'. (*P,* 16–17)

All this is worked out, demonstrated, and will live on in the pages that will be read and reread on *The Severed Head,* concerning *The Death of Pompey* by Corneille, where the "deadly mirror"—analyzed earlier in the chapters on the idol, narcissism, and the "position of the I"—lets us see, in some sense, the very origin of the political and shows how the "great politician then converts the phantasmic object, the head of the Medusa, emblem of the violent origins of the State, the severed head of Pompey, into its own face, the disquieting and cold mask of political power" (*P,* 157).

Yet the reading of *The Tempest* exceeds this purely political dimension. For it shows how the recognition that the king discovers in the gaze that representation turns toward him is also *cosmic* (*P,* 175). Had I had the time, I would have tried to venture into the current space of this *cosmopolitics.* But the pages that, while just as convincing and forceful as all the others, nonetheless moved me the most, I would even say overwhelmed me, are those that—in a reading of whiteness that is quite properly dazzling, in the writing of white light, in what one might want to call the photography of certain Gospels—speak about the *potestas filiationis,* about the son in the bosom of the father, the son as the sight of the image of the father. Of the father *in view* of the son, of the father looked upon, judged, made possible by the son. An abyssal thought of inheritance. It would be necessary to cite here the entire gloss 7 on "the son in the bosom of the father" and reread what is said "in the light of the stained-glass window." Marin speaks of this in a dazzling fashion, for he is himself no doubt bedazzled by bedazzlement, by knowledge "through bedazzlement," through the blindness that comes from an excess of vision. Here again is the theme of what Abbot Suger refers to as a "force renewed" through the very renunciation of all restitution, all reconstitution, all postmortem retribution: the gift itself (*P,* 213). And as for the Transfiguration, the event of the absolute visual that constitutes the ground without ground of the foundation of power, the bedazzlement of whiteness is there associated with this anticipation of death that also marks the time of this book, "as if," says Marin, "the extreme, final, image, that of the absolutely white figure or face, could only anticipate the taste of an exquisite death" (*P,* 239).

We will never have the time.

Had I had the time, had I been able to treat the last six pages of this book, which speak in gloss 9 of "The Reversion of Shadow and Light" and of a certain structural link between "genealogical power" and a supplement of force or "intensification" based on a passage from Nietzsche's *Birth of Tragedy,* I would have tried to situate a bit better what is, to my eyes, Marin's singular place within a hidden tradition, at the heart of a secret lineage, one that is inadmissible to every church or chapel. I am speaking of this heretical filiation that runs from Pascal to Nietzsche, who was also the thinker of force and of the reciprocal convertibility of the strongest or most forceful and the weakest. These two thinkers have often been associated, especially during the heyday of existentialism. But I do not know of anyone before Louis Marin who has given to this intolerable genealogy, to this heretical heritage, such a force of evidence, such titles, I would even say such a force of law. If this tradition was possible, virtual, dynamic, it did not exist, it never had such an incontestable actuality before the work of Marin, and singularly so in *Pouvoirs de l'image*. That this actuality remains a potentiality without limit—that is what I would have wanted to show.

And that is what secretly links the gift to death.

Why does one give and what can one give to a dead friend? And what does one give oneself with this liberty, when one knows that the relation to oneself, that Narcissus himself, gazes at himself only from the gaze of the other, and precedes himself, answering then only for himself, only from the resonance of Echo, when this latter speaks freely of herself, for herself, by seeming to repeat the last syllables of the other and thus to give in to the jealous dictates of divine law?

Louis knew what I thought of him, he was aware of my admiration and my gratitude; he had countless indications of this in everything that was woven between our gestures, our various itineraries, our respective works as well, and in everything that went unspoken, which did not fail, as always, alas, to resound and resonate in all of this. But while he was aware of this admiration, I never really declared it to him to the extent that I am this evening. I am not saying this only, not only, to confess a mistake, a regret, or an inconsolable sadness. This situation is, in the end, rather common; it is what links me to more than one friend, no doubt to all those one calls "best friends."

But then why? Why wait for death? Tell me why we wait for death. Marin's last book will have again helped me to think this, to think that which in fact regards each of us so singularly, namely, the law of what does not return or come back, of what comes back to us only there where it can no longer come back to us, and so all comes down, like mastery, that is, like the fiction of force, to the incontestable authority of death, to the very inexistence of the image, to its fantastic power, to the impresence of a trace.

Louis Marin knew that this authority begins before death, and that death begins its work before death. Death's watch [*veille*], the time of this book, had begun long ago for Louis Marin, well before the eve [*veille*] of his death.

This is also why this book cannot be closed, why it interrupts itself interminably. And however prepared I might have been for it, I read it too quickly. In a sort of haste that no mourning will be able to diminish or console. It happened to me too quickly, like Louis's death. I feel as if I were still on the eve of reading it.

SARAH KOFMAN

SEPTEMBER 14, 1934—OCTOBER 15, 1994

Professor of philosophy and author of over twenty books on philosophy, psychoanalysis, literature, and art, Sarah Kofman was one of France's most significant contemporary thinkers. She was born in 1934 on Rosh Hashanah in the Tenth Arrondissement of Paris, one of six children of Berek Kofman and Fineza Koenig, who had immigrated to France from Poland in 1929. Though all the children were French citizens, the languages spoken at home remained Yiddish and Polish. On July 16, 1942, Kofman's father, the rabbi of a small synagogue in Eighteenth Arrondissement, was taken by the Vichy police from the family's apartment on rue Ordener and sent to the notorious Drancy camp. He later perished at Auschwitz. Most of the members of Berek Kofman's family in Poland also lost their lives during the infamous Warsaw ghetto roundup of May 16, 1943.

After her father's deportation, Kofman, along with her mother and siblings, spent the rest of the war in hiding at various locations throughout France. The children were also given French names to conceal their identities. Sarah, who was taken in by a family in Merville, was given the name Suzanne. In 1943 she and her mother were housed at rue Labat in Paris with a woman whom Kofman later identified in an autobiographical text as Mémé. After the liberation of Paris, Kofman was entrusted to Mémé, though a court later overturned this decision and awarded custody to her mother.

After the war, Kofman lived in several different institutions for children before returning to live with her mother in Paris. Housed in a building for "disaster victims" near the Porte de la Chapelle in the north of Paris, she prepared for the *baccalauréat* exam at the Lycée Jules-Ferry. She then took two years of preparatory courses at the Lycée Fénelon for admission to the Ecole Normale Supérieure, living in a dormitory for high school girls during this time. Kofman eventually obtained a *diplôme* (now a *maîtrise*) from the Ecole Normale Supérieure for a thesis on Plato and language.

Kofman began her teaching career in Toulouse at the Lycée Saint Sernin (1960–63) before moving back to Paris to teach at the Lycée Claude Monet (1963–70). Her first article, on the question of ethics and the philosophy of the absurd in Sartre, was published in 1963. She began work on her doctoral dissertation, "The Concept of Culture in Nietzsche and Freud," under Jean Hyppolite at the Collège de France in 1966. Gilles Deleuze, whose course on Nietzsche's *On the Genealogy of Morals* had served as an inspiration for Kofman while she was studying for her *agrégation,* took over the directorship of her dissertation in 1971.

Sarah Kofman met Jacques Derrida in 1969 and attended his seminars for many years at the Ecole Normale Supérieure. A number of her texts, among them *Camera Obscura, Nietzsche and Metaphor,* and *Le respect des femmes,* were originally presented as papers at Derrida's seminar. (Kofman later devoted a book, *Lectures de Derrida,* to Derrida's work.) In 1970 Kofman took up the post of *maître-assistant* at the University of Paris I, Sorbonne. Her first book publication, *The Childhood of Art,* a study of Freud's aesthetics, dates from the same year.

The year 1972 saw the publication of *Nietzsche and Metaphor.* In the same year she took part in the famous Cerisy-la-Salle conference on Nietzsche and contributed an essay to the proceedings, published under the title *Nietzsche aujourd'hui?* As the number of her publications on Nietzsche and Freud grew, Kofman abandoned her original dissertation project and earned her doctorate in 1976 on the basis of already published work. She was also eventually awarded a *doctorat d'état* in philosophy.

In the mid-1970s Kofman was a member of GREPH (Groupe de recherches sur l'enseignement philosophique), a group formed with Jacques Derrida, Jean-Luc Nancy, and Philippe Lacoue-Labarthe. A number of collective texts were published under the imprimatur of this organization, notably *Ecarts* (1973), *Mimesis des articulations* (1975), and *Qui a peur de la philosophie?* (1977), which included contributions from Kofman.

The breadth of Kofman's oeuvre is remarkable, treating not only philosophy (ranging from the early Greeks, Socrates and Plato, to Kant, Rousseau, and Comte) but also literature (E. T. A. Hoffmann, Gérard de Nerval, and Shakespeare), aesthetics, psychoanalysis, and feminism (or, as she preferred to say, "the question of woman"). But the impact of her legacy has perhaps most clearly been felt in the study of Freud and Nietzsche, to whom she devoted some of her most important work, including *Freud and Fiction* (1974), *Nietzsche et la scène philosophique* (1979), *The Enigma of Woman: Woman in Freud's Writings* (1980), *Un métier impossible: Lecture de "Constructions en analyse"* (1983), *Pourquoi rit-on? Freud et le mot d'esprit* (1986), *"Il n'y a que le premier pas qui coûte": Freud et la spéculation* (1991), *Explosion I: De l'"Ecce Homo" de Nietzsche* (1992), *Explosion II: Les enfants de Nietzsche* (1993), and *Le mépris des juifs: Nietzsche, les juifs, l'antisémitisme* (1994).

Despite her impressive publication record, Kofman was often passed over for tenure and promotion at the Sorbonne, where she remained a *maître de conférences* (the equivalent of an untenured associate professor) until 1991, when she was finally appointed to a chair. With the publication in the late 1980s of *Smothered Words* (a book dedicated to the memory of her father and to the work of Robert Antelme and Maurice Blanchot), her writing took an increasingly autobiographical turn. Between April and September 1993 Kofman wrote *Rue Ordener, rue Labat,* an account of her childhood between the ages of eight and eighteen.

On October 15, 1994, the one hundred and fiftieth anniversary of Nietzsche's birth, Sarah Kofman took her own life.

. . . .

At first I did not know—and I in fact still do not know—what title to give to these words.

What is the gift of a title?

I even had the fleeting suspicion that such a gift would be somewhat indecent: it would imply the violent selection of a perspective, an abusive interpretative framing or narcissistic reappropriation, a conspicuous signature there where it is Sarah Kofman, Sarah Kofman alone, Sarah Kofman herself, *over there* [*là-bas*],[1] beyond here, well beyond me or us here and now, Sarah Kofman who should be spoken about and whom I hear speaking.

Sarah Kofman

would then be the best title, were I not afraid of being unable to measure up to it.

Finally—since the question remains that of the gift and of what it means to give a title—it seemed to me more just to speak, and for just this reason, of the gift in Sarah Kofman, of her gifts: those she gave us, those she left us, and those she too perhaps received.

The title would then be

Sarah Kofman's Gifts

And here are a few possible subtitles, to give you some idea of what I would like to say:

Here There

Open Book, Closed Book

Protestations

Here and there, we find the body and we find the book, the open book and the closed book. And protestations. Between the two, between here and there, between the body and the book, between the open book and the closed one, there would be, here and there, the third, the witness, the *terstis,* testimony, attestation, and testament—but in the form of protest or protestation.

Reprinted, with changes, from ". . . . . ," translated by Pascale-Anne Brault and Michael Naas, in *A Sarah Kofman Reader,* ed. Georgia Albert and Tom Albrecht (Stanford: Stanford University Press, 2001). First French publication, *Les cahiers du Grif,* no. 3 (Paris: Descartes & Cie, 1997), 131–65 (the issue was devoted to Sarah Kofman). Our thanks to the members of a 1999 French reading group at DePaul University for their many judicious suggestions on an early draft: Christopher Boland, Benjamin Borgmeyer, Pleshette DeArmitt, Matthew Pacholec, Elizabeth Sikes, Samuel Talcott, Peter Wake.

1.   As Derrida will develop later, *là-bas* (over there) sounds like *Labat,* the name of the street in Paris where Sarah Kofman lived as a young girl.—*Trans.*

I

One wonders what is taking place. One wonders what a place is, the right or just place, and what placement is, or displacement, or replacement. One wonders about such things insofar as a book always comes to take the place of the body, insofar as it has always tended to replace the proper body, and the sexed body, to become its name even, and occupy its place, to serve in place of this occupant, and insofar as we collaborate with this substitution, lending or giving ourselves over to it, for this is all we ever really do, we are this, we like this, and each word speaks volumes for lending itself from the very first moment to this spiriting away of the proper body, as if already at the behest of the proper body in question, following its paradoxical desire, its impossible desire, the desire to interrupt itself, to interrupt itself in sexual difference, interrupt itself as sexual difference.

What is a place, then, a right or just place when everything seems to be ordered, and seems to begin, by the mourning of this replacement?

What is a just place when everything takes place and takes its place as if the dying wish of the so-called proper, or lived, or living body—for when I say body, I mean the living body as well as the sexed body—as if the supreme affirmation of this headstrong living being were this testament, the oldest and the newest: "this is my body," "keep it in memory of me," and so, "replace it, in memory of me, with a book or discourse to be bound in hide or put into digital memory. Transfigure me into a *corpus*. So that there will no longer be any difference between the place of real presence or of the Eucharist and the great computerized library of knowledge."

This great eucharistic paradigm was first of all, and perhaps will always remain, what is proper to man, I mean to the son or the father. For is this not a scene of men? No doubt, as long, that is, as we keep to the visibility of the scene.

We will perhaps talk later about the veil of a certain Last Supper scene, I mean the Last Supper [*Cène*] of the Holy Table. We will touch upon the veil of modesty that it lays out or barely lifts over sexual difference, from the promise and the gift of the body, the "this is my body and keep it in memory of me," right up to the laying in the tomb and the Resurrection.

Sarah Kofman knew this; she thought it, I believe, and analyzed it—but she *protested,* yes, she no doubt *protested* with all the strength of a living irredentist against this movement to which, like all of us, and from the very first day, she had to succumb. It is of this protestation that I would like to speak, Sarah Kofman's protestation, such as I hear it and believe myself, in my own way, to share in it.

I am not sure I have the right to assume you would know this, but you should be aware that Sarah Kofman was for me, in her own way, and for more than twenty years, a great friend. Yes, in her own way, but I was her friend in my own way too. I will not be able to speak of our own way, which was certainly different, nor of our ways toward one another, whether good or bad. But were we not the only ones, she and I, and am I not the only one today to know, if not to understand, something about this?

What we shared within the public space, for instance, in places of publication, had to do first with the exercises and interests, the aims and challenges of philosophy, of thinking, teaching, reading, and writing. These interests and exercises go so far beyond the limits of a short narrative, indeed of a terminable analysis, that I will not even attempt to speak of them. Those interested will find innumerable small signs in our respective publications. These remains are little more than elliptical greetings, sometimes just a wink; they remain to be interpreted by anyone, including myself, for I am not always certain from where I stand today that I am still able to decipher them.

I have spent the past few weeks rereading certain of Sarah's texts with the feeling, the certainty even, that for me everything still remains to come and to be understood.

But there is no longer any doubt: such testimonies survive us, incalculable in their number and meaning.

They survive us. Already they survive us, keeping the last word—and keeping silent.

But the place of a survivor is unlocatable. If such a place were ever located, it would remain untenable, unbearable, I would almost say deadly. And if it appeared tenable, the speech to be held or the word to be kept there would remain impossible. Such speech or such a word is thus also untenable—unbearable.

The word kept untenable, held to be unbearable [*parole dé-tenue intenable*].

In a text that I shall cite later, Sarah speaks of a "secret" that is held (a "secret they would hold," she says, the "they" being "doctors," men of science, appointed physicians), and it is the secret of a life, of life, of what she calls "an opening onto life."[2]

2.   Sarah Kofman, "La mort conjurée: Remarques sur La leçon d'anatomie du docteur Nicolas Tulp, 1632 Mauritshuis, La Haye," in *La part de l'oeil*, ed. Alexandre Kyritsos (Brussels: Presses de l'Académie royale des beaux-arts de Bruxelles), no. 11 (1995): 41–45. Translated by Pascale-Anne Brault as "Conjuring Death," in *A Sarah Kofman Reader*, ed. Georgia Albert and Tom Albrecht (Stanford: Stanford University Press, 2001).

How does one give an account of the secret of what is held or kept and so refuses itself in this way? The question is all the more formidable insofar as this unlocatable double, the place *to hold* and the speech *to be held* or the word *to be kept,* the experience of what is twice *held untenable,* is at the same time the most common experience of friendship.

There is nothing exceptional about this.

From the first moment, friends become, as a result of their situation, virtual survivors, actually virtual or virtually actual, which amounts to just about the same thing. Friends know this, and friendship breathes this knowledge, breathes it right up to expiration, right up to the last breath. These possible survivors thus see themselves held to the untenable. Held to the impossible as possible impossible survivors, so that some might be tempted to conclude from this that friends are impossible people.

We are that, we were that. I will talk a great deal, here again today, of the impossible. And of the impossible between Sarah and me.

Impossible: that is no doubt what we were for one another, Sarah and I. Perhaps more than others or in some other way, in innumerable ways that I will not be able to recount here, considering all the scenes in which we found ourselves together, all the scenes we made before one another. I sometimes catch myself again making a scene before her, in order to catch up with her, and I smile at this sign of life, of the life in which I am no doubt still obscurely trying to keep her, that is, keep her alive. To "conjure death," as she says in her last text—which implies both to conjure it up and conjure it away, to summon ghosts and chase them away, always in the name of life, to summon and chase away, and thus to pursue the other as the other dead. As if I were making yet another scene before her in response to hers, just so as to make things last long enough to say to her: you see, life goes on, it's still the same old story. . . .

But since it's all about "being impossible" here, perhaps we must accept this side of things. That is, if we can. We cannot say everything, that's impossible, say everything about Sarah, what she was, what she thought and wrote, everything about a work whose richness, force, and necessity the future will never cease to appreciate. We can only accept this side of things [*en prendre son parti*] and take up sides [*prendre parti*].

I am thus taking up this side of things by taking a side—the side of Sarah.

So here would be another title:

Sarah's Side

Taking a side, then, within this side of things, I finally chose to speak of the art of Sarah. Her art—and this is the side on which I will wager—will have given me the chance to take sides.

I will thus speak of her art but also of her laughter—indissociably. We would thus have two additional subtitles.

Since the death of Sarah, and I owe it to her, as I owe it to the truth, to say this, assuming that I might at last be able to do so, since the death of Sarah—and what a death—it has been impossible for me to speak as I knew I wanted to, impossible to speak *to her, to* her, as one does without pretending to friends who have disappeared, impossible also to speak *of* her, as other friends, who are also mine, have known how to do—and have done so well, and were so right to do.

I thus had to try to relearn everything, and I am still at it.

Let us then not hasten to think of mourning, of an impossible mourning. For we would then run the risk of missing, or actually we would not fail to miss, under some clinical category, some general type of mourning—to which a certain guilt is always associated—this incisive, singular, and unappeasable suffering that I simply could not bear, precisely out of friendship, to transfer onto someone else, and even less onto some conceptual generality that would not be Sarah, Sarah Kofman herself.

For me too, of course, Sarah was unique.

And even if I were still to blame her for my suffering, at least it would be her, and her alone, who would be implicated, and that is my first concern here. There would be nothing very new in this, for over the course of twenty years of a tender, tense, and sometimes stormy friendship, of, dare I say, an impossible friendship, impossible right up to the end, we often blamed one another. She would make fun of me, she in me would once more take me to task, were I to try to deny, transfigure, sublimate, or idealize this long story.

Against such a lie, she would once again be right.

Among all the things we shared (I have already said that I would not be able to count them and, besides, the texts bear witness to them to a certain point), there was this protestation (a word I prefer to accusation), of which I would like to let something be heard through her laughter and her art.

I will thus venture a few words to try to say what I believe I can hear *through* her art and her laughter, as well as through her *interpretation* of both art and laughter, which, it seems to me, *carries through* all her work, and, from her body, carries all the books in the great body of work she has left us.

According to the hypothesis I am going to put before you, Sarah interpreted laughter like an artist, she laughed like an artist but also laughed at art, like an artist and in the name of life, not without knowing that neither art nor laughter saves us from pain, anxiety, illness, and death. For she knew these things better than anyone else: pain, anxiety, illness—and death. Art and laughter, when they go together, do not run counter to suffering, they do not ransom or redeem it, but live off it; as for salvation, redemption, and resurrection, the absence of any illusion shines like a ray of living light through all of Sarah's life and work. We will later hear a few of her texts that say this better than I can right now. This ray of living light concerns the absence of salvation, through an art and a laughter that, while promising neither resurrection nor redemption, nonetheless remain necessary. With a necessity to which we must yield. This ray of living light was her lucidity and what I was tempted to call, a moment ago, by analogy, her irredentism, right up to the end, and even through the end.

Her art and her laughter, themselves indissociable, were also indissociably interpretations of art and laughter. Her interpretations were not only readings or theoretical acts but affirmations, themselves art and laughter, and always affirmations of life. When I insist that they were not *only* readings but also acts and experience itself, my point is not to exclude reading from this. For reading was always on the part of Sarah a firm, unconditional, uncompromising, unrelenting, and implacable demand.

Implacable interpretations, implacable like Nietzsche and Freud, for example, and all those pitiless doctors of arts and of laughter whom she cited and summoned to appear and speak, inexhaustibly, sometimes against themselves, in truth protesting always against themselves, and against one another, while laughing it up.

For she too was without pity, if not without mercy, in the end, for both Nietzsche and Freud, whom she knew and whose bodies of work she had read inside and out. Like no one else in this century, I dare say. She loved them pitilessly, and was implacable towards them (not to mention a few others) at the very moment when, giving them without mercy all that she could, and all that she had, she was inheriting from them and was keeping watch over what they had—what they still have—to tell us, especially regarding art and laughter.

Art and laughter were also for her, no doubt, readings of art and of laughter, but these readings were also operations, experiences or experiments, journeys. These readings [*lectures*] were *lessons* in the magisterial sense of an exemplary lecturing or teaching (and Sarah was a great professor, as so many students throughout the world can testify); they were lessons of the lesson in the sense of an exemplary teaching, lessons in the course of which, life never being interrupted, the teacher experiments: she unveils in the act, through experimentation and performance, giving the example of what she says through what she does, giving of her person, as we say, with nothing held back, throwing herself into it headlong, body and soul. The truth being in the symptom.

One of these lessons of the lesson given by Sarah is, for example, that this tormented being laughed a lot, as her friends know, like a little girl shaken by the irresistible joy of uncontrollable laughter on the verge of tears, a little girl whose kept secret does not age and whose tragedies have not stifled the freshness and sparkle of her innocent laughter.

Another of these lessons of the lesson given by Sarah is that she not only talked about art, painting, and drawing in others—or interpreted by others, for example Nietzsche or Freud—but she painted and drew as well. And among all the things that she gave me, which I keep and keep looking at, there are some of these works.

And then, and those who knew her well know this, Sarah laughed a lot even when she did not laugh, and even when, as was often the case— and others here can also bear witness to this—she did not laugh at all. For she did not laugh everyday, as you know, indeed it was quite often the opposite, but even then she was still laughing—and right away, both during and after. I want to believe that she laughed right up to the end, right up to the very last second.

She would cry *for laughs*—that is my thesis or hypothesis.

I would thus like to imagine that all the meditation we see at work in her work might resemble a long reverie on everything that might be meant by the expression "for laughs," and "to cry for laughs," following the Nietzschean-Freudian interpretation of laughter, on the edge of anxiety, on the edge of the conscious and unconscious ends of laughter, of what is done for laughs, in view of laughing, by virtue of laughing, by virtue of laughter's apotropaic economy or economy of drives (I will come back to this in relation to Freud's *Jokes and the Unconscious* and Sarah's book *Pourquoi rit-on* [*Why Do We Laugh*]?[3]—yes, why do we laugh, and why do we cry?), right up to the post-Platonic or nonmetaphysical structure of fiction or the simulacrum, of what has worth only "for laughs," for example, the simulacrum in art and in literature.

---

3.   Sarah Kofman, *Pourquoi rit-on? Freud et le mot d'esprit* (Paris: Galilée, 1986) (hereafter abbreviated as *PR*).

2

In what sense were these great lessons of art and laughter affirmations of life for Sarah?

The affirmation of life is nothing other than a certain thought of death; it is neither opposition nor indifference to death—indeed one would almost say the opposite if this were not giving in to opposition.

I take as testimony, and as a sign, even before beginning, Sarah's last text, "Conjuring Death," published after her death by Alexandre Kyritsos in *La part de l'oeil.* Like others, perhaps, I am tempted to approach Sarah's last text today so as to take by surprise, in some sense, but also to make linger, these last words leaving her lips, to make them resonate with her first words, as I will later do, and to hear in them a final confidence imparted or confided to us—and notice I am not saying a last wish or last word.

Something for which we must be responsible, a confident confidence barely veiled to which we should also respond or correspond.

This very beautiful text is unfinished. A sketch, then, brought to term—interminably, as if a sign of life. It begins with a sentence of just a couple of words, an incipit that fits on one line alone, it alone on the line:

It is a lesson.

It is a lesson, she says.

She is talking about *The Anatomy Lesson of Doctor Nicolaes Tulp, 1632,* by Rembrandt. Sarah interprets in this painting the strange historical relationship between the book and the body, between the book and the proper or lived body of the mortal, to be sure, but also between the book and the body of the body or corporation of doctors gathered there, a body whose gaze is completely occupied by the book rather than the body.

There is too much to say about this text, so I will choose just a few themes, three or four, to let them speak to us today—of Sarah, from Sarah, mixing my words with hers. I read this both posthumous and living— so very living—text as an ironic autobiography of Sarah Kofman, her *autobiogriffure,* her auto-bi-claw-graphy, as she would have said, but also as a painting that has been re-painted and de-picted by her own hand.

It is, in the first place, the story or history of a *preference* for the book. We can there follow the narrative of a historical fascination with the book when it comes to occupy the place of the dead, of the body-cadaver. Actually, I prefer the English word *corpse* here because it incorporates at once the body [*le corps*], the corpus and the cadaver, and because, when read in French, *la corpse* seems to put the body in the feminine and to become an allusion to sexual difference, if not a respect for it.

Une corpse: here would be the subject; there would be the object.

I say "*historical* fascination" or "*history* of a preference" for the book because all this belongs to a history. It is precisely a reading of this history that this lesson on a lesson offers us.

For what does Sarah Kofman tell us of this *corpse* in *The Anatomy Lesson?* That this image of the *corpse* is *replaced* or *displaced,* its *place taken* by the book (as seems to be happening to us at this very instant), replaced-displaced by "a book wide open at the foot of the deceased." This open book organizes: an organ detached from the body, it has an organizing mission. Detached from the body, this quasi organ, this corpus, in turn organizes space. In an at once centripetal and centrifugal fashion. Decentered with regard to the body, as you look at the body, it centers or recenters in turn a new magnetic field; it irradiates it but also capitalizes upon it and captures all the forces of the painting. An open book attracts all the gazes.

This book [*lui*—masculine pronoun—*Trans.*] stands up to, and stands in for, the body: a *corpse* replaced by a corpus, a *corpse* yielding its place to the bookish thing, the doctors having eyes only for the book facing them, as if, by reading, by observing the signs on the drawn sheet of paper, they were trying to forget, repress, deny, or conjure away death—and the anxiety before death.

[. . .]

But instead of seeing here a simple negativity of *distraction* (negation, denegation, lie, occultation, dissimulation), Sarah Kofman seems to sense in this repression, in a no doubt very Nietzschean fashion, a cunning affirmation of life, its irrepressible movement to *survive,* to *live on* [*survivre*], to get the better of itself in itself, to lie by telling its truth of life, to affirm this truth of life through the symptom of repression, to express the irrepressible as it is put to the test of repression, to get, in a word, the better of life, that is to say, of death, giving an account of life: to defeat death by affirming a "hold on the truth of life," a "science of life and its mastery."

There would thus be a secret of life. Life would hold the secret of the secret, and all secrets would keep life alive. For the claim over such a secret, even if it is not justified, even if it is merely an allegation of anguished scholars, could still be read as a redoubled affirmation of life.

Lessons given: what this lesson on the *Lesson,* this physiological lesson on a lesson of anatomy, gives us would be not only a diagnosis concerning a repression or a denegation (later on, we will also talk about a "conjuring" and a "conspiracy"), not only a thesis on the historicity of this repression and this denegation, but an at least implicit interpretation of the very concepts of repression and denegation, an interpretation of their ultimate function, of the ultimate meaning of their strategy. Under their negative or oppositional appearance, through their grammatical or strategic negativity, repression, suppression, and denegation would be in the service of an affirmation of life. Repression would be yet another ruse of affirmation, a *trop* [too much] and a *trope,* an excess and a figure of the "yes" to life, a number or figure of the *amor fati.* The science of life would itself be an art of living; it would have come from, and would take part in, an art of life. The side or part taken by the artist, the art of the painter (like that of the interpreter), would consist in interpreting the truth of this art of life.

The invincible force of this art of life, a force that is at once irreducible, irredentist, its time literally interminable, even in death, at the moment of death, the élan of an art that is at once all powerful and, in the end, powerless, given to failure, frustrated before what is called death itself, this impotence of the all-powerful, this ineffective-ness of an all-powerful that refuses to let up even though it is really nothing—that is what invites a good laugh: it is truly comical, isn't it, laughable, crazy, off the wall, and we can receive from it, as a lesson, the inheritance of an art of living that knows a thing or two about the art of laughter.

That is at least what I think I hear in the following passage, which mentions *life* three times in this place where *book, cadaver, corpus,* and *corpse* exchange places.

> They have before them not a subject but an object, a purely tech-
> nical instrument that one of them manipulates in order to get a
> hold on the truth of *life.* The dead man and the opening of his body
> are seen only insofar as they provide an opening onto *life,* whose
> secret they would hold. The fascination is displaced and, with this
> displacement, the anxiety repressed, the intolerable made tolerable,
> from the sight of the cadaver to that of the book wide open at the
> foot of the deceased, who might now serve as a lectern.
>
> This opening of the book in all its light points back to the
> opening of the body. For the book alone allows the body to be
> deciphered and invites the passage from the exterior to the interior.
> It is this book (and the opening it provides onto the science of *life*
> and its mastery) that attracts the gazes, much more even than the
> point of the scissors that has begun to peel away the skin from the
> body stretched out there. (My emphasis)

Sarah Kofman thus says: "displacement" of an "anxiety repressed," and the "intolerable made tolerable." In numerous texts, too numerous to cite and analyze here, Sarah Kofman has thoroughly examined the question of the relationship between laughter, jokes, and the economy of repression, the complicated symptomatology of repressed anxiety.
[. . .]

3

Before the diagnosis, after the diagnosis of the diagnosis, before and after the lesson on the *Lesson,* before and after Sarah Kofman's diagnosis of the diagnosing attitude of the doctors, of the anatomical gaze and medical knowledge, the little word *là* comes up, meaning at once *here* [*ici*] and *over there* [*là-bas*], right there, between here and over there, between *da* and *fort.* It comes up, *right there* [*là*], three times. Three times to speak of the presence of the dead person or of the corpse stretched out *right there,* of the *corpse* of man's body [*corps*], of a man's body—and not a woman's.

Three times *right there* [*là*], the same number of times as the word "life."

And the whole lesson on the *Lesson* questions and teaches this here [*cela*], this *right there* [*ce là*], this being-right-there of the body [*corps*] or of *la corpse* in the corpus of the work of art.
[. . .]

What is at stake here is indeed the being-right-there (here and over there) of the *corpse.* Three times the adverb *là* [like the musical note "la"—*Trans.*] comes to set the tone. Three times it comes to localize both the body of death and its taking-place in the work, the work of art, its representation, as we say, in a painting, although it is already, as dead, framed or displayed in the anatomical exhibition, which is also a work or operation between the eye and the hand—gaze, surgery, dissection.

So here are the three *là*'s, and then *voilà,* there it is, a gift of modesty, only a veil there [*un voile est là*] to veil the sex, the *being-right-there* of (the) sex, that is to say, sexual difference: "And with this dissimulation of the body, its fragility, its mortality, comes to be forgotten, even though it is exhibited in full light by the pale cadaver *that is right there* [*là*], purely and simply lying there, naked (only the sex is modestly veiled), in the most absolute anonymity" (my emphasis).

What is most remarkable here is the insistence on anonymity, on the loss of the name in the being-right-there of the *corpse;* it is as if death cut the name off in the midst of life, severed the name from the living one who bore it, and this would be precisely its work as death, the operation proper to it; as if death separated the name and the body, as if it tore the name away from the body, as if, as a result, everywhere the name were detached from the body—and this happens to us all the time, especially when we speak, write, and publish—we were attesting, right there, to death, as if we were witnessing to it, all the while protesting against it:

> Those around him seem to be unmoved by any feelings for him, for someone who, just a short time ago, was still full of life, had a name [and Sarah takes pleasure in recalling in a note the child, the little boy, under the name of this *corpse:* "According to the account, the cadaver is that of a recently hanged man, identified by name and nickname as Abrian Adriaenz, called the kid, *Het Kind*"], was a man just like them. Their gazes display neither pity, nor terror, nor fright. They do not seem to identify with the cadaver stretched out *there.* They do not see in it the image of what they themselves will one day be, of what, *unbeknownst* to themselves, they are in the process of becoming. (My emphasis)

In other words, this *there,* this *right there,* which they hold at a distance to disrupt an identification that they unconsciously fear, is also, right here, the place of their *unbeknowing,* to wit, that which they are here and now unwittingly in the process of becoming—according to the process of life and the process of art, two processes to which they are, in all the senses of this word, *exposed, three times* exposed without knowing it: exposed to gazes or looks when they believe themselves to be looking, exposed as mortals, as living beings destined to die, and exposed in the painting as a work of art and by the work of art. "They do not see in it the image of what they themselves will one day be, of what, unbeknownst to themselves, they are in the process of becoming. They are not fascinated by the cadaver, which they do not seem to see as such."

They are thus seen not seeing, and, visible as nonseeing, visible as blinded, they are being diverted, distracted from the fascination for that thing there, diverted by the distracting distance of this *right there;* and this distraction is their very position of objective knowing or learning, their very gaze, their point of view and their doctoral objectivization:

> and their solemnity is not the sort that can be awakened by the mystery of death.
>
> They have before them not a subject but an object, a purely technical instrument that one of them manipulates in order to get a hold on the truth of life. The dead man and the opening of his body are seen only insofar as they provide an opening onto life, whose secret they would hold. The fascination is displaced.

A moment ago we were told that they are not fascinated, not fascinated by the cadaver, but that did not mean that they are not fascinated at all: they have simply turned from one fascination to another, the fascination simply being displaced:

> and, with this displacement, the anxiety is repressed, the intolerable made tolerable, from the sight of the cadaver to that of the book wide open at the foot of the deceased, who might now serve as a lectern.
> This opening of the book in all its light points back to the opening of the body. For the book alone allows the body to be deciphered and invites the passage from the exterior to the interior. It is this book (and the opening it provides onto the science of life and its mastery) that attracts the gazes, much more even than the point of the scissors that has begun to peel away the skin from the body *stretched out there.* (My emphasis)

"The fascination is displaced." I suggested earlier that "they are not fascinated" still implies fascination. The repression of fascination is a repression fascinated by what it represses, and which it simply submits to a topical translation, to a change of place, in a play between the here and the over there.

[. . .]

This would be another way of saying that the science of life, along with the book, along with the corpus and the corporation, do indeed fascinate, and let themselves be fascinated, and so displace attention, and replace, repress, deny, and divert, distracting one from death as much as from life, to be sure, but always *in the name of life.* These are at once symptoms and affirmations of a life that, in the end, as the unconscious that it is, does not know and does not want to know death, wants not to know it, actively wanting this before reactively doing so.

Here is a lesson, then, concerning what we do, in place of death, when we write or read books, when we talk about one book in lieu of an other. Sarah points a finger at these doctors, denouncing them to some extent, for having suddenly become indifferent, all taken up by the book, apparently "unmoved by any feelings for him, for someone who, just a short time ago, was still full of life, had a name, was a man just like them"—and whom the book of science, just like the effect of the *corpse,* returns to anonymity.

[. . .]

And just as she is about to draw a double lesson, what she calls the "lesson of this *Anatomy Lesson,*" her own lesson, Sarah Kofman makes a gesture that I would regard as a sort of initialing. It's like the short stroke, the economic signature that was always hers, the logic of a testimonial idiom: her affirmation, her protestation in the name of life. She ends up affirming the triumph of life, as Shelley would have said, not the triumph of death but the triumph over death—not through a denegation regarding an anxiety over death (Sarah knew what that could be), not through the relinquishing of a knowledge of death, but, on the contrary, through an active interpretation that renounces neither knowledge nor the knowledge of knowledge, that is to say, the knowledge of the role that occultation or repression might still play in certain forms of knowledge. Whence the deployment of so many types of knowledge, the rigorous analysis of an intersemiotic and intertextual imbrication of speech, writing, and the silence of the body, of the sacred book and the book of science, book and painting, in more than one corpus, and first of all within Rembrandt's corpus, especially in the two *Anatomy Lessons* painted by Rembrandt some twenty years apart.

Twenty years apart, and there is always another anatomy lesson, yet one more lesson.

Here is the conclusion, where you will be able to admire along with me the precision of an analytical scalpel that does not forgo any knowledge but that also does not fail to reaffirm life—operating in fact so as to reaffirm life, but without resurrection or redemption, without any glorious body:

> The doctors of *The Anatomy Lesson* are gazing down at the book of science with the same attentive fervor as that found in other paintings (see, for example, Jordaens's *Four Evangelists,* mentioned by Claudel), where the evangelists are looking down at the sacred books from which they draw the confirmation of their message.
>
> In *The Anatomy Lesson,* the book of science takes the place of the Bible; for one truth another has been substituted, a truth that is no longer simply confined to books since it finds its experimental confirmation in the opening of a cadaver. The cadaver of Christ (for example, the one by Mantegna in the Brera Art Gallery in Milan, alluded to by the second *Anatomy Lesson,* that of Amsterdam) has been replaced by that of a man recently hanged, a purely passive object, manipulated, displaying no emotion, signaling no Resurrection, Redemption, or nobility. The cut into the flayed body thus also cuts into the religious illusion of a glorious body.
>
> The lesson of this *Anatomy Lesson* is thus not that of a *memento mori;* it is not that of a triumph of death but of a triumph over death; and this is due not to the life of an illusion, but to that of the speculative, whose function too is one of occultation.

Though uncompromising in her analysis of a speculation, this ruse of the speculative whose economy remains in the service of occultation and repression, indeed of sublimation or denegation, Sarah Kofman nonetheless detects in it the work of art, that is, art's work. She does so in order both to have some fun with it and subscribe to it, to laugh at it but also to approve in it, love, affirm, and repeat in it, the affirmation of art. She deciphers in it, or once again sees in it, the invincible triumph of life. This becomes clear when the word "life" gets drawn into a strange syntax: not illusory life or, as she says, "life of an illusion," the "religious illusion of a glorious body" which she had just mentioned, but life again, the life of the speculative, insofar as it remains, even in its function of occultation or illusion, the *nonillusory life of an illusion,* manifesting, affirming, and still holding on to life, carrying it living right to its limit.

The subject *denies [dément]*—denegation, and that is perhaps the logic of protestation, of a protestation that says *no(t) without illusion,* that says, not without illusion, no without illusion to the illusion and the denegation of death, no to a death conspired or conjured away. ("Conjuring Death" is the title of this last text on the *Anatomy Lessons,* which shows, in short, the body or corporation of doctors as the gathering of a conspiring or a *conspiracy [conjuration]*: the body of the corporation is the body of a conspiracy, the oath, intrigue, and plot of a social body that will do anything to conjure away death.) But this no to conjuring death is not spoken in the name of death; it speaks still in the name of life, of the work of art and of the book of life. It is inscribed in the book of life, in the book of the living, there where, *it's crazy to deny it, it denies like crazy [ça dément]*—in the name of a life that knows that the name of life, as we have said, is not life. Yes, no(t) without any illusion.

Some might consider my granting such a privilege to this last text, to the reaffirmation of the work of life as work of art, to be a stratagem on my part, a ruse to conjure away death in my turn, and, through this ruse, which I do not deny, a sort of protestation against her death: a protestation, that is to say, a sort of testimony so as to attest to what was in her a constant protestation. A lesson in protestation. In nonnegative protestation. But also a lesson in the fact that "protestation" will have been, I now realize as I listen to all the resonances of this word, the privileged mode, the most constant and most common tonality of our face-to-face encounters.

Throughout our entire friendship, during decades of work and shared concerns, we protested, sometimes even against one another, right up until the end, and I catch myself still protesting. I catch myself still making scenes before her, as I said earlier, and I smile over this, while smiling to her, as if over a sign of life in reconciliation. And when it comes to scenes, I have to say that I'll never be able to make as many as she; I'll never catch up.

I began with the end; I would now like to end with the beginning.

"Some twenty years apart," as I emphasized and repeated earlier when quoting her on the two works of Rembrandt that bear the title *The Anatomy Lesson*.

Some twenty years apart.

Had I the time, I would tell you how I reread today what worked, for more than twenty years, as this protestation of life devoted to art and laughter. More than twenty years ago, Sarah came to see me for the first time already to tell me, among other things, that she protested or objected to something I had ventured in *Plato's Pharmacy*. Everything thus began with this scene. When, after becoming friends, we chose together, or so I thought, the title of her first book, *The Childhood of Art*,[4] I did not understand or recognize what I understand better today, after having read *Smothered Words*[5] (between Blanchot and Antelme, in the wake of Auschwitz), and *Rue Ordener, rue Labat*,[6] namely, that this first book—so rich, so sharp, so perfectly lucid in its reading of Freud— was also the childhood of the art, the child's play, of Sarah Kofman. An autobiographical anamnesis, an *autobiogriffure*. All the places—of the father, of the mothers, of the substitution of mothers, of laughter and life as works of art—were there already acknowledged, rigorously assigned. [. . .]

Instead of spending the time we really ought to around the final pages of *The Childhood of Art* (around what is said there about laughter, about the enigma of art as life, about artistic life, about what Nietzsche calls "laughing at oneself" [*CA*, 224 n. 14], about the phrase "one can either cry or laugh" on the next-to-last page [*CA*, 173], about the world that, for Nietzsche as for Freud, plays "an innocent 'child's game' guided by chance and necessity," when "the true art is the art of life" [*CA*, 174]), instead of all that, I rush toward a scene at the table, and toward laughter, as is often done in the most difficult moments of mourning.

4. Sarah Kofman, *The Childhood of Art: An Interpretation of Freud's Aesthetics*, trans. Winifred Woodhull (New York: Columbia University Press, 1988) (hereafter abbreviated as *CA*).

5. Sarah Kofman, *Smothered Words*, trans. Madeleine Dobie (Evanston: Northwestern University Press, 1998).

6. Sarah Kofman, *Rue Ordener, rue Labat*, trans. Ann Smock (Lincoln: University of Nebraska Press, 1996).

Sarah dedicated a copy of her text "Damned Food" to me in 1980 by circling the title of the volume, *Manger* [Eating], in order to write the words: "in the hopes of *Eating* together."

Six years later, on New Year's Day 1986, the dedication to *Pourquoi rit-on? Freud et le mot d'esprit* still spoke of the table. It read: "For Jacques and Marguerite, recalling the good Jewish jokes we once peddled at table, and hoping we can do it again one day."

Now, what is the last word of this great book that says both everything and the rest about laughter, as well as about the apotropaic economy of laughter according to Freud? It is, precisely, the "last word." The book ends in this way: "By way of conclusion, let's give laughter the last word" (*PR,* 198).

But right before this last word on the last word comes a Jewish joke, a sort of postscriptum. It is a joke we had once told each other. Here is the postscriptum:

> Finishing this book today, September 25, the day of Yom Kippur, I cannot resist peddling [this word was already used, recall, in the dedication, which was itself alluding to a subsection of the book entitled "Peddling," whose subtitle is "The Economic Necessity of the Third"; and I recall that my last conversation with Sarah must have more or less directly concerned, at the time it was interrupted, a story about the peddling of history and the economic necessity of the third] this Jewish joke told by Théodore Reik [who has written much on the Great Atonement and the song of Kol Nidre]: "Two Jews, long-standing enemies, meet at the synagogue on the day of the Great Atonement. One says to the other [by way of forgiveness]: "I wish you what you wish me." And the other replies, giving tit for tat: "See, you're doing it again!" (*PR,* 198).

An unfathomable story, a story that seems to stop in its tracks, whose movement consists in interrupting itself, in paralyzing itself in order to refuse any future, an absolute story of the unsolvable, a vertiginous depthlessness, an irresistible whirlwind that draws forgiveness, the gift, and the giving back of forgiveness right to the abyss of the impossible.

How does one acquit oneself of forgiving? Mustn't forgiveness exclude all acquittal, all acquittal of oneself, of the other? To forgive is certainly not to be quits. Neither with oneself, nor with the other. That would be to repeat the evil, to countersign or consecrate it, to let it be what it is, unalterable and identical to itself. No adequation is here appropriate or tolerable. So what then?

As I said, we must have told this Jewish joke to each other, and probably while eating. And we must have agreed that it was not only funny but memorable, unforgettable, precisely insofar as it treats this treatment of memory called forgiveness. There is no forgiveness without memory, surely, but neither is there any forgiveness that can be reduced to an act of memory. And forgiving does not amount to forgetting, especially not. A joke "for laughs," no doubt, but what about it makes us laugh, laugh and cry, and laugh through our tears or our anxiety?

It is no doubt first a matter of its economy, an economy powerfully analyzed by Freud, and then by Sarah Kofman questioning Freud. In fact, in the chapter "The Three Thieves," in the subsection "Peddling: The Economic Necessity of the Third," a note also speaks of forgiveness. It speaks of the economy of "pleasure given by the superego, the *forgiveness* that it in some sense grants, bringing humor close to the maniacal phase, since, thanks to these '*gifts*,' the diminished 'I' finds itself if not euphoric, at least lifted back up" (*PR,* 104; my emphasis).

Without venturing any further in this direction, let me keep for the moment to a rough analysis of this Jewish joke: two enemies make the gesture to forgive one another, they feign to do so, "for laughs," but by inwardly reopening or pursuing the hostilities. In the process, they admit to this inexpiable war, and blame one another for it reciprocally, as if in a mirror. That the admission should be made by way of a symptom rather than a declaration changes nothing as far as the truth is concerned: they have not disarmed, they continue to wish one another ill.

I will thus venture to say this, to address to you something that once again concerns laughter, art "for laughs" and the art of laughter, and to address this to you as if to Sarah, to Sarah in me. Allegorically: what these two Jews come to experience and what makes us laugh is indeed the radical impossibility of forgiveness.

A Jew, a Jew from time immemorial, and especially in this century, Sarah knew this and lived it better than any of us here, better in the worst of ways, for she was also someone who was put to the test of the impossibility of forgiveness, its radical impossibility.

Who, in fact, could give us the right to forgive? Who could give whom the right to forgive on behalf of the dead, and to forgive the infinite violence that was done to them, depriving them of both a grave and a name, everywhere in the world and not only at Auschwitz? And thus everywhere that the unforgivable would have taken place?

[. . .]

And you know, I bet that this insurmountable limit—surmounted, nonetheless, as insurmountable, in the setting free of what is insuperable in the unsurmounted—is indeed the line that our two Jews have crossed—with or within the confession, though without repentance, of their reciprocal accusation. To admit to, to share, to entrust to one another this insurmountable test of the unforgivable, to deem oneself unforgivable for not forgiving, is perhaps not to forgive—since forgiveness appears impossible, even when it takes place—but it is to sympathize with the other in this test of the impossible.

Here it is, then—the ultimate compassion.

It is to tell the other, or to hear oneself tell the other, and to hear the other tell you: you see, you're doing it again, you don't want to forgive me, even on the day of the Great Atonement, but me too, me neither, a "me" neither, we're in agreement, we forgive ourselves for nothing, for that's impossible, so let's not forgive one another, all right? And then you burst into complicitous, uncontrollable laughter, laughing like crazy, with a laughter gone crazy. For isn't this paradoxical agreement peace? Yes, that's peace, that's life: that, in the end, is the great atonement. And what is more comical than the great atonement or forgiveness as the test of the unforgivable? What could be more alive, what better reconciliation could there be? What an art of living! How to do otherwise, in fact, how to do better, as soon as we live, or live on? Without having chosen to do so? This reconciliation in the impossible is the definition of today, of a today, of life's reprieve.

But I want to imagine that these two Jews in their infinite compassion for one another, at the very moment when they conclude that they do not know how to conclude, at the very moment when they recognize that they cannot disarm, just as life itself never disarms, I want to believe that these two Jews have forgiven one another, but without telling one another. At least they have spoken to one another, even if they haven't said that they forgive one another. They have said to one another, in silence, a silence made up of tacit understanding, where misunderstanding can always find a place, that the forgiveness granted implies neither "reconciliation" (Hegel) nor "the work itself," "the profound work" of discontinuous time, a time that is delivered or that delivers us from continuity through the interruption of the other, with a view to the "messianic triumph" "secured against the revenge of evil" (Levinas).[7]

[. . .]

At what moment does Abraham reawaken the memory of his being-foreign in a foreign land? For Abraham does indeed recall that he is

---

7.   Emmanuel Levinas, *Totality and Infinity,* trans. Alphonso Lingis (Pittsburgh: Duquesne University Press, 1969), 283, 285.

destined by God to be a guest (*gêr*), an immigrant, a foreign body in a foreign land ("Go from your country and your kindred and your father's house," "your offspring shall be guests in a land that is not theirs").[8] Presenting himself as a foreigner who has no home, keeping watch over the body of the dead, his dead, Sarah (the woman who laughs when told she is to have a child, and then pretends not to have laughed),[9] Abraham requests a place for her. A final dwelling, a final resting place. He wants to be able to give her a burial place worthy of her, but also a place that would separate her from him, like death from life, a place "in front of me," says one translation, "out of my sight," says another.[10] And for this—you know the scene—he wants to pay, this husband of Sarah, the woman who laughs; he insists on it, he wants at all costs that this not be given to him. In fact, Abraham had himself also laughed upon hearing the same news, the news of the belated birth of Isaac. (*Yiskhak*: he laughs: Isaac, the coming of Isaac, makes them both shake with laughter, one after the other; Isaac is the name of the one who *comes* to make them laugh, to laugh about his coming, at his very coming, as if laughter should greet a birth, the coming of a happy event, a coming of laughter, a coming to laugh: come-laugh-with-me.) The moment having come to laugh was also the moment when Elohim named Sarah. He gave her a new name, deciding that Abraham, who had himself just received another name (changed from Abram to Abraham), would no longer call her Sarai, my princess, but Sarah, princess.[11] So what then? *Comment s'en sortir?*—How to get out of this?[12] To this question in the form of an aporia, I know of no satisfying answer. Not even crazed

8. *Genesis* 12:1, 15:13, from *The New Oxford Annotated Bible,* ed. Bruce M. Metzger and Roland E. Murphy (New York: Oxford University Press, 1991).

9. When told about the coming of Isaac (*yiskhak*: he laughs), Sarah laughs and then pretends not to have done so. But God becomes indignant that she might be doubting his omnipotence and contradicts her denial: "Oh yes, you did laugh" (*Genesis* 18:15). Later (21:3, 6), at Isaac's birth, "Abraham gave the name Isaac to his son whom Sarah bore him: *Is'hac*—he will laugh!" Sarah says, "God has brought laughter for me; everyone who hears will laugh with me."

10. *Genesis* 23:4.

11. *Genesis* 17:15, 17.

12. Sarah Kofman, *Comment s'en sortir?* (Paris: Galilée, 1983); parts of this book have been translated under the title "Beyond Aporia?" by David Macey in *Post-structuralist Classics,* ed. Andrew Benjamin (New York: Routledge, 1988), 7–44. This text, a short treatise on the aporia, opens and closes with a quote from Blanchot's *Madness of the Day,* trans. George Quasha (Barrytown, N.Y.: Station Hill Press, 1981), 7: "Men want to escape death, strange beings that they are. And some of them cry out 'Die, die' because they want to escape from life. 'What a life. I'll kill myself. I'll give in.' This is lamentable and strange; it is a mistake. Yet I have met people who have never said to life, 'Quiet!,' who have never said to death, 'Go away!' Almost always women, beautiful creatures."

laughter. Nothing is given in advance for an act of forgiveness, no rule, no criterion, no norm. It is the chaos at the origin of the world. The abyss of this nonanswer or nonresponse would be the condition of responsibility—decision and forgiveness, the decision to forgive without any concept, if there ever is any. And always (in) the name of the other.

(Last vertigo, last sigh: to forgive [in] the name of the other—is this only to forgive in their place, for the other, in substitution? Or is it to forgive the other their name, to forgive what is in their name, what survives the *corpse,* to forgive the name of the other as their first wrongdoing?)

The answer must each time be invented, singular, signed, and each time only one time like the gift of a work, a giving of art and of life, unique and, right up until the end of the world, played back.

Given back. To the impossible, I mean right up to the impossible.

This is what Sarah Kofman gives me to think about today, in the overflowing of memory, there where she remains for me unique, and where I want to believe that this reaffirmation of life was hers, right up to when the time came, to when it became time, right up to the end.

GILLES DELEUZE

JANUARY 18, 1925—NOVEMBER 4, 1995

One of France's most important philosophers of the twentieth century, Gilles (Louis René) Deleuze was born on January 18, 1925, to René Deleuze, an engineer, and Odette Camauer. He was born in the Seventeenth Arrondissement of Paris, a neighborhood in which he would spend most of his childhood and much of his adult life. Deleuze's older brother and only sibling was arrested by the Germans for "resistance" activities during World War II and died on the train deporting him to Auschwitz.

Deleuze attended the Lycée Carnot for the last two years of his high school education and did his *khâgne* at the Lycée Henri IV. In 1943 he met Michel Tournier, with whom he would develop a close friendship and on whose work he would later write. Like all the students of his year (the class of 1945 at the Lycée Henri IV), he was exempted from military service as a result of the liberation of France. From 1944 to 1948 he studied philosophy at the Sorbonne with, among others, Ferdinand Alquié, Jean Hippolyte, Georges Canguilhem, and Maurice de Gandillac. He worked in particular on Plato, Malebranche, and Leibniz, all of whom were on the study list for the *agrégation* exam, which he passed in 1948.

During this time he formed close friendships with François Châtelet, Michel Butor, Pierre Klossowski, and Claude and Jacques Lanzmann. In 1947 he received a *diplôme d'études supérieures* for a project on Hume supervised by Hippolyte and Canguilhem; this later became his first book, *Empiricism and Subjectivity,* published in 1953.

After his studies at the Sorbonne, Deleuze taught at lycées in Amiens (1948–52) and Orléans (1953–55) before moving back to Paris to teach at the Lycée Louis-le-Grand. He then became *maître-assistant* in 1957 in the history of philosophy at the Sorbonne, where he stayed until 1960. In 1956 he married (Denise Paul) "Fanny" Grandjouan, one of the French translators of D. H. Lawrence. They had two children, Julien, born in 1960, and Emile, in 1964.

From 1960 to 1964 Deleuze was *attaché de recherches* at the Centre National de la Recherche Scientifique. It was during this time that he met Michel Foucault, with whom he would have a long intellectual friendship. His influential text *Nietzsche and Philosophy* was published in 1962. From 1964 to 1969 Deleuze taught at the University of Lyon. His *thèse de doctorat d'état, Difference and Repetition* (supervised by de Gandillac), and the accompanying secondary thesis, *Spinoza and the Problem of Expression* (supervised by Alquié), were both published in 1968. His pulmonary problems, which led to a lung operation in 1970, also date from this same period. In 1969 he became a professor of philosophy at the University of Paris VIII (initially at Vincennes, and then later at the new campus at Saint Denis), where he remained until his retirement in 1987.

In the early 1970s Deleuze became involved in various political activities, due in part to his friendship with Félix Guattari, whom he had met in 1969. He lent his support to a number of political groups and organizations, among them GIP (Groupe d'information sur les prisons), formed by Foucault and Daniel Defert, FHAR (a movement for homosexual rights), the Maoists, the Italian autonomy movement, and the Palestinian liberation movement. *Anti-Oedipus,* published in 1972, was the first fruit of Deleuze's collaboration with Guattari. The two wrote four more books together: *Kafka* (1975), *Rhizome* (1976), *A Thousand Plateaus* (1980), and *What Is Philosophy?* (1991). (Guattari died on August 29, 1992, at the age of 62.)

During most of the 1970s Deleuze spent his time teaching and writing, traveling rarely and making very few media appearances. He participated in the 1972 Cerisy colloquium on Nietzsche, alongside Jean-François Lyotard, Klossowski, and Derrida, and oversaw, with the help of Foucault, the translation of the Colli-Montinari edition of Nietzsche's works into French. In a book of interviews with Claire Parnet, *Dialogues*

(1977), Deleuze speaks of his long-standing love for Anglo-American literature (in particular, Melville, Fitzgerald, and Lewis Carroll).

In the 1980s Deleuze wrote a number of important books on the visual arts, among them *Francis Bacon: Logique de la sensation* (1981) and two volumes on cinema, *L'image-mouvement* (1983) and *L'image-temps* (1985). A great admirer of the films of Godard, Deleuze was also associated with the *Cahiers du cinéma*. In 1986 he wrote a book devoted to, and in memory of, Foucault. A book on Leibniz and the baroque, *The Fold,* appeared two years later, followed by a collection of interviews, *Negotiations* (1990). His last book, *Critique et clinique,* a series of essays on philosophy and literature, was published in 1993. His influence on the history of philosophy (with works on the Stoics, Spinoza, Leibniz, Hume, Kant, Nietzsche, and Bergson, among others), art and literary criticism (his 1964 book on Proust becoming an authoritative text in the field), psychoanalysis, and film studies continues to grow in English-speaking countries, where the majority of his works have been translated.

By 1993 Deleuze suffered so badly from the pulmonary condition that had plagued him for many years that it became difficult for him to write and even to socialize with friends. He took his own life on November 4, 1995.

I'm Going to Have to Wander All Alone

So much to say, and I don't have the heart for it today. So much to say about what has happened to us, about what has happened to me too, with the death of Gilles Deleuze; so much to say about what happens with a death that was undoubtedly feared—we knew he was very ill—but yet so much to say about what happens with *this* death, this unimaginable image, which, if it were possible, would hollow out within the event the sad infinity of yet another event. More than anything else, Deleuze the thinker is the thinker of the event and always of this event in particular. From beginning to end, he remained a thinker of this event. I reread what he said concerning the event, already in 1969, in one of his greatest books, *The Logic of Sense*. He quotes Joë Bousquet, who says, "For my inclination toward death, which was a failure of the will, I shall substitute a longing for dying which is the apotheosis of the will." Deleuze then adds, "From this inclination to this longing there is, in a certain respect, no change except a change of the will, a sort of leap in place by the whole body, which exchanges its organic will for a spiritual will. It wills now not exactly what occurs, but something *in* what occurs, something to come that conforms to what occurs, in accordance with the laws of an obscure, humorous conformity: the Event. It is in this sense that *Amor fati* is one with the struggle of free men."[1] (One could go on quoting endlessly.)

So much to say, yes, about the time that was allotted to me, as to so many others of my "generation," to share with Deleuze, so much to say about the chance to think, thanks to him, by thinking about him. From the very beginning, all of his books (but first of all *Nietzsche and Philosophy, Difference and Repetition, The Logic of Sense*) have been for me not only, of course, strong provocations to think but each time the flustering, really flustering, experience of a closeness or of a nearly total affinity concerning the "theses," if we can use this word, across very obvious distances, in what I would call—lacking any better term—the "gesture," the "strategy," the "manner" of writing, of speaking, of reading perhaps. As regards these "theses"—but the word doesn't fit—notably the one concerning an irreducible difference in opposition to dialectical

Reprinted, with changes, from "I'm Going to Have to Wander All Alone," translated by Leonard Lawler, *Philosophy Today* 42, no. 1 (spring 1998): 3–5. First French publication, "Il me faudra errer tout seul," *Libération,* November 7, 1995.

1. Gilles Deleuze, *La logique du sens* (Paris: Minuit, 1969), 174; English translation, *The Logic of Sense,* ed. Constantin V. Boundas, trans. Mark Lester with Charles Stivale (New York: Columbia University Press, 1990), 149.

opposition, a difference "more profound" than a contradiction (*Difference and Repetition*), a difference in the joyously repeated affirmation ("yes, yes"), a taking into account of the simulacrum—Deleuze undoubtably still remains, despite so many dissimilarities, the one among all those of my "generation" to whom I have always considered myself closest. I have never felt the slightest "objection" arising in me, not even potentially, against any of his works, even if I happened to grumble a bit about one or another of the propositions found in *Anti-Oedipus* (I told him this one day while we were driving back together from Nanterre, after a thesis defense on Spinoza), or perhaps about the idea that philosophy consists in "creating" concepts. One day, I would like to try to provide an account of such an agreement in regard to philosophic "content," when this same agreement never does away with all those deviations that I, still today, do not know how to name or situate. (Deleuze had agreed to publish at some point a long, improvised discussion between us on this topic, but then we had to wait, to wait too long.) I only know that these differences never left room for anything between us but friendship. There was never any shadow, any sign, as far as I know, that might indicate the contrary. This is rather rare in our milieu, so rare that I want it to go on record right here. This friendship was not based merely on the fact—and this is not insignificant—that we had the same enemies. It's true, we didn't see each other very often, especially in the last years. But I still hear the laughter of his voice, which was a little raspy, saying to me so many things I like to recall exactly as he said them. He whispered to me, "Best wishes, all my best wishes," with a sweet irony back in the summer of 1955 in the courtyard of the Sorbonne as I was in the process of failing the examinations for the *agrégation*. Or with a concern like that of an older brother: "It pains me to see you put so much time into this institution [the Collège International de Philosophie], I would prefer that you write." And I recall so many other moments, among them the memorable ten days at the Nietzsche conference at Cerisy in 1972, which make me feel, along with Jean-François Lyotard, no doubt (who was also there at Cerisy), so alone, surviving and so melancholy today in what we call with that terrible and somewhat misleading word a "generation." Each death is unique, of course, and therefore unusual. But what can be said about the unusual when, from Barthes to Althusser, from Foucault to Deleuze, it multiplies, as in a series, all these uncommon ends in the same "generation"? And Deleuze was also the philosopher of serial singularity.

Yes, we will have all loved philosophy, who can deny it? But, it is true—he said it—Deleuze was the one among all of this "generation" who "was doing" philosophy the most gaily, the most innocently. I don't think he would have liked me using the word "thinker" earlier. He would have preferred "philosopher." In this regard, he once described himself as "the most innocent (the one who felt the least guilt about 'doing philosophy')."[2] Undoubtedly, this was the necessary condition in order to leave on the philosophy of this century the deep and incomparable mark that will always be his. The mark of a great philosopher and of a great professor. This historian of philosophy, who conducted a kind of configural election of his own genealogy (the Stoics, Lucretius, Spinoza, Hume, Kant, Nietzsche, Bergson, etc.), was also an inventor of philosophy who never enclosed himself within some philosophic "field"—he wrote on painting, cinema, and literature, Bacon, Lewis Carroll, Proust, Kafka, Melville, and so on.

I also want to say *right here* [in *Libération*] that I loved and admired the way—which was always just right—he treated images, newspapers, television, the whole public sphere and the transformations it has undergone in recent decades. All with economy and a vigilant retreat. I felt in complete agreement with what he was doing and saying in this regard, for example, in an interview for *Libération* (October 23, 1980) on the occasion of the publication of *A Thousand Plateaus* (in the vein of his 1977 *Dialogues*).[3] He said: "It is necessary to come to understand what is really going on in the field of books. We've been going through a period of reaction in all fields for several years. There's no reason for it not to have affected books. People are setting up a literary space, along with a legal space, and an economic and political space, that's completely reactionary, artificial, and crippling. I think it's a systematic process, which *Libération* should have investigated." It is "far worse than censorship," he added; but "this sterile phase won't necessarily go on indefinitely."[4] Perhaps, perhaps. Like Nietzsche and like Artaud, like Blanchot, others whom we both admired, Deleuze never lost sight of this connection of necessity with the aleatory, chaos, and the *untimely*. When I was writing on Marx, at the very worst moment, in 1992, I was somewhat reassured to find out that Deleuze intended to do the same thing. And I reread this evening what he said in 1990 on this subject: "I think Felix Guattari and I have remained Marxists,

2.   Derrida is referring to comments Deleuze made in *Pourparlers, 1972–1990* (Paris: Minuit, 1990), 122; English translation, *Negotiations, 1972–1990*, trans. Martin Joughin (New York: Columbia University Press, 1995), 89.—*Trans.*

3.   Gilles Deleuze and Claire Parnet, *Dialogues* (Paris: Flammarion, 1977); English translation, *Dialogues*, trans. Hugh Tomlinson and Barbara Habberjam (New York: Columbia University Press, 1987).

4.   Deleuze, *Pourparlers,* 41; *Negotiations,* 26–27.

in two different ways, perhaps, but both of us. You see, we think any political philosophy must turn on the analysis of capitalism and the ways it has developed. What we find most interesting in Marx is his analysis of capitalism as an immanent system that is constantly overcoming its own limitations, and then coming up against them once more in a broader form, because its fundamental limit is Capital itself."[5]

I am going to continue—or begin again—to read Gilles Deleuze in order to learn, and I'm going to have to wander all alone in that long discussion that we should have had together. I think my first question would have concerned Artaud, Deleuze's interpretation of the "body without organs," and the word "immanence," which he always held on to, in order to make him or let him say something that is still for us undoubtedly secret. And I would have tried to say to him why his thought has never left me for nearly forty years. How could it do so now?

5.   Deleuze, *Pourparlers*, 232; *Negotiations*, 171.

CHAPTER 13

EMMANUEL LEVINAS

JANUARY 12, 1906—DECEMBER 25, 1995

Emmanuel Levinas was born on January 12, 1906 (December 30, 1905, according to the Julian calendar), in Kaunas (Kovno), Lithuania, to Jehiel Levinas, a bookseller, and Deborah Gurvic. He had two younger brothers, Boris (born in 1909) and Aminadab (born in 1913). At a very young age Levinas read the Bible (in Hebrew), Shakespeare, and the classic works of Pushkin, Gogol, Dostoyevsky, and Tolstoy (in Russian, which was the language of his formal education). In Kovno he attended the Jewish lycée before the family moved to Kharkov in the Ukraine to escape the German invaders. Levinas attended the Russian high school in Kharkov until the family's return to Lithuania in 1920.

In 1923 Levinas traveled to Strasbourg, France, to study philosophy at the University of Strasbourg, where he counted among his professors Henri Carteron, Charles Blondel, Léon Brunschvicg, and Maurice Pradines (who directed his 1930 doctoral thesis on Husserl). It was also at Strasbourg that Levinas met fellow student Maurice Blanchot, with whom he soon formed a lifelong friendship. Levinas devoted himself to a close study of Husserl's *Logical Investigations* and obtained his *licence* in philosophy. He spent 1928–29 at Freiburg University, where he studied with Husserl and Heidegger, giving a presentation in one of Husserl's last seminars and attending the famous Davos encounter between Heidegger and Ernst Cassirer in 1929. In 1930 Levinas returned to Strasbourg to defend and then publish, at the age of twenty-four, his *thèse de doctorat de troisième cycle,* "Theory of Intuition in the Phenomenology of Husserl." In that same year he became a French citizen and performed his military service in Paris. His translation of Husserl's *Cartesian Meditations* (with Gabrielle Peiffer) appeared in 1931.

In September 1932 Levinas married Raïssa Lévi, a musician who had studied in Vienna and at the Conservatoire National Supérieur de Musique in Paris. The couple had two children, Simone, born in 1935, and Michaël, born in 1949. (The former is a doctor and the latter an accomplished pianist and composer.) In the 1930s Levinas took up a position at the Ecole Normale Israélite Orientale (ENIO) and settled in the Seventeenth Arrondissement of Paris. He attended Léon Brunschvicg's and Alexandre Kojève's lectures at the Ecole des Hautes Etudes, where he also met Sartre and Jean Hyppolite.

During this same period Levinas began work on a book on Heidegger, which he later abandoned, though some of this work appeared in *En découvrant l'existence avec Husserl and Heidegger* (published in 1949). Levinas's 1932 essay "Martin Heidegger et l'ontologie" was one of the very first essays written in French on Heidegger. In 1939 Levinas was drafted into the French army as an interpreter of Russian and German. The following year he became a military prisoner of war in northern Germany (Stalag 11B). His wife and daughter were hidden and protected by Maurice Blanchot, who later arranged for their refuge in a convent of the sisters of Saint Vincent de Paul in Prelfort. Many members of Levinas's family in Lithuania (including his father, mother, and two brothers) were killed by the Nazis during the war.

At the end of the war Levinas became director of the ENIO, an institution with which he would remain associated for most of his life, whether as its director (1945–61) or in other teaching and administrative positions. In 1947 he published *De l'existence à l'existant,* much of which was written during his captivity, along with four lectures given at Jean Wahl's Collège Philosophique in 1946–47 under the title *Time and the Other.* Levinas also began studying the Talmud at this time under the direction of M. Chouchani and, from 1957 onward, gave talmudic lessons at the annual Colloquium of Jewish Intellectuals of French Expression. Several of these talmudic readings were published in *Quatre lectures talmudiques* (1968), *Du sacré au saint* (1977), and *l'Au-delà du verset* (1982).

It was not until after the publication of *Totality and Infinity* (his main thesis for the *doctorat d'état*) in 1961 that the true significance of Levinas's philosophical work began to emerge. In 1963 he was appointed a professor of philosophy at the University of Poitiers, where his colleagues included Mikel Dufrenne and Jeanne Delhomme, who accompanied him in 1967 when he moved to the University of Paris, Nanterre. This university became one of the centers of student political activity during the uprisings of 1968. Beginning in the late 1960s Levinas frequently taught at the University of Fribourg in Switzerland, and in 1972 he visited the United States, teaching a course on Descartes at Johns Hopkins University.

Levinas left Nanterre in 1973 to join Henri Birault, Pierre Aubenque, and Ferdinand Alquié at the University of Paris IV, Sorbonne. His second major work, *Otherwise than Being,* was published the following year. Levinas officially retired from the Sorbonne in 1976, but stayed on three more years as Professor Emeritus. In 1980 he left his official post at the ENIO but still gave regular Saturday lessons there.

With the widespread translation of his work, Levinas's international stature and importance continued to grow during the 1980s and 1990s. Several significant collections of his papers and talks were published during these years, notably *Of God Who Comes to Mind* (1982), *Outside the Subject* (1987) and *Entre Nous* (1991), and a number of major international colloquia were devoted to his work, at Cerisy-la-Salle (1986), University of Essex (1987), and Loyola University of Chicago (1993), among others.

Levinas was the recipient of numerous awards and prizes during his lifetime, among them the Albert Schweitzer award (in 1971, for international philosophy), Officier de l'Ordre National du Mérite (1974), Chevalier de la Légion d'honneur (1976), the Jaspers Prize (1983), Commandeur des Arts et Lettres (1985), and Officier de la Légion d'honneur (1991).

Emmanuel Levinas died in the early hours of December 25, 1995. An homage was paid to him at the Richelieu Amphitheater of the Sorbonne on December 7, 1996.

For a long time, for a very long time, I've feared having to say *Adieu* to Emmanuel Levinas.

I knew that my voice would tremble at the moment of saying it, and especially saying it aloud, right here, before him, so close to him, pronouncing this word of *adieu,* this word *à-Dieu,* which, in a certain sense, I get from him, a word that he will have taught me to think or to pronounce otherwise.

By meditating upon what Emmanuel Levinas wrote about the French word *adieu*—which I will recall in a few moments—I hope to find a sort of encouragement to speak here. And I would like to do so with unadorned, naked words, words as childlike and disarmed as my sorrow.

Whom is one addressing at such a moment? And in whose name would one allow oneself to do so? Often those who come forward to speak, to speak publicly, thereby interrupting the animated whispering, the secret or intimate exchange that always links one, deep inside, to a dead friend or master, those who make themselves heard in a cemetery, end up addressing *directly, straight on,* the one who, as we say, is no longer, is no longer living, no longer there, who will no longer respond. With tears in their voices, they sometimes speak familiarly to the other who keeps silent, calling upon him without detour or mediation, apostrophizing him, even greeting him or confiding in him. This is not necessarily out of respect for convention, not always simply part of the rhetoric of oration. It is rather so as to traverse speech at the very point where words fail us, since all language that would return to the self, to us, would seem indecent, a reflexive discourse that would end up coming back to the stricken community, to its consolation or its mourning, to what is called, in a confused and terrible expression, "the work of mourning." Concerned only with itself, such speech would, in this return, risk turning away from what is here our law—the law as *straightforwardness* or *uprightness* [*droiture*]: to speak straight on, to address oneself directly *to* the other, and to speak *for* the other whom one loves and admires, before speaking *of* him. To say to him

This text was delivered as the funeral oration for Emmanuel Levinas on December 25, 1995. Reprinted, with changes, from "Adieu," translated by Pascale-Anne Brault and Michael Naas, *Critical Inquiry* 23, no. 1 (autumn 1996); and in *Philosophy Today,* fall 1996. Republished in *Adieu to Emmanuel Levinas,* by Jacques Derrida (Stanford: Stanford University Press, 1999), 1–13. First French publication, *Adieu: A Emmanuel Lévinas* (Paris: Galilée, 1997), 11–27.

adieu, to him, Emmanuel, and not merely to recall what he first taught us about a certain *Adieu.*

This word *droiture*—"straightforwardness" or "uprightness"—is another word that I began to hear otherwise and to learn when it came to me from Emmanuel Levinas. Of all the places where he speaks of uprightness, what first comes to mind is one of his "Four Talmudic Readings," where uprightness names what is, as he says, "stronger than death."[1]

But let us also keep from trying to find in everything that is said to be "stronger than death" a refuge or an alibi, yet another consolation. To define uprightness, Emmanuel Levinas says, in his commentary on the Tractate Shabbath, that consciousness is

> the urgency of a destination leading to the Other and not an eternal
> return to self . . . an innocence without naivete, an uprightness
> without stupidity, an absolute uprightness which is also absolute
> self-criticism, read in the eyes of the one who is the goal of my
> uprightness and whose look calls me into question. It is a movement
> toward the other that does not come back to its point of origin the
> way diversion comes back, incapable as it is of transcendence—a
> movement beyond anxiety and stronger than death. This upright-
> ness is called *Temimut,* the essence of Jacob. (*NTR,* 48)

This same meditation also sets to work—as each meditation did, though each in a singular way—all the great themes to which the thought of Emmanuel Levinas has awakened us, that of responsibility first of all, but of an "unlimited" responsibility that exceeds and precedes my freedom, that of an "unconditional yes," as this text says, of a *"yes* older than that of naive spontaneity," a *yes* in accord with this uprightness that is "original fidelity to an indissoluble alliance" (*NTR,* 49–50). And the final words of this Lesson return, of course, to death, but they do so precisely so as not to let death have the last word, or the first one. They remind us of a recurrent theme in what was a long and incessant meditation upon death, but one that set out on a path that ran counter to the philosophical tradition extending from Plato to Heidegger. Elsewhere, before saying what the *à-Dieu* must be, another text speaks of the "extreme uprightness of the face of the neighbor" as the "uprightness of an exposure to death, with defense."[2]

1. Emmanuel Levinas, "Four Talmudic Readings," in *Nine Talmudic Readings,* trans. Annette Aronowicz (Bloomington: Indiana University Press, 1990), 48 (hereafter abbreviated as *NTR*).

2. Emmanuel Levinas, "Bad Conscience and the Inexorable," in *Face to Face with Levinas,* ed. Richard A. Cohen (Albany, N.Y.: SUNY Press, 1986), 38. This essay is included

I cannot, nor would I even try to, measure in a few words the oeuvre of Emmanuel Levinas. It is so large that one can no longer glimpse its edges. And one would have to begin by learning once again from him and from *Totality and Infinity,* for example, how to think what an "oeuvre" or "work"—as well as fecundity—might be. One can predict with confidence that centuries of readings will set this as their task. We already see innumerable signs, well beyond France and Europe, in so many works and so many languages, in all the translations, courses, seminars, conferences, and so on, that the reverberations of this thought will have changed the course of philosophical reflection in our time, and of our reflection *on* philosophy, on what orders it according to ethics, another thought of ethics, responsibility, justice, the State, and so on, according to another thought of the other, a thought that is newer than so many novelties because it is ordered according to the absolute anteriority of the face of the Other.

Yes, ethics before and beyond ontology, the State, or politics, but also ethics beyond ethics. One day, on the rue Michel Ange, during one of those conversations whose memory I hold so dear, one of those conversations illuminated by the radiance of his thought, the goodness of his smile, the gracious humor of his ellipses, he said to me: "You know, one often speaks of ethics to describe what I do, but what really interests me in the end is not ethics, not ethics alone, but the holy, the holiness of the holy." And I then thought of a singular separation, the unique separation of the curtain or veil that is given, ordered and ordained [*donné, ordonné*], by God, the veil entrusted by Moses to an inventor or an artist rather than to an embroiderer, the veil that would *separate* the holy of holies in the sanctuary. And I also thought of how other *Talmudic "Lessons"* sharpen the necessary distinction between sacredness and holiness, that is, the holiness of the other, the holiness of the person, who is, as Emmanuel Levinas said elsewhere, "more holy than a land, even when that land is a holy land. Next to a person who has been affronted, this land—holy and promised—is but nakedness and desert, a heap of wood and stone."[3]

This meditation on ethics, on the transcendence of the holy with regard to the sacred, that is, with regard to the paganism of roots and the

as the final section of "La conscience non-intentionnelle," in *Entre nous: Essais sur le penser-à-l'autre* (Paris: Grasset, 1991) (hereafter abbreviated as *BC*).

3. See Levinas's preface to Marlène Zarader, *Heidegger et les paroles de l'origine* (Paris: Vrin, 1986), 12–13. [See also the interview with Schlomo Malka published in *Les nouveaux cahiers* 18 (1982–83): 71, 1–8; translated by Jonathan Romney in *The Levinas Reader,* ed. Seán Hand (Cambridge, Mass.: Basil Blackwell, 1989), 297.—*Trans.*]

idolatry of place, was, of course, indissociable from an incessant reflection upon the destiny and thought of Israel: yesterday, today, and tomorrow. Such reflection consisted of requestioning and reaffirming the legacies not only of the biblical and talmudic tradition but of the terrifying memory of our time. This memory dictates each of these sentences, whether from nearby or afar, even if Levinas would sometimes protest against certain self-justifying abuses to which such a memory and the reference to the Holocaust might give rise.

But refraining from commentaries and questions, I would simply like to give thanks to someone whose thought, friendship, trust, and "goodness" (and I ascribe to this word "goodness" all the significance it is given in the final pages of *Totality and Infinity*) will have been for me, as for so many others, a living source, so living, so constant, that I am unable to think what is happening to him or happening to me today, namely, this interruption or a certain non-response in a response that will never come to an end for me as long as I live.

The non-response: you will no doubt recall that in the remarkable course Emmanuel Levinas gave in 1975–76 (exactly twenty years ago), "La mort et le temps" [Death and time],[4] where he defines death as the patience of time, and engages in a grand and noble critical encounter with Plato as much as with Hegel, but especially with Heidegger, death is often defined—the death that "we meet" "in the face of the Other"—as *non-response;* "it is the without-response" (*DMT,* 20), he says. And elsewhere: "There is here an end that always has the ambiguity of a departure without return, of a passing away but also of a scandal ('is it really possible that he's dead?') of non-response and of my responsibility" (*DMT,* 47).

Death: not, first of all, annihilation, non-being, or nothingness, but a certain experience for the survivor of the "without-response." Already *Totality and Infinity* called into question the traditional "philosophical and religious" interpretation of death as either "a passage to nothingness" or "a passage to some other existence."[5] It is the murderer who would like to identify death with nothingness; Cain, for example, says Emmanuel Levinas, "must have possessed such a knowledge of death." But even this nothingness presents itself as a "sort of impossibility" or, more precisely,

4.   This is one of two courses Levinas taught at the Sorbonne (Paris IV) during 1975–76. It was first published in 1991 under the title "La mort et le temps" in *Emmanuel Levinas,* Paris Cahiers de l'Herne, no. 60, 21–75, and then in 1993 (with the other course from the same year, "Dieu et l'onto-théo-logie") in Levinas, *Dieu, la mort et le temps* (Paris: Grasset, 1993) (hereafter abbreviated as *DMT*).

5.   Emmanuel Levinas, *Totality and Infinity: An Essay on Exteriority,* trans. Alphonso Lingis (Pittsburgh: Duquesne University Press, 1969), 232 (hereafter abbreviated as *TI*).

an interdiction. The face of the Other forbids me to kill; it says to me, "thou shall not kill," even if this possibility remains presupposed by the interdiction that makes it impossible. This question without response, this question of the without-response, would thus be underivable, primordial, like the interdiction against killing, more originary than the alternative of "to be or not to be," which is thus neither the first nor the last question. "To be or not to be," another essay concludes, "is probably not the question par excellence" (*BC,* 40).

Today, I draw from all this that our infinite sadness must shy away from everything in mourning that would turn toward nothingness, that is, toward what still, even potentially, would link guilt to murder. Levinas indeed speaks of the survivor's guilt, but it is a guilt without fault and without debt; it is, in truth, an *entrusted responsibility,* entrusted in a moment of unparalleled emotion, at the moment when death remains the absolute ex-ception. To express this unprecedented emotion, the one I feel here and share with you, the one that our sense of propriety forbids us to exhibit, so as to make clear without personal avowal or exhibition how this singular emotion is related to this entrusted responsibility, entrusted as legacy, allow me once again to let Emmanuel Levinas speak, him whose voice I would so much love to hear today when it says that the "death of the other" is the "first death," and that "I am responsible for the other insofar as he is mortal." Or else the following, from this same course of 1975–76:

> The death of someone is not, despite what it might have appeared to be at first glance, an empirical facticity (death as an empirical fact whose induction alone could suggest its universality); it is not exhausted in such an appearance.
>
> Someone who expresses himself in his nakedness—the face— is in fact one to the extent that he calls upon me, to the extent that he places himself under my responsibility: I must already answer for him, be responsible for him. Every gesture of the Other was a sign addressed to me. To return to the classification sketched out above: to show oneself, to express oneself, to associate oneself, *to be entrusted to me.* The Other who expresses himself is entrusted to me (and there is no debt with regard to the Other—for what is due cannot be paid: one will never be even). [Further on it will be a question of a "duty beyond all debt" for the I who is what it is, singular and identifiable, only through the impossibility of being replaced, even though it is precisely here that the "responsibility for the Other," the "responsibility of the hostage," is an experience

of substitution and sacrifice.] The Other individuates me in my
responsibility for him. The death of the Other affects me in my very
identity as a responsible I . . . made up of unspeakable responsibility. This is how I am affected by the death of the Other, this is
my relation to his death. It is, in my relation, my deference toward
someone who no longer responds, already a guilt of the survivor.
(*DMT,* 21; quotations in brackets, 31, 199)

And a bit further on:

> The relation to death in its ex-ception—and, regardless of its sig-
> nification in relation to being and nothingness, it is an exception—
> while conferring upon death its depth, is neither a seeing nor even
> an aiming toward (neither a seeing of being as in Plato nor an
> aiming toward nothingness as in Heidegger), a purely emotional
> relation, moving with an emotion that is not made up of the reper-
> cussions of a prior knowledge upon our sensibility and our intellect.
> It is an emotion, a movement, an uneasiness with regard to the
> *unknown. (DMT,* 25–26)

The "unknown" is emphasized here. The "unknown" is not the
negative limit of a knowledge. This non-knowledge is the element of
friendship or hospitality for the transcendence of the stranger, the infinite
distance of the other. "Unknown" is also the word chosen by Maurice
Blanchot for the title of an essay, "Knowledge of the Unknown," which
he devoted to the one who had been, from the time of their meeting in
Strasbourg in 1923, a friend, the very friendship of the friend.

For many among us, no doubt, certainly for myself, the absolute
fidelity, the exemplary friendship of thought, the *friendship* between Maurice Blanchot and Emmanuel Levinas, was a grace, a gift; it remains a
benediction of our time and, for more reasons than one, a good fortune
that is also a blessing for those who have had the great privilege of being
the friend of either of them. In order to hear once again today, right here,
Blanchot speak for Levinas, and with Levinas, as I had the good fortune
to do when in their company one day in 1968, I will cite a couple of lines.
After having named what in the other "ravishes" us, after having spoken
of a certain "rapture" (the word often used by Levinas to speak of death),
Blanchot says:

> But we must not despair of philosophy. In Emmanuel Levinas's
> book [*Totality and Infinity*]—where, it seems to me, philosophy in

our time has never spoken in a more sober manner, putting back
into question, as we must, our ways of thinking and even our facile
reverence for ontology—we are called upon to become responsible
for what philosophy essentially is, by welcoming, in all the radiance
and infinite exigency proper to it, the idea of the Other, that is to
say, the relation with *autrui*. It is as though there were here a new
departure in philosophy and a leap that it, and we ourselves, were
urged to accomplish.[6]

If the relation to the other presupposes an infinite separation, an
infinite interruption where the face appears, what happens, where and
to whom does it happen, when another interruption comes at death to
hollow out even more infinitely this first separation, a rending interruption
at the heart of interruption itself? I cannot speak of interruption without
recalling, like many among you, no doubt, the anxiety of interruption I
could feel in Emmanuel Levinas when, on the telephone, for example,
he seemed at each moment to fear being cut off, to fear the silence or
disappearance, the "without response," of the other, to whom he called
out and held on with an "allo, allo" between sentences, sometimes even in
midsentence.

What happens when a great thinker becomes silent, one whom
we knew living, whom we read and reread, and also heard, one from
whom we were still awaiting a response, as if such a response would
help us not only to think otherwise but also to read what we thought
we had already read under his signature, a response that held everything
in reserve, and so much more than what we thought we had already
recognized there? This is an experience that, as I have learned, would
remain for me interminable with Emmanuel Levinas, as with all thoughts
that are sources, for I will never stop beginning or beginning anew to
think with them on the basis of the new beginning they give me, and I
will begin again and again to rediscover them on just about any subject.
Each time I read or reread Emmanuel Levinas, I am overwhelmed with
gratitude and admiration, overwhelmed by this necessity, which is not
a constraint but a very gentle force that obligates, and obligates us not
to bend or curve otherwise the space of thought in its respect for the
other, but to yield to this other, heteronomous curvature that relates us

6.   This is Maurice Blanchot's text "Knowledge of the Unknown," first published in *La
nouvelle revue française*, no. 108 (1961): 1081–95, then again in *L'entretien infini* (Paris:
Gallimard, 1969), 70–83; see Maurice Blanchot, *The Infinite Conversation*, trans. Susan
Hanson (Minneapolis: University of Minnesota Press, 1993), 51–52.

to the completely other (that is, to justice, as he says somewhere in a powerful and formidable ellipsis: the relation to the other, that is to say, justice), according to the law that thus calls us to yield to the other infinite precedence of the completely other.

It will have come, like this call, to disturb, discreetly but irreversibly, the most powerful and established thoughts of the end of this millennium, beginning with those of Husserl and Heidegger, whom Levinas introduced into France some sixty-five years ago! Indeed, this country, whose hospitality he so loved (and *Totality and Infinity* shows not only that "the essence of language is goodness" but that "the essence of language is friendship and hospitality" [*TI*, 305]), this hospitable France, owes him, among so many other things, among so many other significant contributions, at least two irruptive events of thought, two inaugural acts that are difficult to measure today because they have been incorporated into the very element of our philosophical culture, after having transformed its landscape.

First, to say it all too quickly, beginning in 1930 with translations and interpretative readings, there was the initial introduction of Husserlian phenomenology, which would feed and fecundate so many French philosophical currents. Then—in truth, simultaneously—there was the introduction of Heideggerian thought, which was no less important in the genealogy of so many French philosophers, professors, and students. Husserl and Heidegger at the same time, beginning in 1930. I wanted last night to reread a few pages from this prodigious book, which was for me, as for many others before me, the first and best guide. I picked out a few sentences that have made their mark in time and that allow us to measure the distance he will have helped us cover. In 1930, a young man of twenty-three said in the preface that I reread, smiling, smiling at him: "The fact that in France phenomenology is not a doctrine known to everyone has been a constant problem in the writing of this book."[7] Or again, speaking of the so very "powerful and original philosophy" of "Mr. Martin Heidegger, whose influence on this book will often be felt," the same book also recalls that "the problem raised here by transcendental

---

7.   Emmanuel Levinas, *La théorie de l'intuition dans la phénoménologie de Husserl* (Paris: Vrin, 1963), 7; English translation, *The Theory of Intuition in Husserl's Phenomenology*, 2d ed., trans. André Orianne (Evanston: Northwestern University Press, 1995). [As the translator notes (xlix), Levinas's short preface or *avant-propos*, from which the above quote was taken, was omitted from the translation and replaced by the translator's foreword so as to provide a series of "historical remarks more specifically directed to today's English reader."—*Trans.*]

phenomenology is an ontological problem in the very precise sense that Heidegger gives to this term."

The second event, the second philosophical tremor, I would even say the happy traumatism that we owe him (in the sense of the word "traumatism" that he liked to recall, the "traumatism of the other" that comes from the Other), is that, while closely reading and reinterpreting the thinkers I just mentioned, but so many others as well, both philosophers such as Descartes, Kant, and Kierkegaard and writers such as Dostoyevsky, Kafka, and Proust—all the while disseminating his words through publications, teaching, and lectures (at the Ecole Normale Israélite Orientale, at the Collège Philosophique, and at the Universities of Poitiers, Nanterre, and the Sorbonne)—Emmanuel Levinas slowly displaced, slowly bent according to an inflexible and simple exigency, the axis, trajectory, and even the order of phenomenology or ontology that he had introduced into France beginning in 1930. Once again, he completely changed the landscape without landscape of thought; he did so in a dignified way, without polemic, at once from within, faithfully, and from very far away, from the attestation of a completely other place. And I believe that what occurred there, in this second sailing, this second time that leads us back even further than the first, is a discreet but irreversible mutation, one of those powerful, singular, and rare provocations in history that, for over two thousand years now, will have ineffaceably marked the space and body of what is more or less, in any case something different from, a simple dialogue between Jewish thought and its others, the philosophies of Greek origin or, in the tradition of a certain "here I am," the other Abrahamic monotheisms. This happened, this mutation happened, *through him,* through Emmanuel Levinas, who was conscious of this immense responsibility in a way that was, I believe, at once clear, confident, calm, and modest, like that of a prophet.

One indication of this historical shock wave is the influence of this thought well beyond philosophy, and well beyond Jewish thought, on Christian theology, for example. I cannot help recall the day when, listening to a lecture by André Neher at a Congress of Jewish Intellectuals, Emmanuel Levinas turned to me and said, with the gentle irony so familiar to us: "You see, he's the Jewish Protestant, and I'm the Catholic"—a quip that would call for long and serious reflection.

In everything that has happened here through him, thanks to him, we have had the good fortune not only of receiving it while living, from him living, as a responsibility entrusted by the living to the living, but also the good fortune of owing it to him with a light and innocent debt. One day, speaking of his research on death and of what it owed to Heidegger at the very moment when it was moving away from him, Levinas wrote: "It distinguishes itself from Heidegger's thought, and it does so in spite of the debt that every contemporary thinker owes to Heidegger—a debt that one often regrets" (*DMT,* 16). The good fortune of our debt to Levinas is that we can, thanks to him, assume it and affirm it without regret, in the joyous innocence of admiration. It is of the order of the unconditional *yes* of which I spoke earlier, and to which it responds, "yes." The regret, my regret, is not having said this to him enough, not having shown him this enough in the course of these thirty years, during which, in the modesty of silences, through brief or discreet conversations, writings too indirect or reserved, we often addressed to one another what I would call neither questions nor answers but, perhaps, to use another one of his words, a sort of "question, prayer," a question-prayer that, as he says, would be anterior to all dialogue (*DMT,* 134).

The question-prayer that turned me toward him perhaps already shared in the experience of the *à-Dieu* with which I began. The greeting of the *à-Dieu* does not signal the end. "The *à-Dieu* is not a finality," he says, thus challenging the "alternative between being and nothingness," which "is not ultimate." The *à-Dieu* greets the other beyond being, in "what is signified, beyond being, by the word 'glory.'" "The *à-Dieu* is not a process of being: in the call, I am referred back to the other human being through whom this call signifies, to the neighbor for whom I am to fear" (*BC,* 39–40).

But I said that I did not want simply to recall what he entrusted to us of the *à-Dieu,* but first of all to say *adieu* to him, to call him by his name, to call his name, his first name, what he is called at the moment when, if he no longer responds, it is because he is responding in us, from the bottom of our hearts, in us but before us, in us right before us—in calling us, in recalling to us: *à-Dieu.*

Adieu, Emmanuel.

CHAPTER 14

JEAN-FRANÇOIS LYOTARD

AUGUST 10, 1924—APRIL 21, 1998

Philosopher, writer, and aesthetician Jean-François Lyotard was born in Versailles in 1924 to Jean-Pierre Lyotard, a sales representative, and Madeleine Cavalli. He attended the Lycées Buffon and Louis-le-Grand in Paris. He once said that at various periods of his youth he considered becoming a priest, a painter, and a historian, before finally choosing to study philosophy.

After twice failing the entrance exam to the Ecole Normale Supérieure, Lyotard attended the Sorbonne in the years just after World War II. He there became friends with Michel Butor, Gilles Deleuze, Roger Laporte, and François Châtelet. Lyotard's master's thesis, "Indifference as an Ethical Notion," written at the end of the 1940s, examined various conceptions of indifference, from Epicurean *ataraxia,* to Stoic *apatheia* and *adiaphora,* to Zen "not-thinking" and Taoist nothingness, in conjunction with Pierre Janet's book on madness, *De l'angoisse à l'extase.* He later passed the *agrégation* and obtained his *doctorat d'état* for *Discours, figure,* which was published in 1971.

In 1948 Lyotard married Andrée May, with whom he had two children, Corinne and Laurence. He taught at a boys' lycée in Constantine, Algeria, from 1950 to 1952, before being appointed to a school for the sons of military personnel at La Flèche (1952–59). His first book, *Phenomenology,* was published in 1954. In the 1950s Lyotard was very active in politics; at the suggestion of Pierre Souyri he joined Socialisme ou barbarie, a political organization devoted to combating exploitation and alienation and engaged in a critique of totalitarianism. He was on the editorial board for the journal of the same name and its principal spokesperson on Algeria for several years. Lyotard remained with Socialisme ou barbarie, alongside Claude Lefort and Cornelius Castoriadis, until 1964, when he left to join the offshoot group Pouvoir ouvrier (1964–66). (A collection of pseudonymous articles written for Socialisme ou barbarie was published in 1989 under the title *La guerre des Algériens.*)

From 1959 to 1966 Lyotard was *maître-assistant* at the Sorbonne, before joining the philosophy department at the University of Paris X, Nanterre. During the political upheavals of 1968 Lyotard organized a number of demonstrations in support of the "March 22 Movement." He was *chargé de recherches* at the Centre National de la Recherche Scientifique from 1968 to 1970, before being named to the faculty at the University of Paris VIII, Vincennes, where he became *maître de conférences* in 1972. He taught at Vincennes until 1987, eventually becoming Professor Emeritus. During the mid-1970s Lyotard was a visiting professor at a number of American universities, including the University of California at San Diego and at Berkeley, Johns Hopkins, and the Center for Twentieth Century studies at the University of Wisconsin—Milwaukee.

Lyotard's engagement with Marx and Freud resulted in several important texts in the early 1970s, among them *Des dispositifs pulsionnels* (1973), *Dérive à partir de Marx et Freud* (1973), and *Libidinal Economy* (1974). In 1977 Lyotard published four books, *Instructions païennes, Rudiments païens, Les transformateurs Duchamp,* and *Récits tremblants.* The publication in 1979 of *The Postmodern Condition,* a commissioned report on the status of knowledge in the late twentieth century, led to Lyotard's international fame. *Au juste,* a dialogue with Jean-Loup Thébaud, also published in 1979, signaled Lyotard's turn toward the question of judgment, particularly in Kant.

Throughout his career, Lyotard maintained a keen interest in art, writing books (including *Que peindre? Adami, Arakawa, Buren,* published in 1987) and essays, contributing to exhibition catalogs (on Jacques Monory, Albert Aymé, Henri Maccheroni, Ruth Francken, and Sam Francis) and even organizing an exhibition, *Les immatériaux,* at the Pompidou Center in Paris in 1985. He was one of the founders of the Collège International de Philosophie in 1983 and served as its president from 1984 to 1986. In 1984 he published *The Differend*—a work he refers to as "my book of philosophy"—a dense, sustained engagement with figures such as Plato, Aristotle, Kant, Freud, and Wittgenstein.

Lyotard's *Heidegger and "the jews"* was published in 1989; written against the backdrop of the "Heidegger Affair" in France, the book is an attempt to understand Heidegger's disturbing silence on the topic of Auschwitz. Several significant books were published during the late 1980s and early 1990s, *Peregrinations* (originally delivered as the Wellek Library Lectures at the University of California, Irvine), *The Inhuman* (1988), a collection of essays on time, art, and technology, *Lectures d'enfance* (1991), *Postmodern Fables* (1993), and *Lessons on the Analytic of the Sublime* (1993), an analysis of Kant's third *Critique,* a text that was pivotal to much of Lyotard's later work.

Lyotard lectured and taught extensively in the United States during the 1980s and 1990s. He became a professor of French and Italian at the University of California, Irvine, and, later, the Robert W. Woodruff Professor of French at Emory University (1993–98). He also taught for extended periods at the Universities of Montreal, Sao Paulo, Arhus (in Denmark), Turin, and Siegen (in Germany). In 1993 Lyotard married his second wife, Dolorès Djidzek, with whom he had a son, David.

With his biographical book on Malraux, *Signed, Malraux* (1996), and *The Soundproof Room* (1998), a powerful analysis of Malraux's "anti-aesthetics," Lyotard took on a subject whose intellectual interests (philosophy, literature, art criticism) and political engagements were as varied as his own. *Augustine's Confession,* which was never completed, was published posthumously in 1998.

Lyotard passed away in the early hours of April 21, 1998, in Paris, following a long struggle with leukemia.

I feel at such a loss, unable to find public words for what is happening to us, for what has left speechless all those who had the good fortune to come near this great thinker—whose absence will remain for me, I am certain, forever unthinkable: the unthinkable itself, in the depths of tears. Jean-François Lyotard remains one of my closest friends, and I don't use these words lightly. He will have been so, in my heart and in my thought, *forever*—a word I use to translate more than forty years of reading and "discussion" (he always preferred this word, and even gave it as a title for a major text on Auschwitz—and on the rest).[1] A vigilant, uncompromising "discussion," an amused provocation, always punctuated, it seemed, by a smile, a smile at once tender and mocking, an irony committed to disarming itself in the name of what we did not know how to name but that I today would call "all-out friendship" [*amitié-à-tout-rompre*]. A tone at once light and serious, a burst of philosophical laughter that all the friends of Jean-François can no doubt hear today deep within themselves. A singular combination of cutting laughter (judgment) and infinitely respectful attention, which I always loved and thought I could recognize, even in the moments—which were rare and hard to pin down—of "differend," in all the areas common to us (phenomenology, to begin with, an admiring and indispensable reference to Levinas, even if it wasn't exactly the same one—along with so many other points of reference in the same landscape). But I cannot and do not even wish to try to reconstitute here all the paths on which we have crossed and accompanied one another. These encounters will remain for me forever uninterrupted. They took place but will not cease to seek their place in me, right up until the end. The memories of friends differ greatly from one another; they probably bear no resemblance to one another. And yet I remember today having shared too many things with Jean-François during all those years to try to encompass them in a few words. I did not know him at the time of Socialisme ou barbarie, but I thought I could see traces of a faithful attachment to it in all his great books (for example, to cite only a few, *Discourse, Figure, The Postmodern Condition, The Differend,* which I would relate today, in admiration, to his last writings on childhood and tears: an immense treatise or treaty on absolute disarmament, on

Translated by Pascale-Anne Brault and Michael Naas for this volume. First French publication, "Amitié-à-tout-rompre," *Libération,* March 22, 1998.

1.   Jean-François Lyotard, "Discussion; ou, phraser après 'Auschwitz,'" in *Les fins de l'homme* (Paris: Galilée, 1981), 283–310.

that which links thought to infinite vulnerability). The now worldwide thought on the "postmodern" has him to thank, as we know, for its initial elaboration. Along with so many other innovations. I would say the same thing about what, in our time (proper noun and metonymy: "Auschwitz"), will have shaken the tradition of philosophy, its testimony on testimony. Lyotard there ventured forth, as always, with a courage and independence of thought of which I know few other examples. We will no longer be able to think this disaster, in the history of this century, without engaging with him, without reading and rereading him. Students the world over know this. I can attest to it from the faraway place from which I am writing to you and where, for many years, I have lived in the same house that Jean-François lived in, and where, alone, I cry for him today.

A couple more words before giving up.

Among the things that I like having liked along with him, there was more than one affront against the institution. For example, the Collège International de Philosophie, for which he was a driving force, which owes him so much, and which the rearguard of resentment still finds intolerable. One of the last times I saw Jean-François, he burst into laughter at the pitiful grimaces of certain hidden detractors. As always, he was committed to counterattack. But he also laughed on the phone to reassure me about his health: "It's foolishness that saves me," or something to that effect.

Upon the death of Deleuze, you also asked me to attempt—that time too without delay, and in the midst of my sorrow—a sort of testimony. I seem to recall having said that I could feel us quite alone now, Jean-François Lyotard and I, the sole survivors of what has been identified as a "generation"—of which I am the last born, and, no doubt, the most melancholic of the group (they were all more joyful than I). What can I say today, then? That I love Jean-François, that I miss him, like the words I cannot find, beyond words: I alone, and those dear to him, as well as our common friends. For our best friends, in thought as in life, were, I believe, friends we had *in common*. And that is rather rare. I am going to take refuge in the texts that he wrote here, and I am going to listen to him, on the Pacific Wall, so as to rethink childhood. . . .

When, surviving, and so forevermore bereft of the possibility of speaking or addressing oneself *to* the friend, to the friend himself, one is condemned merely to speak *of* him, of what he was, thought, and wrote, it is nonetheless still of *him* that one should speak.

It is of him we mean to speak, of him alone, of or on his side alone. But how can the survivor speak in friendship of the friend without a "we" indecently setting in, without an "us" incessantly slipping in? Without a "we" in fact demanding—and precisely in the name of friendship—to be heard? For to silence or forbid the "we" would be to enact another, no less serious, violence. The injustice would be at least as great as that of still saying "we."

For who could ever venture a "we" without trembling? Who could ever sign a "we," a "we" as subject in the nominative, or an "us" in the accusative or dative? In French, it is the same, the same *"nous,"* even when the second is reflected in the first: *"nous nous"*—yes, *oui, nous nous sommes rencontrés, nous nous sommes parlé, écrit, nous nous sommes entendus, nous nous sommes aimés, nous nous sommes accordés—ou non* [yes, we met one another, we spoke with, wrote to, and understood one another, we loved and agreed with one another—or not]. To sign a "we," an "us," might thus already seem impossible, far too weighty or too light, always illegitimate among the living. And how much more so in the case of a survivor speaking of his friend? Unless a certain experience of "surviving" is able to give *us,* beyond life and death, what it alone can give, and give to the "we," yes [*oui*], its first vocation, its meaning or its origin. Perhaps its thought, *thinking* itself.

When, again at the last minute, I was asked about a title for this paper, I was roaming about the French and English words "we," *"nous,"* *"oui, nous,"* but someone inside me could not stop, and no doubt did not want to stop, this movement. It was impossible to endorse the strict authority exhibited by every title, even one made up of only two words, for example, *"oui, nous,"* "yes, we." I shall not propose any title here. I have

The title was chosen after the talk was first given; it was originally delivered without a title. The paper was first delivered at the Collège International de Philosophie in Paris in March 1999, and then again, after some minor modifications, in October 1999 at Emory University in Atlanta. Translated by Boris Belay and revised by Pascale-Anne Brault and Michel Naas for this volume. First French publication, *Jean-François Lyotard: L'exercice du différend,* ed. Dolorès Lyotard, Jean-Claude Milnee, and Gérald Sfez (Paris: Presses Universitaires de France, 2001), 169–96.

none to propose. But you are well aware that the *"nous,"* the "we," was one of the most serious stakes of Jean-François Lyotard's thought, particularly in *The Differend.* Let us make as if, for us, the title had to be missing, even if "Lyotard and *Us,"* for instance, would have perhaps not been the most unjust phrase—a phrase to be risked, played out, or played off.

"There shall be no mourning [*il n'y aura pas de deuil*]," Jean-François Lyotard once wrote.

This was about ten years ago.

I would never dare say, despite a couple of indications to be given in a moment, that he wrote this phrase for me. But it is certain that he addressed it to us.

That day, in the singular place where he published this phrase, he was pretending without pretending. The place was a philosophy journal. Perhaps he was then pretending to pretend. He was both pretending to address me and pretending to address some other, indeed any other. Perhaps you, perhaps us. Nobody will ever be able to ascertain this beyond a doubt. It was *as if,* in addressing me, he were addressing some other, or as if, in addressing no one in particular, he were also confiding to me: "there shall be no mourning."

He thus wrote what had to be written, and in the way it had to be written, for the identity of the destination to remain elusive, for the address to any particular addressee never to be, as we say, *proven,* not even by the one who signed it: neither publicly declared, nor obvious enough on its own, nor conclusively ascertained by means of a determining, theoretical judgment. In so doing, he asked publicly, in full light, and practically, but with reference to mourning, the question *of* the Enlightenment or the question *about* the Enlightenment, namely—in that Kantian space he tilled, furrowed, and sowed anew—the question of rational language and of its destination in the public space.

"There shall be no mourning" was thus like a drifting aphorism, a phrase given over, abandoned, exposed body and soul to absolute dispersion. If the tense of the verb in "there shall be no mourning" is clearly the future, nothing in what comes before or after the phrase allows one to decide whether the grammar of this future is that of a description or a prescription. Nothing allows one to decide between, on the one hand, the prediction, "it will be thus" (there will be no mourning, mourning will not take place, one will especially not plan for it, there will be no sign or work of mourning), and, on the other hand, the command or the prohibition of an implicit imperative, the prescription, "it must be thus," "there must be no mourning" (no sign or work of concerted mourning, of instituted commemoration), or even the normative wish, "it would be better if there were no mourning." For wouldn't the institution of mourning run the risk of securing the forgetting? Of protecting against memory instead of keeping it?

These hypotheses will remain forever open: is it a prediction or a prescription, an order, prohibition, or wish? What is more, all these "as if's" in these hypotheses come to be suspended through the detour of a negation. One must first pass through mourning, through the meaning of the word "mourning," enduring a mourning that befits its meaning, its essence, according to the very vision of what it will or must be, one must first cross this threshold and understand the meaning of what a mourning worthy of its name would or should be, in order to be able, afterward or thereupon, but in a second moment, to confer upon mourning or the meaning of mourning a negation, a "no" [*ne pas*]. As for mourning, there shall be none. There shall be *none of* it. And in the French syntax, "il *n'*y aura *pas de* deuil," the *de*, the partitive article, on the verge [*à l'article de*] of death and of mourning, is just as disturbing in the syntax of this extraordinary phrase: *of* mourning [*du deuil*], there shall be none, none of it, none at all, neither a lot nor a little, neither in whole nor in part— no matter how small the part; but also, *as for* mourning [*de deuil*], there shall be none, which means that mourning itself [*le* deuil] shall not be. No mourning, period.

But is there ever mourning itself, any mourning at all? Does such mourning exist? Is it ever present? Does it ever correspond to an *essence?* The very authority of the assertion "there shall be no mourning" can even, in its decontextualized isolation, lead one to think that Jean-François also meant to expose it to an analytical question. What is one saying in the end, what does one mean to say, when one asserts, in a suspended phrase, "There shall be no mourning"?

The impossibility of assigning any one single addressee to this phrase is at the same time the probably calculated impossibility of determining its context, including the meaning or the referent of the statement—which, in fact, *earlier* than a discourse, *before* being a statement, forms and leaves a trace. It is the impossibility of describing a context whose borders would be secure. No border is given, no shore [*rive*] at which to arrive or to allow this phrase to arrive. Later, I will explain what the apparent or manifest context was for this discreet but public and published declaration. Yet, even as I give further surface information about the subject, the context will be far from saturated, far from saturable, secure on all its borders.

And so let us dream: "There shall be no mourning" could have been an apocalyptic repetition, the hidden or playful citation of John's

Apocalypse; "ultra non erit . . . luctus, ouk estai eti . . . penthos": "God shall wipe all tears from their eyes. Death shall be no more. Neither mourning, nor cries nor pain shall be, for the first universe [the first things of the world] has vanished [*quia prima abierunt, oti ta prota apelthan*]." This echo of the Apocalypse is infinitely far from exhausting Jean-François Lyotard's words, but it cannot but accompany, like a precursive double, like an elusive memory, at once clandestine and visionary, this "there shall be no mourning." It could be said that this spectral echo roams about like a thief of the Apocalypse; it conspires in the exhalation of this phrase, comes back to haunt our reading, respires or breathes in advance—like the aura of this "there shall be [*aura*] no mourning," which Jean-François will have [*aura*] nonetheless signed, he alone.

Earlier, I ventured the hypothesis, itself uncertain, that this "there shall be no mourning" may not be a constative but a normative or prescriptive phrase. Yet normative and prescriptive are not the same thing. *The Differend* offers us the means to distinguish them.[1] Speaking about the "We" after Auschwitz, Jean-François insists once more on the heterogeneity of phrases, and particularly on the subtle difference between a normative phrase and a prescriptive one. Whereas the normative phrase "resembles a performative" and in itself, by itself, in its immanence, "effectuates the legitimation of the obligation by formulating it," the prescriptive phrase requires another phrase, a further one. This further phrase is left to the addressee, the reader in this case; it is left to him or her, and thus to us here, to take it up or link on, even if it is, as is said elsewhere, with a "last phrase." Jean-François continues: "That is why it is customary to say that the obligation entails the freedom of the one who is obligated." And he adds—and I imagine him smiling mischievously as he wrote this remark about the freedom of the one obligated, playing with quotation marks—"This is a 'grammatical remark,' one that bears upon the mode of linking called forth by the ethical phrase." If the ethical phrase "there shall be no mourning" is taken as an obligation, it thus implies, in a quasi-grammatical way, that another phrase coming from an addressee responds to it. A phrase already called for in advance.

1.   Jean-François Lyotard, *The Differend: Phrases in Dispute,* trans. Georges Van Den Abbeele (Minneapolis: University of Minnesota Press, 1988), 99 (hereafter abbreviated as *D*). [Georges Van Den Abbeele's translation of *The Differend* has, with just a couple of minor modifications, been used throughout here, and his translation of most key Lyotardian terms retained. For example, the French "*phrase*" is translated throughout here as "phrase" rather than "sentence." See Van Den Abbeele's justification of this choice on 194.—*Trans.*]

I would have followed this last recommendation, let myself be led by such an "obligation," had the phrase "there shall be no mourning" been determinable as a constative, normative, *or* prescriptive phrase, or if it had been possible, by either internal or external means, to identify its addressee. Yet not only is this not the case, but this phrase, unlike any other example of normative or prescriptive phrases given by Jean-François Lyotard, contains no personal pronoun. "There shall be no mourning" is an impersonal phrase, without an I or a you, whether singular or plural, without a we, he, she, or they. This grammar sets it apart from all the other examples given in *The Differend* in the course of the analysis just mentioned.

I thus did not know how to take this phrase, this phrase without a truly personal pronoun, when, about ten years ago, in an issue of *La revue philosophique,* Jean-François pretended to be addressing me by pretending not to address me—or anyone. As if there already had to be some mourning of the addressee of this phrase that says "there shall be no mourning." The reader must already go through mourning [*faire son deuil*] in his very desire to know to whom this phrase is destined or addressed, and above all, with respect to the possibility of being, he or she, or us, its addressee. Readability bears this mourning: a phrase can be readable, it must be able to become readable, up to a certain point, without the reader, he or she, or any other place of reading, occupying the ultimate position of addressee. This mourning provides the first chance and the terrible condition of all reading.

Today, I do not know any better, I still do not know, how to read this phrase, which I nevertheless cannot set aside. I cannot stop looking at it. It holds me. It will not let me go, even while it does not need me as addressee or inheritor, even while it is designed to pass right by me more quickly than it is to pass through me. I will thus turn round, turn back to these five words [seven in French] whose imbrication simply cannot be linked up, whose chain cannot be moored or fastened onto any constraining context, as if it risked—a risk calculated by Jean-François—being given over forever to dispersion, dissipation, or even to an undecidability such that the mourning it speaks of immediately turns back to the mute mumbling of those five [or seven] words. This phrase gets carried away all by itself. It holds itself back or withdraws; one can neither understand it nor be deaf to it, neither decipher it nor understand nothing of it, neither keep it nor lose it, neither in oneself nor outside oneself. It is this phrase itself, the phrasing of this unclassifiable phrase, drifting far from the categories analyzed even by its author, that one feels driven to go through mourning [*faire son deuil*], precisely at the point where this phrasing says to us: over me, there shall be no mourning. Over me, the phrase says, or at least the phrasing of the phrase says, you will not go into mourning. You will especially not organize mourning, and even less what is called the work of mourning. And of course the "no mourning," left to itself, can mean the perpetual impossibility of mourning, an inconsolability or irreparability that no work of mourning shall ever come to mend.

But the "no mourning" can also, by the same token, oppose testimony, attestation, protestation, or contestation, to the very idea of a testament, to the hypothesis of a mourning that always has, unfortunately, as we know, a negative side, at once laborious, guilt ridden and narcissistic, reactive and turned toward melancholy, if not envy. And when it borders on celebration, or *wake,* one risks the worst.

Despite all I have just said, and would wish to reaffirm, about the absence of a definite addressee for a phrase that was above all not addressed to me, in a context in which it may nevertheless have seemed to be, I could not completely avoid a temptation. The temptation to imagine Jean-François, one day in 1990, betting that the phrase "there shall be no mourning," which he wrote as he read it, and which I myself then read in a particular fashion in 1990, would one day, when the time came, be reread by one of the two of us (but which one?) both in the same way and differently, for oneself and in public. For this phrase was published. It remains public even if it is uncertain whether its public character exhausts it and whether there might not be a crypt forever buried and hidden within it. As if, published, it still remained absolutely secret, private, or clandestine—three values (secret, private, clandestine) that I would wish to distinguish carefully. I do not mean that this phrase is testamentary. I take all phrases to have a virtually testamentary character, but I would not rush to give this one, just because it says something about the death of the author, any specificity as a last will, as the instructions of a mortal being, even less of someone dying. Rather, it tells us something about the testamentary—perhaps that what the most faithful inheritance demands is the absence of any testament. In this respect, it says again or dictates another "there shall be no mourning." One would owe it to the loved one or the friend not to go through or even into mourning for them.

I am going to put aside, though just for a time, this strange phrase. It will thus keep all of its reserve. I set it aside for a moment with the odd feeling that it will have been, one day, entrusted to me, intensely, directly, immediately addressed to me, while leaving me with no right over it, especially not that of the addressee. He who signed it is still looking at me with an attention at once watchful and distracted.

Reading Jean-François Lyotard, rereading him so intensely today, I think I can discern a question that would retain a strange, uncanny, quality for him, a power that some might rush to call organizing, a force that I also believe to be radically disruptive. If I were to call it subversive, it would be not so as to take advantage of a facile word but so as to describe in its *tropic* literality (tropic, meaning turning, like the spiraling of a turn or a torment) and sketch out in its figural letter a movement that revolves, evolves, revolutionizes, overturns from the bottom up—as any subversion should. The effect of this question is not to radiate out infinitely from a center of thought but would instead be, if one insists on keeping close to a center, like a whirlwind, like a chasm open as a silent eye, like a *mute* glance, as Jean-François liked to say about music, an eye of silence, even as it summons speech and commands so many words that crowd about the opening of the mouth. Like the eye of a hurricane.

This question of such vertiginous force, this thought like the "eye of a hurricane," would not be the question of evil, not even of radical evil. Worse, it would be the question of the worst. A question that some may deem not only apocalyptic but altogether infernal. And the eye of the hurricane, the hyperbole of the worst, is probably not foreign, in its excessive motion, in its blustery violence, to what sucks down from below, making it turn upon itself, the phrase "there shall be no mourning." That there be no mourning—is that bad? Good? Better? Or is it even worse than mourning, like the mourning without mourning of mourning?

In at least two instances the thought of the worst is mentioned, both times quickly, in *The Differend*. First, through a quotation of Adorno: "In the camps death has a novel horror; since Auschwitz, fearing death means fearing something worse than death" (*D*, 88). I emphasize the word "worse," a comparative that can so easily turn into a hyperbolic superlative. There is worse than radical evil, but there is nothing worse than the worst. There would thus be something worse than death, or at least an experience that, in going further than death and doing more harm than it, would be disproportionate to what is too easily granted just after death, namely, mourning. A little further, the worse appears a second time, once again in relation to the survivors of Auschwitz, to the impossibility of bearing witness, of saying "we," of speaking in the "first person plural." Jean-François Lyotard wonders: "Would this be a case of a dispersion worse than the diaspora, the dispersion of phrases?" (*D*, 98). This would seem to imply that the dispersion of the diaspora is only half-bad; in fact, it is barely a dispersion—and dispersion in itself is not absolute evil. As soon as it receives a proper name, indeed a national name, this historical name, the *diaspora,* interrupts absolute dispersion. The Jews of the diaspora form, or at least think they form, a community of the diaspora; they are gathered together by this principle of dispersion, originary exile, the promise, the idea of a return, Jerusalem, if not Israel, and so on. The dispersion of phrases, however, would be an evil worse than evil since what these phrases forever lack—and this is the point of *The Differend*—is the very horizon of a consensual meaning, of a translatability, of a possible "to translate" (I use the infinitive form here for reasons that will become clear in a moment). What is lacking in this dispersion of phrases, in this evil worse than evil, is the horizon, or even the hope, of their very dispersion ever receiving a common meaning. What is inscribed in this worse, apparently, is the differend as everlasting difference between the wrong and the litigation, for example. But, as we will see, there may be something worse yet than this worse.

It is not certain that the "worse" is actually some thing, that it ever appears, is ever presently present, essentially, substantially, like something that "is." It is thus uncertain whether it can be approached by means of an ontological question. Nevertheless, I shall not refrain from asking, so as to pretend to begin: What is the worse, the worst? Is there an essence of the worst? And does it mean anything else, and worse, than evil?[2]

I would first like, for reasons I shall give later, to surround this old word *deuil,* "mourning," with a few phrases.

As if I were citing it—but I just cited it and I will cite it again.

There come moments when, as *mourning* demands [*deuil oblige*], one feels obligated to declare one's debts. We feel it our duty to duty to say what we owe to the friend. Yet being conscious of such a duty may seem unbearable and inadmissible. Unbearable for me, as I believe it would have also been for Jean-François Lyotard. Unbearable, no doubt, because unworthy of the very thing it means to give itself to unconditionally, the unconditional perhaps always having to endure the trial of death.[3] Inadmissible, not because one would have problems recognizing one's

---

2.   I once heard my friend Serge Margel ask a similar question, but in the context of another space of thinking and set of references. See his essay "Les dénominations orphiques de la survivance: Derrida et la question du pire," in *L'animal autobiographique,* ed. Marie-Louise Mallet (Paris: Galilée, 1999), 441–68.

3.   Outline of the argument I was not able to spell out during the conference: death obligates; it would thus be the other original name of absolute obligation. Unconditional engagement binds only to the one who ("who" rather than "what"), from the place of death, becomes at once the absent origin and the destination of the absolute, unconditional, unnegotiable obligation, beyond any transaction. Absence without return would thus open onto the unconditional. Terrifying. Terror. This would be the meaning of "God is dead," the association of the name of God, as the place of the unconditional, with death. A desperate conclusion, perhaps: the unconditional (which I distinguish here from the sovereign, even if the distinction remains improbable) signifies the death

debts or one's duty as indebted, but simply because in declaring these debts in such a manner, particularly when time is limited, one might seem to be putting an end to them, calculating what they amount to, pretending then to be able to recount them, to measure and thus limit them, or more seriously still, to be able to settle them in the very act of exposing them. The mere recognition of a debt already tends toward its cancellation in a denial. The recognizing, grateful [*reconnaissante*] consciousness, all consciousness in fact, perhaps falls into such sacrificial denial: consciousness in general is perhaps the sacrificial and bereaved denial of the sacrifice it mourns. This may be why there must not be—why there shall be—no mourning.

I also wanted, for reasons that should become clear later, to surround the old word *garder,* "to keep," with a phrase.

As if I were citing it—and I will cite it.

For I know that the debt that binds me to Jean-François Lyotard is in some sense incalculable; I am conscious of this and want it thus. I reaffirm it unconditionally, all the while wondering in a sort of despair why an unconditional engagement binds only at death, or to death, to the one to whom death has come, as if the unconditional still depended on absolute death, if there were such a thing, death without mourning: another interpretation of "there shall be no mourning." I will thus not even begin to give an account of this debt, to give an accounting of it, whether with respect to friendship or to philosophy, or to that which, linking friendship to philosophy, will have *kept us* [*gardés*] together, Jean-François and me (kept us together without synchrony, symmetry, or reciprocity, according to a reaffirmed dispersion), in so many places and so many times that I cannot even begin to circumscribe them. I am not able here, relying on my own memory, to recall all the places, occasions, people, texts, thoughts, and words that, whether we recognized it or not, will have *kept* us together, to this day, together apart, together dispersed into the night, together invisible to one another, to the point that this being-together is no longer assured, even though we were sure of it, I am sure of it, *we* were together [*ensemble*]. We were sure of it, but sure with what was neither an assurance nor the surety of some certainty nor even a common accord [*ensemble*]. (One is never *ensemble,* never together, in an *ensemble,* in a group, gathering, whole or set, for the *ensemble,* the whole, the totality

---

of the dead, death without mourning: there shall be no mourning. One is under an unconditional obligation only toward the dead. One can always negotiate conditions with the living. Upon death, there is a rupture of symmetry: truth, the impossibility of pretending anymore. But does one ever really deal with the dead? Who could swear to it? The impossible death perhaps means that what is living conditions everything.

that is named by this word, constitutes the first destruction of what the adverb *ensemble* might mean: to be *ensemble,* it is absolutely necessary not to be gathered into any sort of *ensemble.*) But sure of being together outside any nameable *ensemble, we* were so, even before having decided upon it, and sure of it with a *faith* [*foi*], a sort of faith, over which we were perhaps together in accord, and in accordance with which we went well together. Yes, a faith, because Jean-François, like all those I like to call my best friends, also remains for me, in a certain way, forever unknown and infinitely secret.

For reasons that should become clear later, I have just surrounded the old word *foi,* "faith," with a few phrases.

As if I were citing it—and I will cite it.

In order to free myself, and you as well, from the narcissistic pathos that such a situation, the exhibition of such a "we," summons up, I was dreaming of being capable at last of another approach. I was dreaming of escaping genres in general, particularly two genres of discourse—and two unbearable, unbearably presumptuous ways of saying "we." First, I wanted to avoid the expected homage to Jean-François Lyotard's thought and oeuvre, an homage taking the form of a philosophical contribution fit for one of the numerous conferences in which *we* took part together, Jean-François and I, in so many places, cities, and countries (and right here, at the Collège International de Philosophie, a place that remains so dear to me for having been, since its origin, desired, inhabited, shared *with him,* as was also the case for other, more faraway places, for example, a particular house on the Pacific Wall). I really do not feel up today to such an homage in the form of a philosophical contribution, and Lyotard's oeuvre certainly does not need me for that. But I also wanted to stay away from an homage in the form of a personal testimony, which always tends toward reappropriation and always risks giving in to an indecent way of saying "we," or worse, "me," when precisely my first wish is to let Jean-François speak, to read and cite him, him alone, standing back without, however, leaving him alone as he is left to speak, since this would amount to another way of abandoning him. A double injunction, then, contradictory and unforgiving. How to leave him alone without abandoning him? How, then, without further betrayal, to disavow the act of narcissistic remembrance, so full of memories to cry over [*pleurer*] or to make us cry [*faire pleurer*]? I have just surrounded these words *pleurer* and *faire pleurer,* "to cry" and "to make cry," for reasons that will become clear later.

As if I were citing them—and I will cite them.

Set on giving in to neither of these two genres, neither of these two "we's," in a hurry to get away from them, knowing nevertheless that both will catch up with me at every instant, resigned to struggle with this fate, to fail before it, so as at least to understand it, if not think it, I had at first considered taking up again a conversation *with* Jean-François, addressing him as if he were here. For let me emphasize that it is *as if* he were here, in me, close to me, in his name, without fooling myself or anyone else in the least with this "as if," bearing in mind that he is not here and that, despite the different modalities, qualities, and necessities of these two incompatible but equally irrefutable propositions (he is here and he is not here, in his name and beyond his name) there is no possible transaction. And what I would have wished at once to discover and invent was the most just language, the most refined, beyond the concept, so as to do even more than describe or analyze without concession, so as to speak as concretely and tangibly as possible of the fact that Jean-François is here, that he speaks to us, sees us, hears us, answers us, and that we can know this, feel it, and say it without impugning any truth of what is called life, death, presence, or absence. And nothing attests to this better than the fact that I want to speak or address myself *to* him also, here, not knowing whether I should address him with the formal *vous,* as I always did, or with the informal *tu*—which will take me some time yet.

Later, perhaps.

This very time, this future, perhaps announces the attestation of which I am speaking. And the question I ask myself trembling, following him, concerns a certain right, always improbable, resistant to proof if not to faith—a certain right to say "we." As we will hear, Jean-François sketches a sort of answer to this question, but it is neither easy nor given in advance.

So I had thought about taking up an interrupted conversation, the strangest of all. In fact, all our conversations were odd and cut short, for all conversations are finite, nothing being less infinite than a conversation, and that is why one is never finished with the interruption of conversations, or, as he preferred to call them, "discussions." I had thus thought about pursuing, as if within myself but taking you as witnesses, a conversation that had ended not with Jean-François's death but well before, for reasons none other than those that knock the wind out of all finite speech. I thought I could take up this thread again in order perhaps to declare, among so much many other debts, one debt that nobody would have considered, not even Jean-François, not even myself, in truth, up until today. As for the many other debts that link us, you do not need me to declare them; they are readable in published texts.

I thus wanted to follow a thread of memory—and a particular rec-ollection waiting for what could, one day to come, come to memory. What guided me, more or less obscurely, was an interweaving of motifs whose economy I came to see as necessary when most of the threads of the phrase "there shall be no mourning" appeared woven together silently within it. First, the thread of singularity, of the event and of the destination—of the "to whom it happens." Next, the thread of repetition, that is, of the intrinsic iterability of the phrase, which divides the destination, suspends it on the trace between presence and absence, beyond both, an iterability that, in dividing its destination, splits singularity: as soon as a phrase is iterable, and it is so right away, it can break loose from its context and lose the singularity of its destined addressee. A technical machinery comes in advance to strip it of the unicity of the occurrence and the destination. The tangled web of these threads (the machine, repetition, chance, and the loss of destinal singularity) is precisely what I would like to entrust to you along with this recollection. An easier choice, more cheerful, more modest, more in keeping with the adolescent modesty that always marked, and from both sides, our friendship. This modesty was characterized by a trait that was not in fact so assured, and left open its destinal singularity. I am speaking of the fact that, in a circle of old friends (in particular in the Collège International de Philosophie), where almost everyone addressed one another with the friendly or familiar *tu* form, we always refrained from this way of speaking by a sort of unspoken agreement. Whereas we both said *tu* to most of our common friends, who had been doing so among themselves, as well as with us, for a long time (such was the case, for example, with Philippe Lacoue-Labarthe and Jean-Luc Nancy, though there were many others), Jean-François and I, for decades, did not quite avoid but were careful *not to say "tu" to one another.* This could have suggested something more than the inherent difficulty I have using this form of address, much more so, to be sure, than Jean-François. It could have simply implied a polite distance, perhaps even a sort of neutralization of intimate singularity, of private intimacy, by means of the proper, plural quasi-generality of the formal *vous.* But this was not the case; if it somehow indicated a respect that also keeps a respectful distance, the exceptional character of this *vous* gave it a sort of transgressive value, like the use of a secret code reserved only for us. In fact one day, somebody in the Collège expressed their surprise about this in front of us ("How is it that after so many years you still say *vous* to one another; no one else here does that!"—or something to that effect). I can still hear Jean-François, who was the first to answer, demurring with that smile I would like to imitate and that you all know so well, speaking what I took right away to be a truth, grateful that he saw it so well and stated it so perfectly: "No, he said, let us keep this; this *vous* belongs solely to us, it is our sign of recognition, our secret language." And I approved in silence. Henceforth, it was as if the *vous* between us had become an elective privilege: "we reserve ourselves the *vous,* that's what we do, we say *vous* to one another; it is our shared anachronism, our exception from time." From then on, this *vous* between us belonged to another language, as if it marked the passage, through a kind of grammatical contraband, in contravention of customary practices, to the idiomatic sign, the *shibboleth* of a hidden intimacy, one that would be clandestine, coded, held back, discreetly held in reserve, held in silence [*tue*].

Among so many other signs of this happy complicity, signs that spoke in silence like a series of winks, I would have liked to recall the moments when Jean-François made fun of me, feigning to take on and imitate the French-Algerian accent and gestures he pretended to recognize in me, precisely because, as you know, he too had his Algerian moment. And I learned rather late about the strange love he shared with me for someone whom I always tend to place back in his native Algeria: Saint Augustine. We were, in the time of these two memories, according to an anachronism of some fifteen centuries, Algerian compatriots of sorts by relation.

If I recall what was said and left unsaid, silenced [*tu*], in this unsaid *tu,* it is because the text from which I earlier drew the phrase "there shall be no mourning" puts center stage what had gone on behind the scenes between this *tu* and *vous.* The phrase appears in the section "Mourning" of a text entitled "Translator's Notes," in a special issue of a journal that was, as they say—dare I say it?—"devoted" to me.[4] In it, Jean-François plays at responding to texts that I had, upon his request, written in 1984 for the exhibition *Les immatériaux.*

Let me simply recall, rather than saying more about the calculated randomness of this exhibition, the chance Jean-François's invitation presented me, namely, the wonderful machinations that led me to learn to use, despite my previous reluctance, a word processor, which I have depended upon ever since. Instead of giving grand narratives about major debts, I prefer to speak of this apparently minor debt that Jean-François perhaps knew nothing about, just as I myself never knew whether he used a typewriter or a computer. This debt would appear to be merely technical

4. *Revue philosophique de la France et de l'étranger,* no. 2, April—June 1990, special issue "Derrida," ed. Catherine Malabou. Translations are modified from "Translator's Notes," trans. Roland-François Lack, in *Pli: The Warwick Journal of Philosophy* 6 (summer 1997): 51–57 (hereafter abbreviated as *T*).

or mechanical, but because of the relationship between these techno-machinations and the effacement of singularity and, thus, of destinal unicity, its essential link will soon become clear with the phrase I had to begin with, the phrase that surrounded and besieged me in advance: "there shall be no mourning." I am thus returning to the important question of *tu*-saying. We never used, as I said, the *tu* form in speaking with one another, but in the serial text I had written for *Les immatériaux* (which consisted of defining and organizing in a computer network, through a more or less virtual discussion on early Olivetti computers among Jean-François's twenty-six guests, a series of words, motifs, concepts selected by Jean-François, the final result being the text later published under the title *Epreuves d'écriture*), I myself had played with a *tu* devoid of any assignable addressee, leaving the chance reader without the possibility of deciding whether the *tu* singularly addressed the receiving or reading position, that is, whoever, in the public space of publication, happened to read it, or, rather, and this is altogether different, altogether other, some particular private, if not cryptic, addressee. The point of all these both sophisticated and naive procedures was, among others, to make tremble, and sometimes, at the limit, tremble with fear, the limit itself, all borders, particularly those between private and public, singular and general or universal, the intimate or inner realm and the outside, and so on. In so doing, I pretended to challenge whoever was addressed by this *tu to translate* the idiomatic phrasing of many of my phrases, to translate it into another language (interlinguistic translation, in Jacobson's terms), or into the same language (intralinguistic translation), or even into another system of signs (music or painting, for instance, intersemiotic translation). Accordingly, after a phrase I considered untranslatable, I would regularly add the infinitive form of the ironic command or the imperative challenge: "to translate." Now, it is this challenge (*to translate,* which, if my memory is correct, was actually one of the words in the selected vocabulary) that Jean-François pretended to take up some five or six years later, in the text from which I took the "there shall be no mourning." The text in its entirety, many of you know it well, I am sure, is thus entitled "Translator's Notes." In it, Jean-François plays seriously not at translating but at imagining the notes of a virtual translator. He does so under four subheadings, which I will only mention, leaving you to read these eight pages worthy of centuries of talmudic commentary. The four headings are "Déjouer" [To frustrate, foil, outmaneuver, evade, play off], "Encore" [Again, more, yet, although, still], "Toi" [You], and "Deuil" [Mourning]. And right from the first phrase of the first heading, right from the incipit, Jean-François plays, plays off, replays the great scene of the *tu* and the *vous,* of the being-to-you [*à tu*] and the being-yours [*à toi*]. He addresses *me* as *vous*. I assume—no doubt rather imprudently, for the reasons I mentioned—that he is playing at answering me and is pretending to address himself to me, for such is the law of the genre and the contractual agreement of this text. Right from the first phrase, then, he addresses me as *vous,* leaving for the two final parts of the text entitled "Translator's Notes" the passage to the *tu.* Here are the first phrases: "Your fear (you have left me the *vous,* for good measure, agreed) on the large and the small scale, of being made captive."

Before returning to the question of the worse, of the "worse than death," toward which all work of mourning tends (when the work of mourning seeks neither to save from death nor to deny it, but to save from a "worse than death"), I would like to follow in this eight-page text the trajectory leading from the first part, "Déjouer," to the fourth, "Deuil," through the second, "Encore," and third, "Toi." I will follow only its main outlines, for to do it justice would require an infinite analysis of the tight interplay of citations, quotation marks, responses, turns, and elliptical questions. Here, then, are but a few white pebbles to lead us from the scene of the *vous* and the *toi* to the scene of mourning, so that we might then come back to what *The Differend* will have already told us concerning a certain "we," one that is difficult to think, a certain "we" after Auschwitz, a "thinking we," a "we" that is neither the one related to what Lyotard calls "the beautiful death" nor the one that undergoes in Auschwitz what is, as he says, "worse than death." This "we," perhaps the last one, or the one before last, is neither that of the "beautiful death" nor worse than death, but—in a very particular sense of the word—a posthumous "we." In a passage I will read in a moment, Jean-François Lyotard says: "We only are 'we' posthumously."

My little white pebbles are only or mostly citations. I will cite Jean-François, and when he cites me in the citation as if playfully to add translation notes, I will make that little two-fingered gesture that mimics quotations marks. What comes between my little white pebbles (which you may think of as either those left by *le Petit Poucet* to mark his path,[5] or those left as tokens on graves by Central European Jews), I leave unspoken [*tu*]; that is, I leave it to you [*vous*] to read or reread on your own this extraordinary work of interwoven writing, this more-than-sublime text.

Four times, then—according to the rhythm he chose to divide these "Translator's Notes."

---

5.   As in Grimm's "Hansel and Gretel," *le Petit Poucet* drops pebbles to mark his path and so avoid becoming lost.—*Trans.*

1. *First time,* in "Déjouer," that of a *ductus,* one could say, or of *duction.* I select these lines, which already point, as it were—*between* the trans*duction* of translation [*traduction*] and se*duction*—to the passage from the *vous* to the *tu,* and, later, from a certain *tu* to a certain *nous.*

He writes:

> The untranslatable leaves something to "transduce," something still to be translated. "That we are expecting one thing or another, on arrival" is not "the essential thing," it is "that we are awaiting each other, you and I, on arrival." Not in the language of arrival, but in "the language of our country." (I defer this "you and I.") To await one another: reflexive, transitive? How to translate this out-maneuvering [*dé-jeu*]? In the language in which it is written. You resist capture thanks only to love of the language that captivates. Since language captures by means of its amphibologies, you mark them. In order to seduce language. (*T*, 51)

2. The *second time* would be time proper, the time of time. Without waiting any longer for the passage to the singular and familiar, to the *toi,* this time announces the passage in what I would call a more "cutting" manner. I excerpt a few lines from "Encore," the title of this second time, by cutting even more brutally. By cutting, though you are going to hear a certain "with you and me it's decisive, cutting" at the end. It decides resolutely with respect to a certain "we" or "us" produced by the mirror that Jean-François claims to hold up before "us":

> You give me your voice, your vote (*Voix*). But you have nothing to give. Except suspense. I try suspense. . . . You will smile. Yet another one who will have gotten it wrong. You watch me watching your gaze in the mirror I hold up before us (*Miroir*). . . . I run on time to Time to see if your desire to bend the matrix (to make it submit?) itself lacks time. . . . and yet you declare your "sentiment," your revolt or your ruse: there is simultaneity, beyond all temporal deferrals. There is some "full speed," some quasi-infinite speed, creating synchronies, political contemporaneities, for example, even "ignoble" ones, but above all there is the reprieved, absolute "at the same time" of a being-together outside the network, as "dyad," which eludes any third party (*Miroir*). That is "*toi*" [you]; I'll come back to this.
>
> The importance of the telephone for this speed. . . . loving caress, diligent too. I wonder whether full speed, your "hollow certainty" (*Simultanéité*) of possible simultaneity, so to speak delivered from *différance,* spirited away from every "*de*"-term, is to be

taken as a free-ness or frankness, a freedom at least expected by the captive of delays and postponements, or else to be taken as a forcing of desire by desire itself, the effacing of its *encore,* a ruse of patience simulating absolute impatience. Resolution. It would decide, cut. With you and me, it's decisive, cutting. (*T*, 53)

3. Entitled "Toi" [You], the *third time* thus cuts; and if its title is, directly, if I may say so, *toi,* it does all it can to avoid, as you will hear, a "thesis on the *toi.*" In a few lines that I should not have the right to isolate in this way, I wish to underscore the theme of simulation and simulacra, the question of right ("the right to address one another as *toi*"), and above all the appearance of a "we" as "posthumous we," a phrase that should, I believe, not only make us hear the testamentary postmortem but inhale [*humer*] in advance the humus, the soil, the earth, the humid earth, humility, the human and the inhuman, the inhumed, which will resonate at the end of the text, in what will be the fourth time and last act. Jean-François writes:

> Frankness or simulation: the opposition must be played off [*déjouer*] against itself. If we simulate suffering it is because we suffer from the infinite possibility of simulation (*Simulation*). . . . I mean: none of these partners could be you [*toi*]. "Do we have the right to address one another as *toi?*" (*Droit*). . . . You are the one who signs, only you. "These words that I address only to you but that you sign, of which you are the addressee, the address-she, or as he would say: the mother" (*Sens*). . . . With you, "I want to take my time, all my time" (*Vitesse*), you [*toi*] who "give me time and tell me what it's like out at the time [*le temps qu'il fait*], *if you see what I mean* [in English in original]" (*Temps*).
>
> There is immortality between you and me, whom we shall see die (*Immortalité*). To translate. But you were translating yourself(?) "The essential thing [is] that we expect, you and I, the arrival, that we await one another, you and I, upon arrival, in the language of our country" (*Traduire*). To translate, again. I am trying. But I'm afraid of forcing, of forcing you and forcing me into a thesis of and on the *toi.* . . . "We shall see us die." You will see me and I will see you die. Or, dying will come [*arrivera*] to the two of us together, and we will know it together. Coming ashore [*La rive*] . . . (*T,* 53–54)

And later (but I suffer so much at not being able, for lack of time, to read everything, rushing as I must toward a certain posthumous "we"):

I pause at this *toi et moi,* "you and me," which you dissect . . . since
the body that's yours and the body that's mine, at which neither
you nor I can arrive, we will not get there, we will arrive at the
other body. It would be another country. Sunk in darkness? To
translate. Where we won't see each other, or ourselves, or the two
of us together. Where we will only see each other, or ourselves,
sinking, being blinded, un-writing, delivered up to translators
and those who guide across borders. We are "ourselves," or "we,"
only posthumously. You and I await it, or ourselves, there. Not
that language will ever sink or go under. It is on the boat of every
transit. But it is its image in me. . . . You sign this desire, with my
signature? (*T,* 55)

4. It is in the last breath of this text, in the *fourth time,* entitled
"Mourning," that one can find at once the words I said I wanted to
cite—"mourning," "keep," "cry," "faith"—and the phrase that is now
slightly more, but still not totally, recontextualizable, "there shall be no
mourning," which keeps silent [*se tait*], mute, and keeps it down [*se terre*]
between humus, inhuman, and inhumed. I tear a few more strains from
this mourning lament. Jean-François writes:

"A sign from you, my everyday tongue. What I cry for. To translate" (*Signe*). Already translated: you make me cry, I cry after
you, I shall always cry, right up to the arrival. There shall be no
mourning. Memory will be preserved. "My luck: that the only form
of unhappiness would be to lose, not to preserve, memory." . . .
It is not for this supposed loss that I cry, but for and after your
presence, language, never deserted. Which will always have happened as long as I write, out of place. This gap gives space and
time for tears. . . . You are asked: "We shall efface the harm." The
harm done by writing. But damages call only for litigation and
a decision, not forgiveness, which escapes rules and settlements.
Forgiveness would forgive only the wrong. But it is not a gesture
and makes no gestures. Forgiveness "has already let it [the wrong]
of itself efface itself: what I call writing." This is why there is no
proof of it. As I write, you do me wrong and I forgive you, but
it will never be proven, not even by my tears. As you haunt my
writing, without holiness asking anything, I do you wrong. Do
you forgive me? Who will prove it? Mute. . . . That is why there
is this gap, "melancholy," a wrong exceeding declared forgiveness,
consuming and consummating itself in writing. Of which you have
no need. That is why mourning is never lifted, the fire never put

out. It is vain to count on acquitting yourself of your unseizability
through incineration . . . through the consumption of writing in an
immediate fire and by a signature in cinders. To satirize, to singe
this signarizing [*singerie de cette signerie*]. Cinders are still matter.
I sign in humus. Of the inhuman, I bear witness inhumed. False
witnesses. "I love only faith, or rather, in faith, its irreligious trial."
(*T,* 55–56)

I still do not know how to interpret these words. I do not know how
to identify them through, in, and despite the dispersion of phrases that he
claims to be worse than a diaspora. My fragmentary citations will have
only made things worse. I do not know how to interpret "there shall be no
mourning," followed at a distance by the phrase "that is why mourning is
never lifted, the fire never put out." The impossibility of interpreting, of
deciding about or disposing of these phrases no doubt comes from their
radical, irreversible dispersion, as well as from their forever undetermined
addressee, whether public or not.

These "Translator's Notes" have the remarkable status of a *response.*
They wish to breathe or exude the "yes" [*oui*] of a response that appeals
to a certain "we" [*nous*], a response with, however, no assignable or
demonstrable addressee. And yet I do not consider this impossibility of
interpreting, which is not a hermeneutical impotence, to be an evil. It is the
very chance of reading. Beyond all destination, it bespeaks the very destiny
or fate of mourning. It offers this destiny over to *thinking,* specifically to
thinking, if that is possible, better than an interpretative decision or an
assignable destination could have.

For if, to reassure myself in this deciphering, I were to seek some
help from *The Differend,* written a decade before these "Translator's
Notes," which are themselves about a decade old, I would be able to
find there all the necessary premises for a thinking of this destiny without
destination. And particularly when it is a question of us, of you and I. *The
Differend* already put to work the very language of these "Translator's
Notes," thus confirming yet again that these *Notes,* and their "there
shall be no mourning," cannot be confined to their context or apparent
destination.

Hence, in closing, let me come back to the three occurrences of the
"worse" I mentioned earlier:

1. Adorno's phrase: "since Auschwitz, fearing death means fearing something worse than death" (*D,* 88).
2. Lyotard's phrase some thirteen pages later, which, commenting upon
   Adorno's phrase, says of the death sentence at Auschwitz: "This death

must therefore be killed, and that is what is worse than death. For, if death can be exterminated, it is because there is nothing to kill. Not even the name Jew" (*D*, 101).

3. And between these two occurrences, this third one: "Would this be a case of a dispersion worse than the diaspora, the dispersion of phrases?" (*D*, 98). There is indeed another name for the worse, for the "worse than death." And when, while preparing for this gathering, I read the title chosen by Jean-Luc Nancy, "From One End to the Infinite" [*D'une fin à l'infini*], I assumed that he would cite the following phrase, which I simply recall here without comment: "What makes death not yet the worst is its being not *the* end but only the end of the finite and the revelation of the infinite. Worse than this magical death would be a death without reversal, an end which is simply the end, including the end of the infinite" (*D*, 89).

In all these pages, which are also powerful readings of Hegel and Adorno, but above all, meditations on Auschwitz, on the impossible possibility of bearing witness, on survival and the "we," a "we" that may go beyond, as Lyotard says so well, what he calls a "transcendental illusion" for which the "we" would be a "vehicle" (*D*, 99), the law of the magical death, that is, the "beautiful death," is opposed to the *exception* of Auschwitz.

In both cases, I will venture to say, there is no—there shall be no—mourning. But for diametrically opposed reasons. What Lyotard calls the "beautiful death" or the "magical death" is the one that gets meaning, and gets it as an order given to an addressee. It is a beautiful death because the order thus given to a dying or mortal addressee, the verdict addressed to him, signifies to him that this death has meaning because it is *preferable*, and since it is preferable, it is, in sum, as if it did not take place and thus can do without mourning. This is the case, Lyotard says, when the private authority of the family, the political authority of the state or the party, the authority of religion, gives its members, that is, its identifiable addressees, the order to die the preferable death, the order to prefer death: "Die rather than escape" (Socrates in prison) (in the background are the analyses of the *Apology* and the *Menexenus* in the "Plato Notice," often with reference to Nicole Loraux's work); "Die rather than be enslaved" (the Paris Commune); "Die rather than be defeated" (Thermopylae, Stalingrad).

This beautiful death does not, in the end, I would say, take place, insofar as it claims to make sense, to remain meaningful, oriented by an end that goes beyond it, and thus by an economy, even if it is an economy of sacrifice: "Die with a view to . . . ," and you shall not die. And Lyotard concludes: "Such is the Athenian 'beautiful death,' the exchange of the finite for the infinite, of the *eschaton* for the *telos:* the *Die in order not to die*" (*D*, 100).

But "this is not the case for 'Auschwitz'" (*D*, 100), Lyotard notes, taking pains—and with very good reason—to put quotation marks around this name that also names the "extinction of that name" (*D*, 101), but which of course—and this is an enormous problem that I must leave open here—can play its role of absolute exception only if it loses the quotation marks that make it a metonymical or exemplary name, and as such not exceptional, able to stand in for other possible "Auschwitzes." At any rate, "Auschwitz" would be the exception to the law of the "beautiful death." This is indicated in section 157, whose title is in fact "Exception," and which begins: "'Auschwitz' is the forbiddance of the beautiful death" (*D*, 100). It is an exception first of all because the victim is not the addressee of the order—and let me note in passing that all the deaths in question here are deaths following an order, "Die," which means that these deaths (whether beautiful of not) are never, as one says of illnesses, natural— supposing that an illness is ever natural. The choice here, if I may use this word precisely where there is no longer a choice, is between "Die, I decree it" and "That s/he die, I decree it" or "That I die, s/he decrees it" (*D*, 100). Both of these deaths, which are no more natural than any other, are also forms of putting to death, ordered deaths, whether we are talking about Socrates, Athenian soldiers, World War II, or Auschwitz. But between these two deaths, these two "Die's," the heterogeneity is absolute, so that "Auschwitz" cannot, except through an abuse of rhetoric, be turned into a "beautiful death," or a sacrificial holocaust in which the Jewish people comes to replace Isaac on Mount Moriah. "Rhetoric" is the word Lyotard uses in his analysis of these terrifying hypotheses in the paragraphs about Abraham (161, 170), which I wish I could have meditated upon at greater length.

In all these pages on the *Result,* on the "after Auschwitz," on the witness, the third party, the survivor, on the enormous question of the "we," on the two "Die's," the two orders of dying and the two orders that say "Die," that of the beautiful death and that of "Auschwitz," mourning never comes up. "Mourning" never appears, and the word "mourning" has no grounds for appearing. As if the phrase "there shall be no mourning" had already been heard, and taken into account, in its most extreme consequences. I wouldn't swear that the word "mourning" never appears in the whole book, but if it does, it is not in the passages dealing with death, the beautiful death, or the death that is worse than death. The word and concept "death" appear twice in the index ("death," "beautiful death"), but "mourning" does not appear at all. If there are no grounds for mourning, if there are no grounds for having to go through mourning these two ordered deaths, it is for diametrically opposed reasons. In the "beautiful death," it is because death has meaning: it brings to fulfillment a life full of meaning; this death gets over itself, overtakes or sublates itself, in this meaning. In the case of "Auschwitz," on the contrary, "worse than death," it is the extinction of the very name that forbids mourning, given that this murder of the name constitutes the very meaning of the order "die," or "that he die," or even "that I die." In both of these orders, the "there shall be no mourning" is implicitly so radical that the word "mourning" does not even need to be uttered. Which would seem to suggest that whenever the word is uttered we are perhaps—we are no doubt—dealing with another case, where mourning is at least possible enough to be averted by the "there shall be no mourning."

I would like to inscribe here, as a programmatic indication of a reflection to come, a reference to two of Jean-François Lyotard's remarks, apparently quite distant from one another (*D*, 106, 56), which, without referring to mourning, give us a great deal to think about the empty place left to mourning in *The Differend* and about what is worse than death. It is as if—or at least this will be the hypothesis of my reading—mourning implied either a litigation concerning damages, or else some kind of wrong, that is, some differend. Without litigation or differend, there can be no mourning. In a way, then, what is worse than death, as well as non-mourning, is that there *not even be a differend*. As if what is "worse than death" were what comes, if not to erase, at least to marginalize or subordinate the nevertheless unerasable limit between a wrong and damages, differend and litigation: an alternative or alternation that, as you know, marks the rhythm, pulse, and heartbeat of this great book, *The Differend*.

I take the risk of sketching this hypothesis about mourning based on what Lyotard himself says, without mentioning mourning, about a certain duel, or even divorce, between "Auschwitz" and "Israel." In establishing damages that can be repaired, in thinking that it can translate the wrong into damages and the differend into a litigation, which is and remains impossible, it is as if Israel had wished to go through mourning. The state of Israel would have sought to signify the mourning of Auschwitz, precisely there where mourning has no meaning. All I can do here is juxtapose these two series of statements from *The Differend*:

1. First, "Auschwitz":

> Between the SS and the Jew there is *not even* a differend, because
> there is not even a common idiom (that of a tribunal) in which

damages could at least be formulated, be they in place of a wrong. Thus there is no need of a trial, not even a parodic one. (This is not the case with the communists.) The Jewish phrase has not taken place. (*D*, 106; I emphasize "not even")

2. Now Israel, the state that bears or takes this name, signifying something like the mournful mis-understanding of this truth, namely, the absence of a common idiom and the impossibility of translating a wrong into damages. Some fifty pages earlier, we read:

> By forming the State of Israel, the survivors transformed the wrong into damages and the differend into a litigation. By beginning to speak in the common idiom of public international law and of authorized politics, they put an end to the silence to which they had been condemned. But the reality of the wrong suffered at Auschwitz [no quotation marks here] before the foundation of this state remained and remains to be established, and it cannot be established because it is in the nature of a wrong not to be established by consensus. (*D*, 56)

I now want to recall something obvious throughout: the absence of the word "mourning," the alternative between the "beautiful death" and the exception of the "worse than death," are related to an institution of *ordered* death, to some imperious verdict: "die," "that he die," or "that I die." Should we deduce from this that mourning, the experience of mourning or simply the hypothesis and the naming of mourning—even if it is only to say "there shall be no mourning"—are reserved for the endurance of a death that, while never natural, would nevertheless not be murder, not the terrifying result of some order to die, whether given to oneself or the other? Yes, of course, and this is precisely what we are discussing tonight. Whether we accept it or not, whether we endure it or not, whether we name it or not, mourning here does not follow an order to die. If mourning does still follow, hypothetically, some order, wish, prayer, request, or desire, it would instead be, still tonight, a "do not die" or a "that he not die." And the "there shall be no mourning" could thus be heard as a response to, or echo of, some "do not die," "that he not die." To go into mourning, on the contrary, and even more so, to organize mourning, would always run the risk of confirming the order or the wish ("die," "be dead," "stay dead," "that you die, that you be or remain in death"). (We should never forget, however, that what *happens* to us, what comes to *affect* us, at the death of the friend, goes beyond the order, the wish, even the promise, beyond any performative project. As does any event worthy of this name.)

But we know that this "do not die," which nothing will silence, even when it would not be heard, even when it would forgo mourning, is *threatened* on all sides: threatened by the "beautiful death" itself, with its consoling image, like the figure of a life that was indeed fulfilled, successful, so full of accomplishments and reminders left for future generations, so abundant in meaning and work in the service of thinking, of loved ones, of humanity, and so on, but threatened too by the always open risk of a "worse than death," the disguised extinction of the name always lying in wait. For there are a thousand different ways, as we know, for a name to vanish; it can lose itself at the point where there would no longer even be a differend, as in the "not even a differend" I just recalled. But the name can also be effaced, in another perversion of the worse, precisely insofar as it is kept or keeps itself back, *through* what it keeps for itself or *through* the one who keeps it, or insofar, as we read in *Signed, Malraux,* in the last chapter entitled "Witness," as "the names remain," or what remains is the "Signature from beyond the tomb. As always. The only one."[6] Names keep, watch over, but these spectral sentinels remain always as threatened as they are threatening; "In and around names, vengeance is on the prowl," says *The Differend* (*D,* 56) on the same page as the passage about Israel I cited a moment ago. Consequently, would this threat be "worse than death"? Would the "worse than death" be this, and worse than the worst? Would what is worse than the worst be this threat of the *contamination* of all these deaths, and all the forms that might be taken on—and yet also denied—by this mourning of mourning?

This is why, in his "Translator's Notes," Jean-François linked with so much insight his reflection on mourning to the question of wrong and forgiveness. Faced with the threat of equivocation, forever pressing and necessary, between all these orders of death, we are all, we, Jean-François's friends, in the impossible—some may even say unforgivable—situation of those third parties or surviving "we's" who must survive not only death but the disappearance or disqualification of the "witness," of a certain "we" and a certain "third."

In the guise of a conclusion, I would like to read an extraordinary passage, the passage to hyperbole in *The Differend,* in the apparently furtive moment in which, so to speak, Jean-François Lyotard signs his book by giving us to think what is perhaps here thought, the very thinking of thought. It is also precisely the moment of the leap toward a thinking "we" that signs, seals, leaves its seal and its legacy, goes on to survive or

6.   Jean-François Lyotard, *Signed, Malraux,* trans. Robert Harvey (Minneapolis: University of Minnesota Press, 1999), 286, 288.

live on beyond all the "we's" that it demystifies. This "we" will have been, in the end, the only one to have inspired me tonight, to have whispered to me everything I say and address to Jean-François, to those who love him and those whom he loves. The fact that Lyotard almost always (though there are exceptions) puts this "we" into quotation marks does not mean that he is neutralizing it. It is simply being torn out of an all-too-easy understanding of so many other "we's" and given over to a type of thinking that should be called reflection, the reflexive thinking of an impossibility. What happens when one thinks and reflects an impossibility? Is this possible? For instance, so close to the experience of the worse, whenever it becomes nearly impossible to distinguish between a wrong and damages, between a differend and a litigation? Does this experience of the impossible become possible? What possibility is there for another *we* announcing itself to us through the impossibility of the *we*? And even through the "affirmation of nothingness"?

Here is the passage to the hyperbole of the "we." It comes at the end of section 158, entitled "Third Party?" in the course of a powerful reflection on the coexistence of two secrets and on the troubling equivalence between the third and fourth party. These pages deserve a much closer analysis than I can provide here. As you will hear, this thinking *we* is *presupposed* by the critique, by the overcoming or sublating [*relevante*] disappearance of all the other *we's*. Rhetoric here develops an "objection" attributed to the "speculative." But it is unclear whether the speculative gains or loses itself here, whether it wins or loses its head. This thinking *we* survives all the *we's* it thinks. It thus indeed resembles a Hegelian presupposition (*Voraussetzung*), a speculative *we*. But does it not also survive this survival? Does it not survive as survival itself, through a subtle and infinitesimal excess of thinking? Does it not rather think the speculative, even before thinking in a speculative mode? A beautiful risk to run, once again, at the instant of death. With or "without a result" ("Without a Result" is the title of the following section, which I would have wanted to follow step by step). Let us listen:

> But the third is there, objects speculation. The dispersion without
> witnesses that "we" have characterized as the extinction of the third
> needed to be expressed by a third. That *we* [in italics, while most
> of the other "we's" are within quotation marks] has vanished at
> Auschwitz, "we," at least, have said it. There is no passage from the
> deportee's phrase universe to the SS's phrase universe. In order to
> affirm this, however, we needed to affirm one universe and then
> the other as if "we" were first the SS and then the deportee. In

doing this, "we" effected what "we" were looking for, a we [this time, neither italics nor quotation marks]. In looking for it, this we was looking for itself. It is expressed then at the end of the movement as it had effected itself since the beginning. For, without the presupposition of this permanence of a thinking "we," there would have been no movement in search of a whole. This we is certainly not the totalization of the I's, the you's, and the s/he's in play under the name of "Auschwitz," for it is true that this name designates the impossibility of such a totalization. Instead, it is the reflective movement of this impossibility, that is, the dispersion that comes to self-consciousness and is sublated out of the annihilation and into the affirmation of nothingness. The we composed at least of *I* who write and *you* who read. (*D*, 102–3)

There it is. Running the risk of what *The Differend* elsewhere calls the "last phrase" (*D*, 11), that is what I would have wanted to say. Perhaps I was still speculating.

And yet would I have stopped addressing myself to you?
    To "us"?
    Would I be abusing fiction or desire if I were to say to Jean-François, here and now, as if for the first time in my life, still not daring to address him as *tu*, still keeping to the *vous*, keeping it, keeping him faithfully alive in our *vous*, there it is, Jean-François, this is what, I tell myself, I today would have wanted to try to tell you.

COMPILED BY KAS SAGHAFI

LOUIS ALTHUSSER

1959   *Montesquieu: La politique et l'histoire.* Paris: Presses Universitaires de France. English translation, "Montesquieu: Politics and History," trans. Ben Brewster. In *Politics and History: Montesquieu, Rousseau, Hegel and Marx.* London: New Left Books, 1972.

1965   *Pour Marx.* Paris: Maspero. Reprint, Paris: La Découverte, 1996. English translation, *For Marx,* trans. Ben Brewster. London: New Left Books, 1969.

1965   *Lire le Capital I.* With Pierre Macherey and Jacques Rancière. Paris: Maspero.

1965   *Lire le Capital II.* With Etienne Balibar and Roger Establet. Paris: Maspero. Later appeared as *Lire le Capital,* by Louis Althusser, Etienne Balibar et al. Edited by Etienne Balibar, Pierre Bravo Gala, and Yves Duroux. Paris: Presses Universitaires de France, 1996. English translation, *Reading Capital,* trans. Ben Brewster. London: New Left Books, 1970.

1969   *Lénine et la philosophie.* Paris: Maspero. 2d ed., rev., 1972. English translation, *Lenin and Philosophy and Other Essays,* trans. Ben Brewster. London: New Left Books, 1971. Reprinted in *Philosophy and the Spontaneous Philosophy of the Scientists and Other Essays.* London: Verso, 1990.

1973   *Réponse à John Lewis.* Paris: Maspero. English translation in *Essays in Self-Criticism,* trans. Grahame Lock. London: New Left Books, 1976. Reprinted in *Essays in Ideology.* London: Verso, 1984.

1974   *Philosophie et philosophie spontanée des savants.* Paris: Maspero. English translation, *Philosophy and the Spontaneous Philosophy of the Scientists and Other Essays,* ed. Gregory Elliott, trans. Ben Brewster, James H. Kavanagh, Thomas E. Lewis, Grahame Lock, and Warren Montag. London: Verso, 1990.

1974   *Éléments d'autocritique.* Paris: Hachette. English translation, *Essays in Self-Criticism,* trans. Grahame Lock. London: New Left Books, 1976.

1976   *Positions.* Paris: Editions Sociales.

1978   *Ce qui ne peut plus durer dans le parti communiste.* Paris: Maspero. English translation, "What Must Change in the Party," trans. Patrick Camiller. *New Left Review* 109 (May/June 1978): 19–45.

Posthumous Texts

1992   *L'avenir dure longtemps,* followed by *Les faits: Autobiographies.* Edited by
Olivier Corpet and Yann Moulier Boutang. Paris: Stock/IMEC. 2d ed.,
expanded, Le Livre de Poche, 1994. English translation, *The Future Lasts
Forever: A Memoir,* trans. Richard Veasey. New York: New Press, 1993.

1992   *Journal de captivité: Stalag XA/1940–1945: Carnets—Correspondances—
Textes.* Edited by Olivier Corpet and Yann Moulier Boutang. Paris:
Stock/IMEC.

1993   *Écrits sur la psychanalyse: Freud et Lacan.* Edited by Olivier Corpet and
François Matheron. Paris: Stock/IMEC. English translation, *Writings
on Psychoanalysis: Freud and Lacan,* trans. Jeffrey Mehlman. New York:
Columbia University Press, 1996.

1994   *Sur la philosophie.* Paris: Gallimard.

1994   *Ecrits philosophiques et politiques.* Vol. 1. Edited by François Matheron.
Paris: Stock/IMEC. English translation, *The Spectre of Hegel: Early
Writings,* trans. G. M. Goshgarian. London: Verso, 1997.

1995   *Ecrits philosophiques et politiques.* Vol. 2. Edited by François Matheron.
Paris: Stock/IMEC. Partial English translation, *Machiavelli and Us,* ed.
François Matheron, trans. Gregory Elliott. New York: Verso, 1999.

1995   *Sur la reproduction.* Paris: Presses Universitaires de France.

1996   *Psychanalyse et sciences humaines: Deux conférences (1963–1964).* Edited
by Olivier Corpet and François Matheron. Paris: Le Livre de Poche.

1998   *Lettres à Franca (1961–1973).* Edited by François Matheron and Yann
Moulier Boutang. Paris: Stock/IMEC.

ROLAND BARTHES

1953   *Le degré zéro de l'écriture.* Paris: Seuil. 2d ed. (followed by *Nouveaux essais
critiques*), Paris: Seuil, 1972. English translation, *Writing Degree Zero,*
trans. Annette Lavers and Colin Smith. New York: Hill and Wang,
1968.

1954   *Michelet par lui-même.* Paris: Seuil. English translation, *Michelet,* trans.
Richard Howard. New York: Hill and Wang, 1987. Reprint, Berkeley:
University of California Press, 1992.

1957   *Mythologies.* Paris: Seuil. English translation, *The Eiffel Tower and Other
Mythologies,* trans. Richard Howard. New York: Hill and Wang, 1979.

1963   *Sur Racine.* Paris: Seuil. English translation, *On Racine,* trans. Richard
Howard. New York: Hill and Wang, 1964. Reprint, Berkeley: University
of California Press, 1992.

1964   *Éléments de sémiologie.* Paris: Seuil. English translation, *Elements of
Semiology,* trans. Annette Lavers and Colin Smith. New York: Noonday
Press, 1968.

1964   *Essais critiques.* Paris: Seuil. English translation, *Critical Essays,* trans. Richard Howard. Evanston: Northwestern University Press, 1972.

1966   *Critique et vérité.* Paris: Seuil. English translation, *Criticism and Truth,* trans. Katrine Pilcher Keuneman. Minneapolis: University of Minnesota Press, 1987.

1967   *Système de la mode.* Paris: Seuil. English translation, *The Fashion System,* trans. Matthew Ward and Richard Howard. New York: Hill and Wang, 1983. Reprint, Berkeley: University of California Press, 1990.

1970   *S/Z.* Paris: Seuil. English translation, *S/Z,* trans. Richard Miller. New York: Hill and Wang, 1970.

1970   *L'empire des signes.* Paris: Skira. English translation, *Empire of Signs,* trans. Richard Howard. New York: Hill and Wang, 1982.

1971   *Sade, Fourier, Loyola.* Paris: Seuil. English translation, *Sade/Fourier/Loyola,* trans. Richard Miller. New York: Hill and Wang, 1976. Reprint, Baltimore: Johns Hopkins University Press, 1997.

1973   *Le plaisir du texte.* Paris: Seuil. English translation, *The Pleasure of the Text,* trans. Richard Miller. New York: Noonday Press, 1975.

1975   *Roland Barthes par Roland Barthes.* Paris: Seuil. English translation, *Roland Barthes by Roland Barthes,* trans. Richard Howard. New York: Noonday Press, 1977.

1977   *Fragments d'un discours amoureux.* Paris: Seuil. English translation, *A Lover's Discourse: Fragments,* trans. Richard Howard. New York: Hill and Wang, 1978.

1978   *Leçon.* Paris: Seuil. English translation, "Inaugural Lecture, Collège de France." In *A Barthes Reader,* ed. Susan Sontag. New York: Hill and Wang, 1982.

1979   *Sollers, écrivain.* Paris: Seuil. English translation, *Sollers, Writer,* trans. Philip Thody. Minneapolis: University of Minnesota Press, 1987.

1980   *La chambre claire: Note sur la photographie.* Paris: Cahiers du cinéma, Gallimard, and Seuil. English translation, *Camera Lucida: Reflections on Photography,* trans. Richard Howard. New York: Hill and Wang, 1981.

Posthumous Texts

1981   *Le grain de la voix.* Paris: Seuil. English translation, *The Grain of the Voice: Interviews 1962–1980,* trans. Linda Coverdale. New York: Hill and Wang, 1985. Reprint, Berkeley: University of California Press, 1991.

1982   *L'obvie et l'obtus: Essais critiques III.* Paris: Seuil. English translation, *The Responsibility of Forms,* trans. Richard Howard. New York: Hill and Wang, 1985. Reprint, Berkeley: University of California Press, 1991.

1984   *Le bruissement de la langue: Essais critiques IV.* Paris: Seuil. English translation, *The Rustle of Language,* trans. Richard Howard. New York: Hill and Wang, 1986.

1985   *L'aventure sémiologique.* Paris: Seuil. English translation, *The Semiotic Challenge,* trans. Richard Howard. New York: Hill and Wang, 1988. Reprint, Berkeley: University of California Press, 1994.

1987   *Incidents.* Paris: Seuil. English translation, *Incidents,* trans. Richard Howard. Berkeley: University of California Press, 1992.

1993–95 *Oeuvres complètes.* Edited by Eric Marty. Vol. 1, *1942–1965.* Paris: Seuil, 1993. Vol. 2, *1966–1973.* Paris: Seuil, 1994. Vol. 3 *1974–1980.* Paris: Seuil, 1995.

JEAN-MARIE BENOIST

1970   *Marx est mort.* Paris: Gallimard.

1975   *La révolution structurale.* Paris: Grasset. 2d ed., Paris: Denöel-Gonthier, 1980. English translation, *The Structural Revolution,* trans. Jean-Marie Benoist, Arnold Pomerans, and Robert Olorenshaw. New York: St. Martin's Press, 1978.

1975   *Tyrannie du logos.* Paris: Minuit. 2d ed., Paris: Presses Universitaires de France, 1993.

1976   *Pavane pour une Europe défunte.* Paris: Denöel-Gonthier.

1977   *L'identité: Séminaire interdisciplinaire.* Edited by Claude Lévi-Strauss and Jean-Marie Benoist. Paris: Grasset. 2d ed., 1979.

1977   *Garache.* Texts by Jean-Marie Benoist and John E. Jackson. Paris: Maeght.

1978   *Les nouveaux primaires.* Paris: Hallier-Albin Michel.

1978   *Un singulier programme: Le carnaval du Programme commun.* Paris: Presses Universitaires de France.

1979   *Chronique de décomposition du PCF.* Paris: La Table Ronde.

1981   *La génération sacrifiée.* Paris: Denöel. French Academy award.

1982   *Le devoir d'opposition: Chroniques 1981–1982 parues dans "Le Quotidien de Paris" et autres textes, précédés d'une préface et suivis d'un envoi au Président de la République.* Paris: Robert Laffont.

1983   *Figures du baroque.* Edited by Jean-Marie Benoist. Paris: Presses Universitaires de France.

1985   *Les outils de la liberté.* Paris: Robert Laffont.

1990   *Après Gorbatchev: Les chances d'une Europe libre: Un dossier de la revue Politique internationale.* Edited by Jean-Marie Benoist and Patrick Wajsman. Paris: La Table Ronde.

GILLES DELEUZE

1953   *Empiricisme et subjectivité: Essai sur la nature humaine selon Hume.* Paris: Presses Universitaires de France. English translation, *Empiricism and Subjectivity: An Essay on Hume's Theory of Human Nature,* trans. Constantin V. Boundas. New York: Columbia University Press, 1991.

1962   *Nietzsche et la philosophie.* Paris: Presses Universitaires de France. English translation, *Nietzsche and Philosophy,* trans. Hugh Tomlinson. New York: Columbia University Press, 1983.

1963   *La philosophie critique de Kant: Doctrine des facultés.* Paris: Presses Universitaires de France. English translation, *Kant's Critical Philosophy: The Doctrine of the Faculties,* trans. Hugh Tomlinson and Barbara Habberjam. Minneapolis: University of Minnesota Press, 1984.

1964   *Proust et les signes.* Paris: Presses Universitaires de France. 3d ed., 1976. English translation, *Proust and Signs,* trans. Richard Howard. Minneapolis: University of Minnesota Press, 2000.

1965   *Nietzsche.* Paris: Presses Universitaires de France.

1966   *Le Bergsonisme.* Paris: Presses Universitaires de France. English translation, *Bergsonism,* trans. Hugh Tomlinson and Barbara Habberjam. New York: Zone, 1988.

1967   *Présentation de Sacher-Masoch.* Paris: Minuit. Reprint, Paris: Union Générale d'Editions, 1974. English translation, *Masochism* ("Coldness and Cruelty," by Deleuze; "Venus in Furs," by Leopold Sacher-Masoch), trans. Jean McNeil. New York: George Braziller, 1971. Reprint, New York: Zone, 1991.

1968   *Différence et répétition.* Paris: Presses Universitaires de France. English translation, *Difference and Repetition,* trans. Paul Patton. New York: Columbia University Press, 1994.

1968   *Spinoza et le problème de l'expression.* Paris: Minuit. English translation, *Expressionism in Philosophy: Spinoza,* trans. Martin Joughin. New York: Zone, 1990.

1969   *Logique du sens.* Paris: Minuit. Reprint, Paris: Union Générale d'Editions, 1973. English translation, *The Logic of Sense,* ed. Constantin V. Boundas, trans. Mark Lester with Charles Stivale. New York: Columbia University Press, 1990.

1970   *Spinoza: Philosophie pratique.* Paris: Presses Universitaires de France. 2d ed., 1981. English translation, *Spinoza: Practical Philosophy,* trans. Robert Hurley. San Francisco: City Lights, 1988.

1972   *Capitalisme et schizophrénie.* Vol. 1, *L'Anti-Oedipe.* With Félix Guattari. Paris: Minuit, 1972. English translation, *Anti-Oedipus: Capitalism and Schizophrenia,* trans. Robert Hurley, Mark Seem, and Helen R. Lane. New York: Viking Press, 1977. Reprint, Minneapolis: University of Minnesota Press, 1987.

1975   *Kafka: Pour une littérature mineure.* With Félix Guattari. Paris: Minuit. English translation, *Kafka: Toward A Minor Literature,* trans. Dana Polan. Minneapolis: University of Minnesota Press, 1986.

1976   *Rhizome: Introduction.* With Félix Guattari. Paris: Minuit. *On the Line,* trans. John Johnston. New York: Semiotext(e), 1983.

1977   *Dialogues.* With Claire Parnet. Paris: Flammarion, 1977. English translation, *Dialogues,* trans. Hugh Tomlinson and Barbara Habberjam. New York: Columbia University Press, 1987.

1977   *Politique et psychanalyse.* With Félix Guattari. Alençon: Des Mots Perdus.

1979   *Superpositions.* With Carmelo Bene. Paris: Minuit.

1980   *Capitalisme et schizophrénie.* Vol. 2, *Mille plateaux.* With Félix Guattari. English translation, *A Thousand Plateaus: Capitalism and Schizophrenia,* trans. Brian Massumi. Minneapolis: University of Minnesota Press, 1987.

1981   *Francis Bacon: Logique de la sensation.* Paris: La Différence. English translation, Daniel W. Smith, University of Chicago Press, forthcoming.

1983   *Cinéma-1: L'image-mouvement.* Paris: Minuit. English translation, *Cinema 1: The Movement-Image,* trans. Hugh Tomlinson and Barbara Habberjam. Minneapolis: University of Minnesota Press, 1986.

1985   *Cinéma-2: L'image-temps.* Paris: Minuit. English translation, *Cinema II: The Time-Image,* trans. Hugh Tomlinson and Robert Galeta. Minneapolis: University of Minnesota Press, 1989.

1986   *Foucault.* Paris: Minuit. English translation, *Foucault,* trans. Seàn Hand. Minneapolis: University of Minnesota Press, 1988.

1988   *Le pli: Leibniz et le baroque.* Paris: Minuit. English translation, *The Fold: Leibniz and the Baroque,* trans. Tom Conley. Minneapolis: University of Minnesota Press, 1993.

1988   *Périclès et Verdi: La philosophie de François Châtelet.* Paris: Minuit.

1990   *Pourparlers, 1972–1990.* Paris: Minuit. English translation, *Negotiations, 1972–1990,* trans. Martin Joughin. New York: Columbia University Press, 1995.

1991   *Qu'est-ce que la philosophie?* With Félix Guattari. Paris: Minuit. English translation, *What Is Philosophy?* trans. Hugh Tomlinson and Graham Burchell. New York: Columbia University Press, 1994.

1992   "L'épuisé," postface to Samuel Beckett, *Quad et autres pièces pour la télévision.* Paris: Minuit. English translation in *Essays Critical and Clinical,* trans. Daniel W. Smith and Michael A. Greco. Minneapolis: University of Minnesota Press, 1997.

1993   *Critique et clinique.* Paris: Minuit. English translation, *Essays Critical and Clinical,* trans. Daniel W. Smith and Michael A. Greco. Minneapolis: University of Minnesota Press, 1997.

1995   "L'immanence: Une vie . . ." *Philosophie* 47 (septembre 1): 3–7.

PAUL DE MAN

1971   *Blindness and Insight: Essays in the Rhetoric of Contemporary Criticism.* New York: Oxford University Press. 2d rev. ed., with five additional essays, ed. Wlad Godzich, Minneapolis: University of Minnesota Press, 1983.

1979 *Allegories of Reading: Figural Language in Rousseau, Nietzsche, Rilke, and Proust.* New Haven: Yale University Press.

Posthumous Texts

1984 *The Rhetoric of Romanticism.* New York: Columbia University Press.

1986 *The Resistance to Theory.* Edited by Wlad Godzich. Minneapolis: University of Minnesota Press.

1988 *Wartime Journalism, 1939–1943.* Edited by Werner Hamacher, Neil Hertz, and Tom Keenan. Lincoln: University of Nebraska Press.

1989 *Critical Writings, 1953–1978.* Edited by Lindsay Waters. Minneapolis: University of Minnesota Press.

1993 *Romanticism and Contemporary Criticism: The Gauss Seminar and Other Papers.* Edited by E. S. Burt, Kevin Newmark, and Andrzej Warminski. Baltimore: Johns Hopkins University Press.

1996 *Aesthetic Ideology.* Edited by Andrzej Warminski. Minneapolis: University of Minnesota Press.

MICHEL FOUCAULT

1954 *Maladie mentale et personnalité.* Paris: Presses Universitaires de France. Revised as *Maladie mentale et psychologie.* Paris: Presses Universitaires de France, 1962. English translation, *Mental Illness and Psychology,* trans. Alan Sheridan. New York: Harper and Row, 1976.

1961 *Folie et déraison: Histoire de la folie à l'âge classique.* Paris: Plon. 2d ed., with a new preface and two appendices, *Histoire de la folie à l'âge classique.* Paris: Gallimard. Abridged English translation as *Madness and Civilization: A History of Insanity in the Age of Reason,* trans. Richard Howard. New York: Pantheon, 1965.

1962 *Raymond Roussel.* Paris: Gallimard. English translation, *Death and the Labyrinth: The World of Raymond Roussel,* trans. Charles Ruas. Garden City, N.Y.: Doubleday, 1986.

1963 *Naissance de la clinique: Une archéologie du regard médical.* Paris: Presses Universitaires de France. 2d rev. ed., 1972. English translation, *The Birth of the Clinic: An Archaeology of Medical Perception,* trans. Alan Sheridan Smith. New York: Pantheon, 1973.

1966 *Les mots et les choses: Une archéologie des sciences humaines.* Paris: Gallimard. English translation, *The Order of Things: An Archaeology of the Human Sciences,* trans. Alan Sheridan. New York: Vintage, 1973.

1969 *L'archéologie du savoir.* Paris: Gallimard. English translation, *The Archaeology of Knowledge,* trans. A. M. Sheridan. New York: Pantheon, 1972.

1971   *L'ordre du discours*. Paris: Gallimard. English translation, "The Discourse on Language," trans. Rupert Swyer, as an appendix to *The Archaeology of Knowledge*. Also translated by Ian McLeod as "The Order of Discourse." In *Untying the Text: A Post-structuralist Reader*, ed. Robert Young. New York: Routledge, 1981.

1973   *Ceci n'est pas une pipe*. Montpellier: Fata Morgana. English translation, *This Is Not a Pipe*, trans. James Harkness. Berkeley: University of California Press, 1983.

1975   *Surveiller et punir: Naissance de la prison*. Paris: Gallimard. English translation, *Discipline and Punish: The Birth of the Prison*, trans. Alan Sheridan. New York: Pantheon, 1977.

1976   *La volonté de savoir*. Vol. 1 of *Histoire de la sexualité*. Paris: Gallimard. English translation, *The History of Sexuality: An Introduction*. Vol. 1 of *The History of Sexuality*, trans. Robert Hurley. New York: Pantheon, 1978.

1984   *L'usage des plaisirs*. Vol. 2 of *Histoire de la sexualité*. Paris: Gallimard. English translation, *The Use of Pleasure*. Vol. 2 of *The History of Sexuality*, trans. Robert Hurley. New York: Pantheon, 1985.

1984   *Le souci de soi*. Vol. 3 of *Histoire de la sexualité*. Paris: Gallimard. English translation, *The Care of the Self*. Vol. 3 of *The History of Sexuality*, trans. Robert Hurley. New York: Pantheon, 1986.

Posthumous Texts

1989   *Résumé des cours au Collège de France, 1970–1982*. Paris: Julliard.

1994   *Dits et écrits*. Edited by Daniel Defert and François Ewald. 4 vols. Vol. 1, 1954–69. Vol. 2, 1970–75. Vol. 3, 1976–79. Vol. 4, 1980–88. Paris: Gallimard. Selections from these volumes translated in *Essential Works of Michel Foucault* as follow: *Ethics: Subjectivity and Truth*. Vol. 1 of *Essential Works of Michel Foucault, 1954–1984*. Edited by Paul Rabinow. Translated by Robert Hurley and others. New York: New Press, 1997. *Aesthetics, Method, Epistemology*. Vol. 2 of *Essential Works of Michel Foucault, 1954–1984*. Edited by James D. Faubion. Translated by Robert Hurley and others. New York: New Press, 1998. *Power*. Vol. 3 of *Essential Works of Michel Foucault, 1954–1984*. Edited by James D. Faubion. Translated by Peter T. Hoffer. New York: New Press, 2000.

1997   *"Il faut défendre la société": Cours au Collège de France, 1975–1976*. Paris: Seuil and Gallimard.

1999   *Les anormaux: Cours au Collège de France, 1974–1975*. Paris: Gallimard and Seuil.

2001   *L'herméneutique du sujet: Cours au Collège de France, 1981–1982*. Paris: Gallimard and Sevil.

EDMOND JABÈS

1936 *L'obscurité potable.* Paris: Guy Lévis Mano.

1945 Preface to *Lettres de Max Jacob à Edmond Jabès.* Alexandria: Scarabée.

1947 *Chansons pour le repas de l'ogre.* Paris: Pierre Seghers.

1947 *Le fond de l'eau.* Cairo: La Part du Sable.

1948 *Trois filles de mon quartier.* Paris: Guy Lévis Mano.

1949 *La voix d'encre.* Cairo: La Part du Sable.

1950 *La clef de voûte.* Paris: Guy Lévis Mano.

1951 *Les mots tracent.* Paris: L'Âge d'Or.

1953 *Paul Eluard.* Cairo: La Part du Sable.

1955 *L'écorce du monde.* Paris: Pierre Seghers.

1959 *Je bâtis ma demeure: Poèmes, 1943–1957.* Paris: Gallimard. 2d ed., 1975. Preface by Gabriel Bounoure. A selection of these poems was translated by Anthony Rudolf as *A Share of Ink.* London: Menard, 1979. Another selection was included in *If There Were Anywhere but Desert: The Selected Poems of Edmond Jabès,* trans. Keith Waldrop. Barrytown, N.Y.: Station Hill Press, 1988.

1963 *Le livre des questions.* Vol. 1. Paris: Gallimard.

1964 *Le livre de Yukel.* Vol. 2 of *Le livre des questions.* Paris: Gallimard.

1965 *Le retour au livre.* Vol. 3 of *Le livre des questions.* Paris: Gallimard. These first three volumes of *Le livre des questions* were translated by Rosmarie Waldrop as *The Book of Questions,* vol. 1 (*The Book of Questions, The Book of Yukel, Return to the Book*). Hanover: Wesleyan University Press, 1991.

1967 *Yaël.* Vol. 4 of *Le livre des questions.* Paris: Gallimard.

1969 *Elya.* Vol. 5 of *Le livre des questions.* Paris: Gallimard.

1972 *Aely.* Vol. 6 of *Le livre des questions.* Paris: Gallimard.

1973 *. (El ou le dernier livre).* Vol. 7 of *Le livre des questions.* Paris: Gallimard. These last four volumes of *Le livre des questions* were translated by Rosmarie Waldrop as *The Book of Questions,* vol. 2 (*Yaël, Elya, Aely, El or the Last Book*). Hanover: Wesleyan University Press, 1991.

1975 *Ça suit son cours.* Vol. 1 of *Le livre des marges.* Montpellier: Fata Morgana.

1976 *Le livre des ressemblances.* Vol. 1 of *Le livre des ressemblances.* Paris: Gallimard. English translation, *The Book of Resemblances.* Vol. 1 of *The Book of Resemblances,* trans. Rosmarie Waldrop. Hanover: Wesleyan University Press, 1990.

1978 *Le soupçon le désert.* Vol. 2 of *Le livre des ressemblances.* Paris: Gallimard. English translation, *Intimations, the Desert.* Vol. 2 of *The Book of Resemblances,* trans. Rosmarie Waldrop. Hanover: Wesleyan University Press, 1991.

1980   *L'ineffaçable l'inaperçu.* Vol. 3 of *Le livre des ressemblances.* Paris: Gallimard. English translation, *The Ineffaceable, the Unperceived.* Vol. 3 of *The Book of Resemblances,* trans. Rosmarie Waldrop. Hanover: Wesleyan University Press, 1992.

1981   *Du désert au livre: Entretiens avec Marcel Cohen.* Paris: Pierre Belfond. English translation, *From the Desert to the Book: Dialogues with Marcel Cohen,* trans. Pierre Joris. Barrytown, N.Y.: Station Hill Press, 1989.

1981   *Récit.* Montpellier: Fata Morgana.

1982   *Le petit livre de la subversion hors de soupçon.* Vol. 1 of *Le livre des limites.* Paris: Gallimard. English translation, *The Little Book of Unsuspected Subversion,* trans. Rosmarie Waldrop. Stanford: Stanford University Press, 1996.

1984   *Dans la double dépendance du dit.* Vol. 2 of *Le livre des marges.* Montpellier: Fata Morgana. Both volumes of *Le livre des marges* (see 1975 for volume 1) were translated by Rosmarie Waldrop as *The Book of Margins.* Chicago: University of Chicago Press, 1993.

1984   *Le livre du dialogue.* Vol. 2 of *Le livre des limites.* Paris: Gallimard. English translation, *The Book of Dialogue,* trans. Rosmarie Waldrop. Hanover: Wesleyan University Press, 1988.

1985   *Ce qui m'appartient.* Paris: Marcel Duchamp.

1985   *Le parcours.* Vol. 3 of *Le livre des limites.* Paris: Gallimard.

1986   *Aigle et chouette.* Montpellier: Fata Morgana.

1987   *Le livre du partage.* Vol. 4 of *Le livre des limites.* Paris: Gallimard. English translation, *The Book of Shares,* trans. Rosmarie Waldrop. Chicago: University of Chicago Press, 1989.

1987   *La mémoire et la main.* Paris: Galerie Lelong.

1987   *L'Inferno di Dante.* Sienna: Barbablù.

1989   *Un étranger avec, sous le bras, un livre de petit format.* Paris: Gallimard. English translation, *A Foreigner Carrying in the Crook of his Arm a Tiny Book,* trans. Rosmarie Waldrop. Hanover: Wesleyan University Press, 1993.

1990   *Pages nouvelles.* Sienna: Barbablù.

1990   *Le seuil le sable: Poésies complètes, 1943–1988.* Paris: Gallimard.

1990   *La mémoire des mots: Comment je lis Paul Celan.* Paris: Fourbis.

1991   *Le livre de l'hospitalité.* Paris: Gallimard.

1991   *Désir d'un commencement, angoisse d'une seule fin.* Montpellier: Fata Morgana.

1991   *L'enfer de Dante.* Montpellier: Fata Morgana.

Posthumous Texts

1992   *Un regard.* Montpellier: Faga Morgana.

1993   *Cela a eu lieu.* Paris: Fourbis.

1997   *Bâtir un quotidien: Esquisse.* Vol. 3 of *Le livre des marges.* Montpellier: Fata Morgana.

SARAH KOFMAN

1970   *L'enfance de l'art: Une interprétation de l'esthétique freudienne.* Paris: Payot. 3d ed., Paris: Galilée, 1985. English translation, *The Childhood of Art: An Interpretation of Freud's Aesthetics,* trans. Winifred Woodhull. New York: Columbia University Press, 1988.

1972   *Nietzsche et la métaphore.* Paris: Payot. 2d ed., Paris: Galilée, 1983. English translation, *Nietzsche and Metaphor,* trans. Duncan Large. Stanford: Stanford University Press, 1993.

1973   *Camera obscura: De l'idéologie.* Paris: Galilée. English translation, *Camera Obscura: Of Ideology,* trans. Will Straw. Ithaca: Cornell University Press, 1998.

1974   *Quatre romans analytiques.* Paris: Galilée. English translation, *Freud and Fiction,* trans. Sarah Wykes. Cambridge: Polity Press, 1991.

1976   *Autobiogriffures: Du chat Murr d'Hoffmann.* Paris: Christian Bourgois. 2d ed., Paris: Galilée, 1984.

1978   *Aberrations: Le devenir-femme d'Auguste Comte.* Paris: Aubier-Flammarion.

1979   *Nerval: Le charme de la répétition: Lecture de "Sylvie."* Lausanne: L'Âge d'Homme.

1979   *Nietzsche et la scène philosophique.* Paris: Union Générale d'Editions. Paris: Galilée, 1986.

1980   *L'énigme de la femme: La femme dans les textes de Freud.* Paris: Galilée. English translation, *The Enigma of Woman: Woman in Freud's Writings,* trans. Catherine Porter. Ithaca: Cornell University Press, 1985.

1982   *Le respect des femmes (Kant et Rousseau).* Paris: Galilée.

1983   *Comment s'en sortir?* Paris: Galilée.

1983   *Un métier impossible: Lecture de "Constructions en analyse."* Paris: Galilée.

1984   *Lectures de Derrida.* Paris: Galilée.

1985   *Mélancolie de l'art.* Paris: Galilée.

1986   *Pourquoi rit-on? Freud et le mot d'esprit.* Paris: Galilée.

1987   *Paroles suffoquées.* Paris: Galilée. English translation, *Smothered Words,* trans. Madeleine Dobie. Evanston: Northwestern University Press, 1998.

1987   *Conversions: Le Marchand de Venise sous le signe de Saturne.* Paris: Galilée.

1989   *Socrate(s).* Paris: Galilée. English translation, *Socrates: Fictions of a Philosopher,* trans. Catherine Porter. Ithaca: Cornell University Press, 1998.

1990   *Séductions: De Sartre à Héraclite.* Paris: Galilée.

1991   *Don Juan ou le refus de la dette.* With Jean-Yves Masson. Paris: Galilée.

1991   *"Il n'y a que le premier pas qui coûte": Freud et la spéculation.* Paris: Galilée.

1992   *Explosion I: De l'"Ecce Homo" de Nietzsche.* Paris: Galilée.

1993   *Explosion II: Les enfants de Nietzsche.* Paris: Galilée.

1994   *Rue Ordener, Rue Labat.* Paris: Galilée. English translation, *Rue Ordener, Rue Labat,* trans. Ann Smock. Lincoln: University of Nebraska Press, 1996.

1994   *Le mépris des juifs: Nietzsche, les juifs, l'antisémitisme.* Paris: Galilée.

Posthumous Texts

1995   *L'imposture de la beauté.* Paris: Galilée.

1995   "La mort conjurée." *La part de l'oeil* 11:41–45.

1997   *Sarah Kofman.* Edited by Françoise Collin and Françoise Proust. *Les cahiers du Grif,* no. 3. Paris: Descartes & Cie.

EMMANUEL LEVINAS

1930   *La théorie de l'intuition dans la phénoménologie de Husserl.* Paris: Alcan. Reprint, Paris: Vrin, 1963. English translation, *The Theory of Intuition in Husserl's Phenomenology,* trans. André Orianne. Evanston: Northwestern University Press, 1973. 2d ed., 1995.

1934   *Quelques réflexions sur la philosophie d'hitlérisme.* Paris: Payot et Rivages, coll. "Rivages poche," 1997. English translation, "Reflections on the Philosophy of Hitlerism," trans. Seàn Hand. *Critical Inquiry* 17, no. 1 (autumn 1990): 63–71.

1935   *De l'évasion.* Published as a book, annotated by Jacques Rolland, Montpellier: Fata Morgana, 1982. Reprint, Le Livre de Poche, 1998.

1947   *De l'existence à l'existant.* Paris: Fontaine. Reprint, Paris: Vrin, 1973. English translation, *Existence and Existents,* trans. Alphonso Lingis. The Hague: Martinus Nijhoff, 1978.

1948   *Le temps et l'autre.* Published as a book, Montpellier: Fata Morgana, 1979. Reprint, Paris: Presses Universitaires de France, 1983. English translation, *Time and the Other,* trans. Richard A. Cohen. Pittsburgh: Duquesne University Press, 1987.

1949   *En découvrant l'existence avec Husserl et Heidegger.* Paris: Vrin. 2d ed., expanded, 1967. Partially translated as *Discovering Existence with Husserl and Heidegger,* trans. Richard A. Cohen. Evanston: Northwestern University Press, 1998.

1953   *Liberté et commandement: Transcendance et hauteur* (originally published in 1953 and 1962). Cognac: Fata Morgana, 1994. Reprint, Le Livre de

Poche, 1999. Partial English translation, "Transcendance and Height," trans. Tina Chanter, Simon Critchley, and Nicholas Walker. Translation revised by Adriaan Peperzak in *Basic Philosophical Writings,* ed. Adriaan Peperzak, Simon Critchley, and Robert Bernasconi. Bloomington: Indiana University Press, 1996.

1961   *Totalité et infini: Essai sur l'extériorité.* The Hague: Martinus Nijhoff. Reprint, Le Livre de Poche, 1988. English translation, *Totality and Infinity: An Essay on Exteriority,* trans. Alphonso Lingis. Pittsburgh: Duquesne University Press, 1969.

1963   *Difficile liberté: Essais sur le judaïsme.* Paris: Albin Michel. 2d enlarged ed., 1976. Reprint, Le Livre de Poche, 1984. *Difficult Freedom: Essays on Judaism.* trans. Seàn Hand. Baltimore: Johns Hopkins University Press, 1990.

1968   *Quatre lectures talmudiques.* Paris: Minuit. English translation in *Nine Talmudic Readings,* trans. Annette Aronowicz. Bloomington: Indiana University Press, 1990.

1972   *Humanisme de l'autre homme.* Montpellier: Fata Morgana. Reprint, Le Livre de Poche, 1972. Translated as three separate essays without "Avant-propos" in *Collected Philosophical Papers,* trans. Alphonso Lingis. The Hague: Kluwer Academic, 1993. Reprint, Pittsburgh: Duquesne University Press, 1998.

1974   *Autrement qu'être ou au-delà de l'essence.* The Hague: Martinus Nijhoff. Reprint, Le Livre de Poche, 1991. English translation, *Otherwise than Being or Beyond Essence,* trans. Alphonso Lingis. The Hague: Martinus Nijhoff, 1981. Reprint, Pittsburgh: Duquesne University Press, 1998.

1975   *Sur Maurice Blanchot.* Montpellier: Fata Morgana. English translation, *On Maurice Blanchot,* in *Proper Names,* trans. Michael B. Smith. Stanford: Stanford University Press, 1996.

1975   *Noms propres.* Montpellier: Fata Morgana. English translation, *Proper Names,* trans. Michael B. Smith. Stanford: Stanford University Press, 1996.

1977   *Du sacré au saint: Cinq nouvelles lectures talmudiques.* Paris: Minuit. English translation, *From the Sacred to the Holy,* in *Nine Talmudic Readings,* trans. Annette Aronowicz. Bloomington: Indiana University Press, 1990.

1982   *L'au-delà du verset.* Paris: Minuit. English translation, *Beyond the Verse,* trans. Gary D. Mole. Bloomington: Indiana University Press, 1994.

1982   *De Dieu qui vient à l'idée.* Paris: Vrin. English translation, *Of God Who Comes to Mind,* trans. Bettina Bergo. Stanford: Stanford University Press, 1998.

1982   *Ethique et infini: Dialogues avec Philippe Nemo.* Paris: Fayard. Reprint, Le Livre de Poche, 1984. English translation, *Ethics and Infinity:*

Conversations with Philippe Nemo, trans. Richard A. Cohen. Pittsburgh: Duquesne University Press, 1985.

1984   *Transcendance et intelligibilité.* Geneva: Labor et Fides. English translation, "Transcendence and Intelligibility," in *Basic Philosophical Writings,* ed. Adriaan T. Peperzak, Simon Critchley, and Robert Bernasconi. Bloomington: Indiana University Press, 1996.

1987   *Hors sujet.* Montpellier: Fata Morgana. Reprint, Le Livre de Poche, 1997. English translation, *Outside the Subject,* trans. Michael B. Smith. Stanford: Stanford University Press, 1993.

1988   *A l'heure des nations.* Paris: Minuit. English translation, *In the Time of Nations,* trans. Michael B. Smith. Bloomington: Indiana University Press, 1994.

1990   *De l'oblitération: Entretien avec Françoise Armengaud à propos de l'oeuvre de Sosno.* Paris: La Différence. Excerpts translated in "On Obliteration: Discussing Sacha Sosno," trans. Richard A. Cohen. *Art & Text* 33 (winter 1989): 30–41.

1991   *Entre nous: Essais sur le penser-à-l'autre.* Paris: Grasset. Reprint, Le Livre de Poche, 1993. English translation, *Entre nous: On Thinking-of-the-Other,* trans. Michael B. Smith and Barbara Harshav. New York: Columbia University Press, 1998.

1993   *La mort et le temps.* Edited by Jacques Rolland. Paris: L'Herne.

1993   *Dieu, la mort et le temps.* Edited by Jacques Rolland. Paris: Grasset. Reprint, Le Livre de Poche, 1995. English translation, *God, Death and Time,* trans. Bettina Bergo. Stanford: Stanford University Press, 2000.

1994   *Les imprévus de l'histoire.* Cognac: Fata Morgana. Reprint, Le Livre de Poche, 2000.

1995   *Altérité et transcendance.* Cognac: Fata Morgana. English translation, *Alterity and Transcendence,* trans. Michael B. Smith. New York: Columbia University Press, 1999.

1996   *Nouvelles lectures talmudiques.* Paris: Minuit. English translation, *New Talmudic Readings,* trans. Richard A. Cohen. Pittsburgh: Duquesne University Press, 2000.

2000   *Positivité et transcendance: Suivi de Lévinas et la phénoménologie.* Edited by Jean-Luc Marion. Paris: Presses Universitaires de France.

MAX LOREAU

1964   *Catalogue des travaux de Jean Dubuffet.* Edited by Max Loreau. Paris: J.-J. Pauvert.

1966   *Dubuffet et le voyage au centre de la perception.* Paris: La Jeune Parque.

1967   *Vers une peinture péremptoire: Asger Jorn.* Catalog. Paris: Galerie Jeanne Bucher. Later reprinted in *La part de l'oeil* 14 (1988): 201–8.

1967   *Cerceaux 'sorcellent.* Illustrated by Jean Dubuffet. Paris: Galerie Jeanne Bucher.

1971   *Jean Dubuffet: Délits, déportements, lieux de haut jeu.* Lausanne: Weber.

1973   *Jean Dubuffet: Stratégie de la création.* Paris: Gallimard.

1973   *Cri: Eclat et phases.* Paris: Gallimard.

1975   *Les logogrammes de Christian Dotrement.* Paris: Fall.

1976   *Nouvelles des êtres et des pas.* Paris: Gallimard.

1978   *Chants de perpétuelle venue.* Paris: Gallimard.

1980   *La peinture à l'oeuvre et l'énigme du corps.* Paris: Gallimard.

1980   *Michel Deguy: La poursuite de la poésie tout entière.* Paris: Gallimard.

1986   *Vue d'intérieur (Le drame de la naissance du globe).* Montmorency: Carte Blanche.

1986   *Florence portée aux nues.* Paris: L'Astrée.

1987   *En quête d'un autre commencement.* Brussels: Lebeer-Hossmann.

1988   *L'attrait du commencement.* Brussels: Les Editions du Botanique.

1989   *La genèse du phénomène: Le phénomène, le logos, l'origine.* Paris: Minuit.

1989   *L'épreuve.* Illustrated by Pierre Alechinsky. Montpellier: Fata Morgana.

Posthumous Texts

1991   *Max Loreau, 1928–1990.* Volume d'hommage. Brussels: Lebeer-Hossmann.

1996   "Dans l'éclat du moment: Le matin d'Orphée." In *In forma di parole* 16, no. 2:114–39.

1998   Special issue, "Dossier: Hommage à Max Loreau." *La part de l'oeil,* vol. 14.

1998   *Max Loreau: De la création, peinture, poésie, philosophie.* Brussels: Labor.

JEAN-FRANÇOIS LYOTARD

1954   *La phénoménologie.* Paris: Presses Universitaires de France. English translation, *Phenomenology,* trans. Brian Beakley. Albany, N.Y.: SUNY Press, 1991.

1971   *Discours, figure.* Paris: Klincksieck.

1973   *Dérive à partir de Marx et Freud.* Paris: Union Générale d'Editions. 2d ed., Paris: Galilée, 1994.

1973   *Des dispositifs pulsionnels.* Paris: Union Générale d'Editions. 2d ed., Paris: Galilée, 1994.

1974   *Economie libidinale.* Paris: Minuit. English translation, *Libidinal Economy,* trans. Iain Hamilton Grant. Bloomington: Indiana University Press, 1993.

1975   *Le mur du Pacifique.* Paris: Christian Bourgois. 2d ed. Paris: Galilée, 1979. English translation, *Pacific Wall,* trans. Bruce Boone. Venice, Calif.: Lapis Press, 1990.

1976   *Sur cinq peintures de René Guiffrey.* Paris: Galerie Stevenson and Palluel.

1977   *Les transformateurs Duchamp.* Paris: Galilée. English translation, *Duchamp's Transformers,* trans. Ian McLeod. Venice, Calif.: Lapis Press, 1990.

1977   *Instructions païennes.* Paris: Galilée. English translation, "Lessons in Paganism," trans. David Macey. In *The Lyotard Reader,* ed. Andrew Benjamin. Cambridge, Mass.: Basil Blackwell, 1989.

1977   *Récits tremblants.* Illustrated by Jacques Monory. Paris: Galilée.

1977   *Rudiments païens: Genre dissertatif.* Paris: Union Générale d'Editions.

1979   *La condition postmoderne: Rapport sur le savoir.* Paris: Minuit. English translation, *The Postmodern Condition: A Report on Knowledge,* trans. Geoff Bennington and Brian Massumi. Minneapolis: University of Minnesota Press, 1984.

1979   *Au juste: Conversations.* With Jean-Loup Thébaud. Paris: Christian Bourgois. English translation, *Just Gaming,* trans. Wlad Godzich. Minneapolis: University of Minnesota Press, 1985.

1980   *Sur la constitution du temps par la couleur dans les oeuvres récentes d'Albert Aymé.* Paris: Traversière.

1980   *La partie de peinture.* Illustrated by Henri Maccheroni. Cannes: Editions Maryse Candela.

1981   *Daniel Buren, les couleurs, les formes, peintures.* Edited by Benjamin H. D. Buchloh. Paris: Centre Georges Pompidou.

1981   *Monory: Ciels—Nébuleuses et galaxies, les confins d'un dandysme.* Paris: Galerie Maeght.

1982   *Monogrammes/Loin du doux.* Paris: Catalogue Baruchello, Galerie Le dessin.

1983   *Le différend.* Paris: Minuit. English translation, *The Differend: Phrases in Dispute,* trans. Georges Van Den Abbeele. Minneapolis: University of Minnesota Press, 1988.

1983   *L'histoire de Ruth.* With Ruth Francken. Paris: Le Castor Astral. English translation, "The Story of Ruth," trans. Timothy Murray. In *The Lyotard Reader,* ed. Andrew Benjamin. Cambridge, Mass.: Basil Blackwell, 1989.

1984   *L'assassinat de l'expérience par la peinture: Monory.* Paris: Le Castor Astral. English translation, *The Assassination of Experience by Painting: Monory,* trans. Rachel Bowlby. London: Black Dog, 1998.

1984   *La peinture du sacré à l'ère postmoderne.* Paris: Centre Georges Pompidou.

1984   *Tombeau de l'intellectuel et autres papiers.* Paris: Galilée. English translation, "Tomb of the Intellectual," trans. Bill Readings and Kevin Geiman.

In *Political Writings*, trans. Bill Readings and Kevin Geiman. Minneapolis: University of Minnesota Press, 1993.

1985   *Les immatériaux*. Edited with Thierry Chaput. Paris: Centre Georges Pompidou.

1986   *Le postmoderne expliqué aux enfants: Correspondance, 1982–1985*. Paris: Galilée. English translation, *The Postmodern Explained*, trans. Julian Pefanis, Morgan Thomas, et. al. Minneapolis: University of Minnesota Press, 1992.

1986   *L'enthousiasme: La critique kantienne de l'histoire*. Paris: Galilée.

1987   *Que peindre? Adami, Arakawa, Buren*. Paris: La Différence.

1988   *Heidegger et "les juifs."* Paris: Galilée. English translation, *Heidegger and "the jews,"* trans. Andreas Michel and Mark S. Roberts. Minneapolis: University of Minnesota Press, 1990.

1988   *L'inhumain: Causeries sur le temps*. Paris: Galilée. English translation, *The Inhuman: Reflections on Time*, trans. Geoffrey Bennington and Rachel Bowlby. Stanford: Stanford University Press, 1991.

1988   *Peregrinations: Law, Form, Event*. New York: Columbia University Press. French version, *Pérégrinations: Loi, forme, événement*. Paris: Galilée, 1990.

1989   *La guerre des Algériens: Ecrits, 1956–1963*. Paris: Galilée. Collected in *Political Writings*, trans. Bill Readings and Kevin Geiman. Minneapolis: University of Minnesota Press, 1993.

1991   *Leçons sur l'analytique du sublime*. Paris: Galilée. English translation, *Lessons on the Analytic of the Sublime*, trans. Elizabeth Rottenberg. Stanford: Stanford University Press, 1994.

1991   *Lectures d'enfance*. Paris: Galilée.

1991   *La face des choses*. Le Havre: Catalogue Laponge.

1992   *Sans Appel: La geste d'Appel en quête d'un commentaire*. Paris: Galilée.

1993   *Moralités postmodernes*. Paris: Galilée. English translation, *Postmodern Fables*, trans. Georges Van Den Abbeele. Minneapolis: University of Minnesota Press, 1997.

1993   *Sam Francis: Lessons of Darkness—"Like the Paintings of a Blind Man."* Translated by Geoffrey Bennington. Los Angeles: Lapis Press.

1993   *Un trait d'union*. With Eberhard Gruber. Sainte-Foy, Quebec: Le Griffon d'Argile, 1993. English translation, *The Hyphen: Between Judaism and Christianity*, trans. Pascale-Anne Brault and Michael Naas. New York: Humanity Books, 1999.

1996   *Signé Malraux*. Paris: Grasset. English translation, *Signed, Malraux*, trans. Robert Harvey. Minneapolis: University of Minnesota Press, 1999.

1997   *Flora danica: La sécession du geste dans la peinture de Stig Brøgger*. Paris: Galilée.

| 1997 | *Corinne Filippi: Photographie . . .* Texts by Jean-François Lyotard and Nicole Vitre. Reims: Editions du Paysage. |

1997   *Corinne Filippi: Photographie . . .* Texts by Jean-François Lyotard and Nicole Vitre. Reims: Editions du Paysage.

1998   *Chambre sourde: L'antiesthétique de Malraux.* Paris: Galilée.

1998   *La confession d'Augustin.* Paris: Galilée.

2000   *Misère de la philosophie.* Paris: Galilée.

LOUIS MARIN

1971   *Etudes sémiologiques: Écritures, peintures.* Paris: Klincksieck.

1971   *Sémiotique de la Passion: Topiques et figures.* Paris: Desclée de Brouwer, Aubier-Montaigne. English translation, *The Semiotics of the Passion Narratives: Topics and Figures,* trans. Alfred M. Johnson, Jr. Pittsburgh: Pickwick Press.

1973   *Utopiques: Jeux d'espaces.* Paris: Minuit. English translation, *Utopics: The Semiological Play of Textual Spaces,* trans. Robert A. Vollrath. Atlantic Highlands, N.J.: Humanities Press International, 1990.

1974   *Le récit évangélique.* With Claude Chabrol. Paris: Desclée de Brouwer, Aubier-Montaigne.

1975   *La critique du discours: Sur la "Logique de Port-Royal" et les "Pensées" de Pascal.* Paris: Minuit.

1977   *Détruire la peinture.* Paris: Galilée. English translation, *To Destroy Painting,* trans. Mette Hjort. Chicago: University of Chicago Press, 1995.

1978   *Le récit est un piège.* Paris: Minuit.

1978   *Le roi s'en va-t-en guerre; ou, Les pièges du récit historique.* Strasbourg: Université II, Groupe de recherches sur les théories du signe et du texte.

1979   *La voix excommuniée: Essais de mémoire.* Paris: Galilée.

1981   *Le portrait du roi.* Paris: Minuit. English translation, *The Portrait of the King,* trans. Martha M. Houle. Minneapolis: University of Minnesota Press, 1988.

1986   *La parole mangée et autres essais théologico-politiques.* Paris: Klincksieck. English translation, *Food for Thought,* trans. Mette Hjort. Baltimore: Johns Hopkins University Press, 1989.

1988   *Jean-Charles Blais: Du figurable en peinture.* Paris: Blusson.

1989   *Opacité de la peinture: Essais sur la représentation au Quattrocento.* Paris: Usher.

1992   *Lectures traversières.* Paris: Albin Michel. English translation, *Cross-Readings,* trans. Jane Marie Todd. Atlantic Highlands, N.J.: Humanities Press, 1998.

Posthumous Texts

1993   *Des pouvoirs de l'image: Gloses.* Paris: Seuil.

1994 *De la représentation*. Edited by Daniel Arasse, Alain Cantillon, Giovani Careri, Danièle Cohn, Pierre-Antoine Fabre, and Françoise Marin. Paris: Seuil and Gallimard.

1995 *Philippe de Champaigne; ou, La présence cachée*. Paris: Hazan.

1995 *Sublime Poussin*. Paris: Seuil. English translation, *Sublime Poussin*, trans. Catherine Porter. Stanford: Stanford University Press, 1999.

1997 *De l'entretien*. Paris: Minuit.

1997 *Pascal et Port-Royal*. Edited by Alain Cantillon. Paris: Presses Universitaires de France.

2000 *L'écriture de soi*. Paris: Presses Universitaires de France.

JOSEPH RIDDEL

1965 *The Clairvoyant Eye: The Poetry and Poetics of Wallace Stevens*. Baton Rouge: Louisiana State University Press. 2d ed. with new postscript, 1991.

1971 *C. Day Lewis*. New York: Twayne.

1974 *The Inverted Bell: Modernism and the Counterpoetics of William Carlos Williams*. Baton Rouge: Louisiana State University Press.

Posthumous Texts

1995 *Purloined Letters: Originality and Repetition in American Literature*. Edited by Mark Bauerlein. Baton Rouge: Louisiana State University Press.

1996 *The Turning Word: American Literary Modernism and Continental Theory*. Edited by Mark Bauerlein. Philadelphia: University of Pennsylvania Press.

1996 *American Modernisms: Revaluing the Canon: Essays in Honor of Joseph N. Riddel*. Edited by Kathryne V. Lindberg and Joseph G. Kronick. Baton Rouge: Louisiana State University Press.

MICHEL SERVIÈRE

1974 "Ponctuation de Nietzsche." In *Motifs et figures*. Rouen: Publications de l'Université de Rouen.

1974 "Gradiva/Gravida" (excerpt). In *Psychanalyse et anthropologie prospective*. Rouen: Publications de l'Université de Rouen.

1982 "Ex Libris." In *Catalogue de l'exposition de Déclinaisons*. Rouen: Musée des Beaux-Arts de Rouen.

1985 "Le lisible et le visible." *Le cahier du Collège international de philosophie* 1:163–67.

1985 "Wagner dans le texte de Nietzsche." In *L'opéra*. Rouen: Centre d'Art, Esthétique et Littéraire de Rouen.

1986   "De la signature: Hésitations, circulations du sujet." *Le cahier du Collège international de philosophie* 2:166–70.

1986   "La création adoucit les moeurs." In *Vie musicale et courants de pensée (1780–1830)*. Haute Normandie: DRAC de Haute-Normandie.

1986   "Peinture et grossesse: La signature 'géné-rationnelle.'" In *Le Bucentaure*. Paris: Osiris.

1987   *Portrait, autoportrait.* Edited by Michel Servière, Eric Van de Casteele, and Jean-Louis Déotte. Paris: Osiris. Includes Servière's "L'imaginaire signé: Référence et sujet dans le portrait."

1987   "Portrait-charge de philosophie, Grandville avec Nietzsche." *Le cahier du Collège international de philosophie*, no. 3.

1988   "Le livre d'artiste ou la double vue." In *Livres délivrés*. Haute Normandie: FRAC de Haute-Normandie.

1989   "Le discours polygraphique de Jacques Derrida." In *Encyclopédie philosophique universelle (L'univers philosophique)*, ed. A. Jacob. Paris: Presses Universitaires de France.

1990   "Beethoven était-il sourd? Beethoven war nicht hörig!" In *Révolution(s), politique et musique*. Rouen: Les cahiers du Centre international de recherches en esthétique musicale.

1997   *Le sujet de l'art.* Paris: L'Harmattan.